WITHDRAWN

Compara **Y0-AAF-516**

ETHNICITY

AND

LANGUAGE

* * * * *

VOLUME VI

ETHNICITY AND PUBLIC POLICY
SERIES

ETHNICITY AND PUBLIC POLICY
SERIES

*　　　*　　　*　　　*　　　*

ETHNICITY

AND

LANGUAGE

WINSTON A. VAN HORNE
EDITOR

THOMAS V. TONNESEN
MANAGING EDITOR

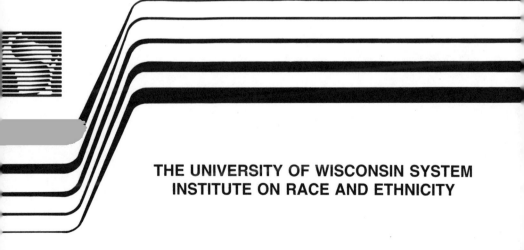

THE UNIVERSITY OF WISCONSIN SYSTEM
INSTITUTE ON RACE AND ETHNICITY

v

The University of Wisconsin System
Institute on Race and Ethnicity
P. O. Box 413, Milwaukee, WI 53201

International Standard Book Number ISBN 0-942672-10-0 (cloth)
International Standard Book Number ISBN 0-942672-11-9 (paper)
Library of Congress Catalog Card Number: 87-50468

[I]f two men, each ignorant of the other's language, meet, and are not compelled to pass, but, on the contrary, to remain in company, dumb animals, though of different species, would more easily hold intercourse than they, human beings though they be.

Saint Augustine
The City of God, XIX, 7

PREFACE

One need not be a prophet nor even a demographer to foresee that as the United States approaches the twenty-first century, the percentage of its people who are members of ethnic or racial minority groups, and the number of those whose first language is other than English, will continue to increase. That much is certain. What is far from certain, though, is how well this nation will react and adapt to these changes. Addressing these issues, especially the one regarding language diversity, is the raison d'être of this volume.

No single characteristic in the United States, except for skin color, serves to distinguish individuals and groups as being "different" as does language. When we hear others speak a language different than our own, and this is especially so in the United States for English monolinguals, a kind of uneasiness, in the extreme case a paranoia, immediately arises. What language is that? What are they saying? Why are they laughing? Are they talking about me/us? Why don't they speak English (or go back to where they came from)? Questions of this sort race through our minds as we struggle with ourselves either to tune in or ignore the conversation. Despite official pronouncements that this nation makes regarding the diversity and pluralism that have made us great, many of us as individuals, and not just members of the white majority, react defensively and even negatively to strangers and their strange languages within our midst. This is true even for many of us who, *intellectually*, accept language diversity and pluralism as a plus— it is especially so for the great many who do not, or at least are not sure.

Why is this so? The answer is—pure and simple—ignorance. Not, of course, ignorance in its pejorative sense, meaning a lack of intelligence, but the kind of ignorance that denotes a lack of knowledge and information. We tend to fear the unknown and, unfortunately, the majority of us, our race and/or ethnicity notwithstanding, are inclined to fear people who are culturally (and *linguistically*) different than ourselves. This type of ignorance only can be overcome by education and exposure to others as equals, and the chapters in this volume both implicitly and explicitly make this plea, while pointing toward means how this can, through the use of language, be accomplished.

For too long the United States publicly has trumpeted heterogeneity, diversity, and pluralism, while it privately has danced to the tune of homogeneity, assimilation, and Anglo-Saxon conformity. To achieve what this nation espouses to be, we must all strive to divorce the connection in our minds between cultural assimilation (e.g., English monolingualism) and political loyalty. Just as the eyes are the window to our soul, so too can language be the window to other cultures. When our windows are open and knowledge, like the wind, can flow freely, our social environment will be cleansed of fear and suspicion. To spread knowledge of *all* cultures *to* all, rather than to demand knowledge of only *one* culture *from* all, surely should be our goal.

Those readers who are familiar with the previous five volumes in the *Ethnicity and Public Policy* series might have already noticed a significant change. Whereas the preceding volumes were published under the rubric of the University of Wisconsin System American Ethnic Studies Coordinating Committee (AESCC), you will note that this volume, *Ethnicity and Language*, is published under that of the University of Wisconsin System Institute on Race and Ethnicity. The University of Wisconsin System Board of Regents has recently combined the AESCC and the former Systemwide Center for the Study of Minorities and the Disadvantaged to form the new Institute, and this action is more than a mere change in nomenclature. The creation of the Institute on Race and Ethnicity signifies an expanded effort on the part of the University of Wisconsin System to pursue scholarly inquiry, both nationally and internationally, on the issues of race and ethnicity, and as such all involved are enthusiastic about pursuing this mission. As we do so, you can be sure that the *Ethnicity and Public Policy* series will continue to be a significant part of our efforts.

Because of the above change, the list of people to thank this year is a lengthy one. We trust that our readers will bear with us, though, for none of the individuals are undeserving. Beginning with the book itself, the individuals are primarily familiar ones. Sharon Gutowski again has been the quintessential organizer in piecing together the colloquium, and Joanne Brown continues to juggle masterfully her law career with her substantial copy editing abilities. Ellen Baugher has played a key role in bringing the chapters to a camera-ready state, and neither can we forget Cathy Mae Nelson in this capacity. The varied skills of Claire Parker have been vitally important to the completion of this book, and her role in marketing and sales also cannot go unmentioned. Linda Jallings, with a pinch hitting performance by Gary Polzen, has been, as always, our source of guidance through the labyrinths of production and printing.

Turning our attention to the creation of the University of Wisconsin System Institute on Race and Ethnicity, we have first to thank the members of the Board of Regents, President Kenneth Shaw, Executive Vice President Katharine Lyall, and Vice President Eugene Trani, who collectively possessed the vision to launch this venture. Associate Vice Presidents Vernon Lattin and Dallas Peterson have been critical to the Institute's inauguration, and the roles of Urban Corridor Consortium Director William Murin, its former director, W. Werner Prange, AESCC members Peter Kellogg, William Leffin, Marvin Dawkins, and Susan Takata, and the members of the UW System American Ethnic Studies Advisory Committee cannot go unheralded. On the University of Wisconsin-Milwaukee campus, where the Institute is housed, we look forward to the continued support of Chancellor Clifford Smith, Vice Chancellor John Schroeder, and Dean George Keulks and Associate Dean Ronald Hedlund of the Graduate School. Without the involvement and counsel of all these individuals and others, past, present, and future, the *Ethnicity and Public Policy* series and the Institute on Race and Ethnicity would surely flounder.

Thomas V. Tonnesen

University of Wisconsin-Milwaukee

CONTENTS

INTRODUCTION

Richard Ruiz

University of Arizona

Language and Society

Language both unifies and separates, at once includes and excludes. This is in the very nature of language, as well as in the ways language is used. Language is inseparable from community, even in its most individuated forms: "private languages," to the extent we accept such a combination of terms, still involve community—the "I" and the "me." Community shares with language (one could even say that language serves community by reinforcing) this simultaneous inclusion/exclusion function: however wide we may consider our community circle to be, it is still the marker that distinguishes "us" from "them." This is noted by the great Spanish philosopher Ortega, who reminds us that the pronoun *nosotros* in Spanish, commonly translated "we" in English, is literally "we-others."[1] To the extent that a particular language is intimately related to a particular community, it serves to define the members of the group, at the same time that it marks others as outsiders.

Illustrations of this quality of language are numerous; we shall cite only a few. In ancient Palestine, when the Gileadites wanted to identify their fraternal enemies, the Ephraimites, they asked any suspect to say "shibboleth." They killed anyone who slurred over the initial /sh/, since this was a distinguishing feature of Ephraimite dialect.[2] In Thai Buddhist exorcism rituals, the monk will inquire of the patient about the illness in the native vernacular, but the illness itself is always addressed in a "demon language" unknown to the patient. This sort of language behavior fixes the distinction between patient and healer, and thus makes therapy possible.[3] Chicanos of the southwestern United States, even those who are English monolinguals, will occasionally interject a Spanish word into their speech (e.g. tag questions, such as *ves?* or *verdad?*) when conversing with other Chicanos, but never when speaking to Anglos. In this case, language, even when minimally shared, points to a common basis for identification.[4]

These cases illustrate a particular quality in the nature of language: those who share the language (i.e., those who understand) are included in the relationship I have called "community," and those who do not are excluded. Short of the creation of a universal language, or the spread of a universal *lingua franca*, this situation is unavoidable. Just as important, and just as interesting, as the issue of the nature of language, however, is the matter of how language is used to create particular kinds of communities or societies. How does language contribute to the building of nationhood? What is the role of language in intergroup relations? How do linguistic considerations enter into the affirmation or denial of civil and political rights? What is the role of language in the creation of equal educational opportunity? Although the nature of language is not irrelevant to the answers one might give to these questions, more to the point would be a consideration of the uses to which language is put.

This is a major underlying theme of this volume. It is not language, but language and society (or, more accurately, language-and-society) which occupies the attention of the authors. The sole exception to this contention might be Kai Nielsen's chapter on undistorted discourse. His is a philosophical treatment of an essentially political question: Can we through our language and culture come to a self-definition which is oriented to the universally-human, or must local attachments to particular languages and ethnicities be surrendered in the interests of the development of a national or international polity? Does, in other words, the putative need for self-identification (the "sense that we are a *we*") negate the possibility that we might become "citizens of the world"? His answer will be taken up presently; for the moment it is important to see that these questions are not so much about language as about the interrelation of language and society.

It is perhaps easier to see this concern in the other chapters. Interestingly, all of the other writers give central importance to Nielsen's main topic—self-definition. And like Nielsen, they understand that self-definitions are matters which go far beyond linguistic considerations. Lambert and Taylor begin their essay by suggesting that people in the United States demonstrate a persistent preoccupation with self-definition—with determining what is and is not "American." It is a question which has confronted newcomers to the United States as well. It is a question the answer to which is conceptually prior to any movement toward or program of assimilation: What is one assimilating into? We have assumed that there is a consensus which has developed around the question of what is and is not American, and so we have imposed on the newcomers the ideal of Anglo-conformity. Lambert and Taylor present evidence that such a consensus, if it ever existed, has changed significantly. They see an acceptance of ethnicity and of bilingualism, at least within the immigrant communities themselves. Two factors may account for this change. First, the immigrant may have a more realistic picture of American society now than in the past (they "come with fewer stars in their eyes"). The attractiveness of this society, which some have suggested as a powerful motive for discarding "old world" attachments such as language, religion, and ethnicity,[5] may no longer be irresistible. Second, successive waves of immigration and differential birth rates have changed significantly the demographics of American society. We are coming upon an era, perhaps we have already reached it, when racial/ethnic minority groups will constitute a numerical majority in the United States. Americans, Lambert and Taylor suggest, are becoming more ethnic. As they state, "The hard-line Anglo-Saxons who are prone to worry about all this may soon become too few in number to be worried about."

But can the mere fact of demographic change itself be sufficient to alter self-definitions in American society? This point is take up by Sauling Wong and Shirley Williams in two chapters which, at least on this issue, serve as a counterpoint to Lambert and Taylor. Wong shows how the groups which are the focus of her study, Chinese, Filipinos, Koreans, Vietnamese, Cambodians, and others have very different histories and characteristics and perhaps should be treated separately. But these groups are generally denied the authority of self-definition in this society; they are therefore lumped together as "Asians" or, more recently, "Asian and Pacific Americans." This kind of lumping has a long history: the Chinese Exclusion Act of 1882 included all "orientals"; the Chinese Bookkeeping case of 1921 was about Filipinos; before that, the "yellow peril" included Japanese and Chinese explicitly, but other groups as well. These cases and many others show that Asians have always been defined by others; this situation persists up to now, as Wong observes.

Williams makes a similar point about Black English. Whether or not a linguist is in favor of the continued use of Black English, or of its teaching and learning, the debate has until very recently been conducted almost exclusively outside the black community. Judging from the number of studies of Black English, one might conclude with justification that it is the most thoroughly researched of all the varieties of English. The weight of the scholarly evidence is that there is no linguistic reason to consider Black English anything less than a rule-governed system of communication—a language. Yet, as Williams notes, it is still the only major variety of English consistently referred to as a "dialect." While there is no negative connotation attached to this term from a linguistic point of view, its social meaning stains Black English with a negative marker. Will the growth of the black, Asian, and other minority communities eventually change these negative attitudes, and allow for the positive self-definition of these communities, as Lambert and Taylor seem to imply? One can only hope that this will happen. Aside from that presented by Lambert and Taylor, there is little evidence that would encourage such a hope. Even in "model" programs which seem to encourage multiculturalism and ethnic and linguistic diversity, such as some in Canada, the reality may be something less than the image:

> The French to be taught in Quebec schools is the "good" French, that is, standard Québecois French, which is very close to the fiction called standard international French, itself quite similar to the educated middle class French spoken in France; local peasant dialects or working class dialects such as the Montreal "joual" are not given any prestige.[6]

This state of affairs is due to the fact that social evaluations of language have little to do with the languages themselves. Instead, they have to do with the social, economic, and political power of the communities to which they are attached. This power may be enhanced by numerical strength, but it is rarely caused by it.

Frank Grittner and Ricardo Fernandez also take up the matter of definitions, and in an indirect way get at the issue of self-definition as well. Grittner's topic is foreign language education. He suggests that part of the appeal of the study of Latin in public schools was that it is an "academically respectable and ethnically neutral" language. With the emergence of modern languages as a course of study, the criterion of ethnic neutrality remained central. This implied that the study of a second language for academic purposes gained primacy over the study of one's own language in school, the purpose of which presumably was the strengthening of ethnic heritage. Even recent legislation on bilingual-bicultural education, such as that enacted in Wisconsin, stipulates that such programs are for the purpose of teaching English, not maintaining ethnic mother tongues, and makes scant mention of the cultural component of the curriculum.

Fernandez notes these same concerns in his analysis of the federal Bilingual Education Act. There, as in the state legislation, the nature and purpose of the programs have been determined largely by those outside the communities which are to be served. How else can one explain the indifference to mother tongue loss and the concern for rapid transition into a school system that has served the targeted groups so badly? The message of this legislation is that foreign languages are good as long as they are devoid of ethnic encumbrances, and ethnic languages are acceptable only to the extent that they allow a rapid transition to English. The impact of these messages on self-esteem and efforts at self-definition within ethnic communities must be considerable.

Donald Larmouth's chapter treats the matter of self-definition by expanding Lambert and Taylor's question, What is "American"?, into a more general consideration, What is a "nation"? Borrowing some of his analysis from Joshua Fishman, he highlights three factors in nationalism: historicity, autonomy, and authenticity. Language serves to strengthen these factors when it enjoys a high social status. The international examples he presents demonstrate an important proposition: concern for the status of a language in society is almost always a concern for nation-building. Whether an indigenous or outside language is chosen as the official language, whether a language is declared acceptable for school use, whether a language is promoted through funding its study or encouraging its use in the media ultimately are matters not of language, but of society. Many "emerging" or "developing" nations have had to decide how language decisions will lend authenticity to the new society by, for example, creating access to a high technology or aligning it with a glorious tradition. The United States, not a new society, has a comparatively secure sense of national identity. Its language enjoys high status internationally and virtual hegemony domestically. Still, it is occasionally concerned with such issues as language status. Those are most often periods of perceived threat to the nation—threat of internal conflict or of external enemies. The 1980s have been such a period, although the source of the perceived threat is not as clear as in other times. Perhaps an administration obsessed with promulgating anti-communist fervor has increased our sense of insecurity. Perhaps the recent public debates on the magnitude of illegal immigration, legislative measures aimed at "controlling our borders," and media reports on the flow of "economic refugees" from Mexico and Central America have created anxieties about what this nation is becoming. This, no doubt, is what is behind much of the support for a Constitutional amendment declaring English the official language in the United States: there exists a threat to the nation *from the inside*. It is not so much aliens who concern us, but *aliens among us*—people, as Lambert and Taylor describe them, who are in the United States, but whose hearts are elsewhere. This is the threat of uncontrolled immigration;

but it is also the threat of the separate and self-sustaining ethnic community that survives through a series of concessions and accommodations by the larger society—bilingual education, bilingual voting materials, bilingual health services, and more. How can the nation survive such separtism? The response to initiatives that would make English official demonstrates the extent to which many in the United States are convinced of the threat to the nation and are prepared to undertake new efforts at self-definition.

Language and Power

Nielsen's treatment of the notion of self-definition leaves unattended the issue of the power to self-define. Perhaps he is saying that the power and authority for self-definition inhere in the individual, that each person ultimately decides how he or she will be identified. But Wong and Williams in this volume, and countless others elsewhere, have demonstrated that some people apparently have their identities circumscribed for them by others; such an imposition entails not merely names—"Asians," "Indians," "Mexican-Americans," "Negroes," and others—but also a configuration of values and attitudes embodied in such adjectives as "shiftless," "lazy," "savage," and "inscrutable." The fact that some members of minority groups have set out explicitly to change in order to conform to the majority ideal lends credence to the possibility that they have accepted such a characterization of their ethnic selves. Cultural assimilation and linguistic assimilation become in those cases an effort at power sharing.

Indeed, language minority groups in the United States know very well the power differential between their languages and the language of the dominant society. It is for the purpose of gaining access to that power, principally, that they set out to learn English. But is it necessary, in the process, to lose their first language? What would incline anyone to answer this question in the affirmative? There is, even in relatively enlightened societies, a prevailing attitude that linguistic difference is sometimes, perhaps often, a strong contributing factor to the disadvantage and disenfranchisement of minority group members. In other words, the native language of the minority group member is a problem to be overcome on the road to social and economic mobility, rather than an asset which might help in the advance along that road. Consider this comment by the director of the Mother Tongue Project in England on why there is relatively little interest in research on bilingualism in that country:

LMP [the Linguistic Minorities Project] attributes this lack of research information to the international role of English, the inferior status of minority languages and their speakers, the dominant view of minorities as problems, and the historical development of policies on immigration which viewed the acquisition of English by non-native speakers to be hindered rather than helped by supporting the first language.[7]

Sau-ling Wong argues that much of the public policy in the United States which is directed at minority groups has developed out of such a "problem orientation." This accounts for the predominance of compensatory education programs for minority group members, as well as for their overrepresentation in special education classrooms. It also explains why the dominant model for bilingual education—transitional bilingual education—gives no attention to the development of mother tongue skills. This model perpetuates "subtractive" as opposed to "additive" bilingualism, in the words of Lambert and Taylor: it merely replaces the mother tongue with English, instead of developing advanced proficiency in both the mother tongue and English. This orientation is played out so that it extends even to the labels we use for those who participate in bilingual education. In the Wisconsin state law on bilingual-bicultural education, for example, students in these programs are referred to not as "bilingual," but as "limited-English proficient." But *everyone else* whose role is defined in the statute, including teachers, aides, counselors, and counselor's aides, are call "bilingual." This is curious, since certification as a bilingual teacher does not guarantee proficiency, yet the law confers status on the teacher because of previous training, while it marks the child negatively because of previous and intimate experience with a non-English language. It is this sort of irony that causes Fishman to note the "totally unnatural, shameful, and, indeed, slanderous relationship between bilingual education and poverty or other social dislocation which is still *required* by much of the Bilingual Education legislation in the United States."[8]

Ricardo Fernandez's chapter chronicles much of this legislation, as well as many of the major court decisions on bilingual education. He also notes the heavy transitional bias of federal bilingual education policy. In addition, while the courts have not always prescribed specific remedies for the education of language minority groups, they have sometimes contributed to the problem orientation of the policymakers and the general public. Note the language in the *Castaneda* decision, in which the court contended that educational agencies have "an obligation to overcome the direct obstacle to learning which the language barrier itself imposes."[9] Consider, also, that the premier decision on bilingual education in the United States, *Lau* v. *Nichols*, reinforced in the public mind the conceptualization of bilingual education as a compensatory program designed to teach English to students with limitations:

> [T]he Supreme Court did nothing to counter the prevailing concept of bilingual education, a concept already embodied in federal and state law, as a concept of remedial provision for linguistically handicapped children. The image of bilingual education as a remedy rather than an opportunity was reinforced by the Court.[10]

Fernandez acknowledges the political compromises that were necessary to get any sort of bilingual education policy. The latest attacks on the effectiveness of bilingual education have created an atmosphere conducive to even more compromise, away from even transitional bilingual education and increasingly toward English-only approaches. What will be the response of the minority communities to such proposals? It may be time, as Wong, Lambert and Taylor, and Fernandez suggest, to mount a frontal attack on the old problem orientation. A first step might be to acknowledge that transitional bilingual education has significant problems, but that these problems derive not from the fact that it is bilingual, but from the fact that it is not bilingual enough. Put differently, the failings of transitional bilingual education are accounted for by the fact that it represents an implicit acceptance of the contention that the child's first language and ethnic culture are problems to be overcome, rather than assets to be developed. What is needed is another kind of program representing a different orientation. Lambert and Taylor would say that the task is one of "transforming subtractive forms of bilingualism into additive ones"; Wong would agree, but put it slightly differently: in the development of public policy, the major need is to proceed from a resource orientation rather than a problem orientation.

But how is such an orientation to be articulated? What will be its major arguments? Fernandez gives a good starting point. He asks us to recall the 1979 report of the President's Commission on Foreign Language and International Studies, which highlighted the major problems the United States encounters in international trade, foreign affairs, and cross-national communication because of our general ineptitude in foreign languages. Important political figures such as Senator Paul Simon and Representative Leon Panetta have also taken an interest in this subject. Why not try to develop a coalition of interest with professional foreign language organizations and educators to integrate bilingual education into discussions of a need for foreign language competence? This would serve the interest of both groups, and need not hurt either. It would also help to round out the resource orientation which, as Wong says in her chapter, is now biased in favor of resource development (the acquisition of foreign language competence) and against resource conservation (the maintenance of non-English mother tongues).

Such an approach has its problems; two will be mentioned. First, there is a tradition of treating foreign languages and ethnic languages differently in this country, as Grittner points out in his chapter. The study of a foreign language is seen as academically respectable in large part because it is ethnically and politically neutral; the study of one's own ethnic language, so the argument goes, leads to ethnic separatism and political conflict. The one is seen as a valuable academic exercise, the other a potentially dangerous act of political confrontation that could be a hindrance to academic achievement, besides. One only need be reminded of Secretary of Education William Bennett's many speeches against bilingual education, and of his appointment of anti-bilingual education foreign language specialists to the National Advisory Council on Bilingual Education, to understand how those deeply committed to foreign language education can also be enemies of bilingual education.

Second, one needs to understand that many people are against bilingual education not because they know anything about it, but merely because they are against bilingual education: it is sometimes a question of ideology pure and simple. No amount of research or linkage with positive results will convince them otherwise. Fernandez reminds us of this when he says that the debate about bilingual education will continue because "it is based on deeply held values and attitudes by opponents and advocates which transcend research evidence and established policy." One should not expect widespread acceptance of bilingual education merely because one can now make new arguments for its value. Perhaps the best case showing the irrelevance of positive research to social evaluations of a linguistic phenomenon is that of Black English. After decades of research demonstrating that Black English is indeed a language, the most that can honestly be said is that there is reluctant acceptance of its use as a transition to Standard English literacy, and isolated affirmations of the right of black students and communities to use and foster it. Very few would venture to suggest that it is an asset to the black child and/or to the nation.

Still, the resource development approach holds promise for the start of a reorientation. The programs that would result from seeing language communities as resources would likely approximate those that Lambert and Taylor and their Canadian colleagues have developed. These include the white English-speaking child, the language minority child, and the black child. Pedagogically, these "multi-group" programs would provide language opportunities not possible in other arrangements. More important, they would give a real chance to the provision of equal educational opportunity. This is also important politically, as Lambert and Taylor and Fernandez all observe. What is important, after all, is to provide a good education, not merely a particular kind of language experience. This is consistent, as well, with the suggestions Wong gives for possible programmatic alternatives. In arrangements that accommodate whole communities as equal participants, the social conflicts that result from unequal distribution of resources, along with the concomitant threat of litigation, are transcended. What is more, they serve as a prototype for schools who want to empower students and communities rather than incapacitate them.

Language and Politics

Much of what has been said up to now concerns the political implications of the relationship of language and society. Certainly the questions of the differential evaluations of language and the association of language with social power involve political considerations. In addition, Frank Grittner's analysis of the development of foreign language study in the United States presents a powerful lesson in the connection of language and politics. In this section, the more explicit connections between language and politics as presented by several of the contributors to this volume, most obviously Fernandez and Larmouth, will be discussed.

Both pay significant attention to the topic of language rights, conceived of quite literally as guarantees given or denied by authoritative decrees. Fernandez addresses the issue in two contexts: entitlements conveyed by judicial and legislative authorities, and constitutional amendments prescribing (and proscribing) certain kinds of language behavior. Larmouth takes up the topic in the context of movements toward language officialization, internationally and within the United States.

Their discussion converges in the analysis of English Language Amendments (ELA) in the United States. In November 1986, voters in California passed an ELA to their state constitution. The measure makes English the official language of the state. While other states have enacted similar legislation, California's is important for several reasons. First, it is aimed at substantive reforms in key areas of public policy, and creates mechanisms for implementation of the new policy.

In other states such as Indiana, designation of an official language has been more symbolic than substantive—similar to the adoption of a state bird or flower. There it has changed little in the everyday work of the state government or in the implementation of public policy, and it does not appear to be aimed at restricting language behavior in any significant way. In California, on the other hand, the new amendment is designed to eliminate such things as bilingual voting materials and many programs of non-English language instruction in the public schools. Furthermore, it gives any citizen the right to bring legal action to prevent violations of the new policy. Second, the amendment was passed by an overwhelming majority of the voters, including a substantial percentage of Hispanics. As Fernandez indicates, this shows the political and economic strength of U.S. English, the lobbying group most closely identified with the ELA movement. The triumph in California has invigorated U.S. English and other similar groups in their efforts in other states. Third, passage of such an amendment to the constitution of the largest state serves to break down the resistance to amending the federal Constitution in a similar fashion. There is little doubt that a Constitutional amendment is the ultimate goal of U.S. English.

Larmouth's international perspective on this issue is instructive. His principal question is the title of his chapter: Does linguistic heterogeneity erode national unity? His answer is, sometimes yes, sometimes no. Several factors combine to determine the effects of linguistic diversity on national unity—the size of the language minority communities, their integration into the economic life of the society, the status of their languages. But one crucial factor appears to be the nature of language rights embodied in statements of language officialization. Generally, oppressive and restrictive language policies create conflict, while tolerant and supportive policies are conducive to harmony. Larmouth brings this analysis to bear on the case of the United States. Movements for an ELA by groups like U.S. English are partly a reaction to the demands of ethnic groups for bilingual education and voting materials. U.S. English conceives of these demands as an affirmation of the right to cultural and social separation. Larmouth sees this reading as a distortion of the language minority group's position. He sees the desire for bilingual education, for example, as "mainly a demand for greater participation in the educational system and as a way to prevent further attrition of these languages, not as a strategy for gaining greater autonomy or to authenticate a separatist effort." Similarly, bilingual voting materials are a way of integrating into the political system, rather than an effort to remain separate from it.

The ultimate purpose of the ELA movement appears to be greater national unity through the promotion of a common language. This is most efficiently achieved, says U.S. English, through a federal amendment to the Constitution declaring English to be the official language of the nation. But such a law will almost surely be seen by non-English speakers as a restriction of their language behavior. There is a very real prospect that the unity and cohesiveness that is the explicit goal of the members of U.S. English may be undermined by the very measures they would have us take to effect it. If nation-building and the development of social and cultural unity are the goals, the international case studies presented by Larmouth clearly suggest that restrictive English language amendments are just what should be avoided.

Language and Pluralism

In discussing the chapters of this volume, a former colleague posed a haunting question: If we were to find that pluralism *is* a detriment to national unity, should we be willing to work against it? This volume addresses this question only implicitly; let me discuss what I have concluded is its essential answer. The dilemma that would have one choose between pluralism and unity is a conceptual phantom. How, in the real world, could one find out conclusively that pluralism is a threat to national unity? Where would be the irrefutable demonstration of this? One could point to cases—Quebec, Belgium, perhaps India—to support the existence of problems. But one could also point out as many cases and more where linguistic pluralism and national unity coexist. One could point to social conflict in our own society, conflict which seems to be fueled by language differences. But one could no doubt suggest other factors that are as likely the causes of such conflict. One could also respond, following Nielsen, that the question poses a phantom dilemma because there is no such thing as a homogeneous society. If national unity exists now, it must coexist with some level of pluralism.

The question can be answered for ourselves by understanding that it does not demand from us an empirical demonstration, but rather an existential commitment. We should return now to a question which was put off at the outset. It is Kai Nielsen's question: Can we retain such local attachments as ethnic identification and mother tongue and still become "citizens of the world"? His answer, and ours, must be "yes." I say "must be" because, as Nielsen says, it is not possible to live unless one lives as a particular human being, in a particular time and place. So, if universalism is an ideal to be striven for, it must accommodate itself to our particularism. How does such a striving take place? Perhaps it is by cultivating what Michael Novak calls the "pluralistic personality":

> The pluralistic personality has two strengths: (a) clarity and depth about its own roots and particularity; (b) openness to and interest in sources of strength beyond its own traditions. A system of education designed to nourish the pluralistic personality must itself comprehend the diversity of the moral roots of the American people. It should not attempt to develop a "common culture" that would represent a watering down of each participant culture, but rather a "common culture" that arises out of a shared, common knowledge of the analogies and differences between moral traditions.[11]

One need not be a radical Whorfian to understand how language pluralism—especially as to a language which is intimately tied to an ethnic community—can contribute immeasurably to the sort of common culture that Novak describes. It is clear that the contributors to this volume have themselves made the existential commitment to advance the conditions which promote the pluralistic personality. One can only hope that their efforts help nurture that same commitment in those who read their words.

NOTES

[1]Jose Ortega y Gasset, *Man and People*, trans. Willard R. Trask (New York: W. W. Norton and Company, 1957), pp. 110-111.

[2]Judges 12:6, NIV.

[3]S. J. Tambiah, "The Magical Power of Words," *Man* 3:2 (June 1968):175-208.

[4]George C. Barker, "Social Functions of Language in a Mexican-American Community," in Eduardo Hernandez-Chavez, Andrew D. Cohen, and Anthony F. Beltramo, eds., *El Lenguaje de los Chicanos: Regional and Social Characteristics of Language Used by Mexican Americans* (Arlington, VA: Center for Applied Linguistics, 1975), p. 177.

[5]Joshua A. Fishman, "The Historical and Social Contexts of an Inquiry into Language Maintenance Efforts," in Joshua A. Fishman, et al., *Language Loyalty in the United States: The Maintenance and Perpetuation of Non-English Mother Tongues by American Ethnic and Religious Groups* (The Hague: Mouton, 1966), pp. 21-33.

[6]Michel Laferrière, "Languages, Ideologies, and Multicultural Education in Canada: Some Historical and Sociological Perspectives," in Ronald J.

Samuda, John W. Berry, and Michel Laferrière, eds., *Multiculturalism in Canada: Social and Educational Perspectives* (Toronto: Allyn and Bacon, Inc., 1984), p. 181.

[7]Paula Tansley, *Community Languages in Primary Education* (Philadelphia: NFER-NELSON, 1986), p. 12.

[8]Joshua A. Fishman, *Bilingual Education in International Sociological Perspective* (Rowley, MA: Newbury House, 1976), p. x.

[9]*Castaneda* v. *Pickard*, 648 F.2d 989 (5th Cir. 1981).

[10]Barry MacDonald, Clem Adelman, Saville Kushner, and Rob Walker, eds., *Bread and Dreams: A Case Study of Bilingual Schooling in the U.S.A.* (Norwich, U.K.: Center for Applied Research Education, F. Crowe and Sons, Ltd., 1982), p. 249.

[11]Michael Novak, "Conclusion: Social Trust," in *Parents, Teachers, and Children* (San Francisco: Institute for Contemporary Studies, 1977), p. 276.

UNDISTORTED DISCOURSE, ETHNICITY, AND THE PROBLEM OF SELF-DEFINITION

Kai Nielsen

University of Calgary

I

Self-definition in any society must be difficult, but in complex societies and particularly in ones with such layered and involuted ethnic mixes as present-day North American societies, it must be extraordinarily difficult. We want to know who we are, who we were, and who we might become. Indeed, we not only want the right to say "we," we want to have some coherent understanding of what this means. We North Americans may, because of our life conditions, feel this more—speaking now in the anthropological present—than do the Kaluli of the southern highlands of Papua New Guinea, though even here we need to be careful about the assumptions we make about Stone Age people. That such caution is in order can be seen from a reading of Herbert Read's sensitive and lyrical account of the Susuroka of the central highlands of New Guinea, where, as Read makes plain, the Susuroka indeed have problems of self-definition, problems admittedly exacerbated by the fact that the Susuroka he wrote about were living through a period of dramatic and traumatic transition.[1]

Perhaps all human beings feel this need for self-definition, though, of course, unless we are to make some kind of intellectualist fallacy, we should recognize that often it is frightfully inarticulate. But articulate or inarticulate, the quest for self-definition is intimately bound up with culture, and culture and language are like hand and glove. Self-definition involves cultural identification. But here we get something which deeply skews us from the very start. Language acquisition plainly has its biological parameters, still, from tribe to tribe there are wide differences in how the acquisition of language takes place and in how children are molded in different societies, so that they are able to display and understand behavior appropriate to various social situations. There are in some instances radical differences between cultures here.

The way language is instilled in children varies greatly with the different ways their caregivers respond to them in different cultures. Some ethnographic approaches to the development of language have made a powerful case for this.[2]

We could be as innatist as Noam Chomsky is about language acquisition and still recognize that the adult world, with all its cultural skewing, remains a very vital source of linguistic knowledge for the child. The innatist position makes the important point that the verbal environment of the adult is not a sufficient source for a child inductively to learn a language. Neither can we account for language acquisition behavioristically, á la B. F. Skinner. But this does not, of course, eliminate the need for the adult linguistic environment in coming to understand a language and, with that, in being socialized into a particular culture and, in complex cultures, in being socialized as well into a particular subculture with its distinctive ways of viewing the world. And there the socialization and cultural skewing cut very deep indeed. It goes right down to the very different ways in which linguistic competence is attained in different cultures.[3] Indeed, we gain this as a kind of knowledge by *wont*. But just as we native speakers of various languages cannot, in the typical case, state the grammatical principles which actually guide our speech, so we do not, to put it minimally, find it easy to isolate and make explicit these cultural principles. So we all have deeply ingrained a cultural identity by which the parameters of our self-definition are set.

A segment (a subculture, if you will) of the intelligentsia in Western culture has a belief, inherited from the Enlightenment but held firmly by Karl Marx and the Marxist tradition generally, and by liberals such as John Dewey and Jürgen Habermas as well, that notwithstanding cultural and subcultural identities, the depth of our distinctive and particular socialization, and the closeness of the tie between socialization and language acquisition, we need not suffer from a conceptual imprisonment in which there are just these different and not infrequently incommensurable belief systems like cultural monads which so differently structure our understandings of ourselves (our self-definition). While there may be some brute facts and simple truths, much of our world is culturally mediated such that we do not have a common world or an Archimedian point in virtue of which we could gain one.[4] The counter-Enlightenment belief is that we have our local attachments and that they simultaneously fetter us and define us in ways that are inescapable: They are in part given in our very language and thought structures with their distinctive and culturally differentiated categories and ways of seeing the world.

Are we so conceptually imprisoned? Is this even the right way—the right metaphor—for viewing our local attachments or ethnic identities? Is the Enlightenment belief that human emancipation and a truly adequate self-definition are to be achieved only by setting aside, or at least by transcending, such local attachments and ethnic identities, the correct way of viewing things? Or should we, to make sense of our lives and to feel at home in the world, maintain those local attachments and ethnic or subcultural identities? Or may it be the case that these particular attachments cannot but blinker us and that enlightenment and emancipation, if they are to be thorough, require that we set aside such things and become citizens of the world in which the object of our identification and the object of our deep loyalties become humankind rather than just or principally those particular kinds of people with whom we come of age? For many who have read their Herder and studied social anthropology, this Enlightenment conception will seem utterly naive, and to some in effect an unfortunate and perhaps even a dangerously persuasive definition of "emancipation" and "enlightenment" as well, and as something that in reality makes impossible anything like an even remotely adequate self-definition. These are big, hedgehoggish questions, blending, in what could be a confusing way, descriptive, explanatory, and normative considerations. We need to make a start at sorting this out a bit.

II

Where we have, as we all have, local attachments, we have various culturally-defined legitimating beliefs. To have a set or a cluster of legitimating beliefs is to have a set or a cluster of attitudes and norms which constitutes a world picture. This collection not only interprets our experience but commends as legitimate, or at least as necessary and accepted, a network of social institutions and practices. If we could adequately characterize a set of legitimating beliefs which would have to be accepted by any rational person in what Jürgen Habermas calls an ideal speech situation, then we would have the grounds for the vindication of the Enlightenment's ideal of emancipation. If it were ever to take place, it would be an emancipation that would be without mystification and thus, at last in the long annals of history, be a genuine emancipation.

Perhaps we can show what a self-definition would look like that was not fettered by local attachments and ideological discourse. What Habermas seeks to do is to define a set of unique circumstances which would have to obtain for communication and speech (discourse generally) to be undistorted. He is not, of course, claiming that these conditions do obtain or perhaps even could obtain, but he is characterizing what it would be like for there to be ideologically undistorted discourse. For legitimating beliefs to be rational, morally-justified legitimating beliefs—to be a part of undistorted discourse—they would (a) have to be formed in conditions of absolutely free and unlimited critical discussion, and (b) be formed by participants who were capable, vis-à-vis the institutions and social practices being set up, of recognizing that they were freely consenting to the establishment of these institutions and practices under conditions in which the only constraints on their consent were those that came from the distinctive force of the better argument.

Habermas, rather pedantically and in considerable detail, spells out this idea in a theory of speech-acts. But, as Quentin Skinner rightly observes, the core of the proposal can be put quite simply and untechnically: ". . . [I]f potentially repressive institutions are rightly to be regarded as legitimate, it must be possible to imagine their creation under conditions of freedom and equality and their acceptance by the unforced consent of all those subsequently liable to be affected by their behaviour."[6]

Our actual beliefs, as Habermas is perfectly aware, including our various local attachments and ethnic loyalties, were not at all formed this way. Moreover, they could not be so formed. We do not discuss things or make our decisions in anything that even approximates the ideal speech situation. Indeed, ideological distortion is rife throughout. If, counterfactually, our beliefs were formed under such ideal speech conditions, we would find our present beliefs, beliefs not so formed, reflectively unacceptable. It is essential to the very idea of what it is to be moral that human beings be capable of arriving at reasons for action that consider impersonally what actions are most likely to achieve the greatest good, and where the interests of everyone count equally.[7] No one, from the moral point of view, can simply be ignored or not given an initially equal position; no one simply because of race, sex, class, caste, or ethnic identity can be discounted. The very nature of what moral discourse has become in Western societies does not allow this as even a conceptual possibility. Even severe antiegalitarians such as Robert Nozick, Antony Flew and Robert Nisbet will not sanction *moral* inequality. From the moral point of view, the life of every human being counts equally, though, of course, what exactly this comes to in practice will be given different readings by different people with different conceptions of what the world is like and what the world can be. If our discourse is to conform to the canons of an ideal speech situation, then we as moral agents need not only be capable of so reasoning but *must* reason in this way. Our decisions must be such that we will be willing to have them assessed ultimately from an external point of view, in which we will appear just as one person among others. If people actually come to reason in this way, we will have escaped the distorting effects of ideology and the conceptual imprisonment that in turn lead to the moral impoverishment of ethnocentrism which results from making our self-definitions in purely ethnic terms, rather than in universal terms as members of the family of humankind (what once was called in unwittingly sexist terms, "the family of man"). Here what matters is not that you are Albanian or American, Franco-Manitoban or Boston Irish or Boston Brahmin, but that you are a human being—a member of the human race in which, for people with those universalistic attitudes, nothing human is foreign. This is the liberating claim of the Enlightenment, and it gets a new and distinct articulation in the work of Jürgen Habermas and again, in a somewhat different idiom and in a different conceptual framework, by such progressive liberal philosophers in the Anglo-American analytic tradition as John Rawls and Thomas Nagel.[8]

But are things as clear-cut as that? The question is whether we, in seeking a humanly adequate self-definition in the tradition of the Enlightenment, can set aside local attachments or indeed even rightly see them merely as local attachments. Let us try to get something of a purchase on this.

III

It is here that relativism, to put it tendentiously, again raises its ugly head. Consider again the question of culture, socialization, and language acquisition. Consider, that is, the way we see the world, the way we react to our conceptions of ourselves and others, the way we come to possess the very categories of understanding and appreciation that we do. They are all deeply conditioned and structured by the culture, and even to a degree by the subculture, in which we find ourselves. The language, and with it the conceptual scheme we acquire and the way we acquire it, differs radically over cultural space and historical time. As Quentin Skinner taxes Habermas: How is it "possible limited as we are by our local concepts and canons of evidence to encompass such a transcendent entity as the truth about the good society itself?"[9] Habermas's answer is that we gain access to such truths in the ideal speech situation. We can know these putative truths are true, and thus have universal validity, by virtue of the fact that the ideal speech situation must free itself from all cultural particularities and local assumptions in order to be labeled such.

Is this transcendental turn at all possible even as a heuristic ideal? Can we give any substantive content to it, or is it as empty as Kant's categorial imperative? Consider where the medieval people portrayed, say, in the *Laxdaela Saga* start, and by contrast where a contemporary *New York Times*-reading or *Globe and Mail*-reading New York or Toronto professional starts. Is it at all plausible to believe that, even if both groups were placed in an ideal speech situation and came to share the same full information and with that reflected fully on their culturally-created desires, they would then come to share the same, or even a very similar, conception of the good or make the same, or even very similar, moral judgements? If we start with a peasant from the highlands of Bolivia and a contemporary resident of Zurich or Stockholm, are we likely, even under ideal speech conditions, to get such a consensus about the right and the good and about how one is to live one's life? Two generally sympathetic critics of Habermas, Raymond Geuss and Quentin Skinner, think Habermas is being thoroughly unrealistic here.[10] As Skinner puts it, echoing Geuss:

> Does Habermas really mean that everyone in the ideal speech situation would arrive at exactly the same moral as well as cognitive judgements? Does he mean to include "pre-dynastic Egyptians, ninth-century French serfs and early-twentieth-century Yanomano tribesmen" on exactly the same terms as each other and as ourselves? Is it really plausible to suppose that all of us would agree on what counts as coercion and what as true liberty? What possible grounds are there for such a belief? As Geuss rather tartly concludes, all that Habermas seems able to offer us at this crucial stage in his argument is "a transcendental deduction of a series of non-facts."[11]

Being skeptical here is understandable, so is even being patronizingly ironical. This is particularly true when we take to heart the cultural facts about language acquisition and socialization referred to earlier in this chapter. Still one is somewhat ambivalently inclined to conclude that this criticism moves too fast and too easily and does not sufficiently take into consideration the deliberately counterfactual nature of Habermas's ideal speech situation and the role it plays. He is asking us to suppose that we could get people of all this great cultural diversity into the ideal speech situation, where they had undistorted and full factual information about the world including, of course, the human world. They would in such a world know about the cultural pecularities of their personality formation, their own ideals of the self as well as those of others; they would know about how ideology functions and about other distorting factors. Habermas asks us to carry out a thought experiment and ask whether it is likely that culturally peculiar beliefs, beliefs that would appear arbitrary and groundless in the light of such knowledge, would wither away and be psychologically extinguished with such knowledge.

Habermas's Marxist critics rightly tax him with being, in a bad sense, utopian in not attending to the mechanics of how in our class-divided, ideologically-penetrated, and mystified societies we can get within even a country mile of a simulation of such conditions. We should contrast Habermas unfavorably here with Hans Magnus Enzensberger.[12] Habermas has given us a model without any of the *causal mechanisms*. Still the model has its uses. It is fair enough to say that the phenomenon of modernity, and with it more extensive contacts between peoples, has made our world increasingly more of a global village and, as Edward Westermarck has shown more generally—his ethical relativism to the contrary notwithstanding—there is, with an ever greater knowledge of one another and an acquaintance with each other, an expanding circle of ethical concern away from tribalism and nationalism and toward a more extensive consensus.[13] (The ferocious and barbaric nationalism emerging in the twentieth century is a reaction which runs against structurally modernizing tendencies, and it is not unreasonable to believe that it will not prevail.) Habermas makes an ideal extrapolation from that. Why is that extrapolation so totally unrealistic? If we could get in the conditions of an ideal speech situation, if those conditions were to prevail, we would, it is reasonable to expect, attain such a consensus. The idealization is in assuming that we could somehow place ourselves in such an ideal speech situation. However, if, counterfactually, we were in it, that we should get such a consensus is not so evidently unrealistic.

We sometimes use idealizations to good effect in physics and economics. Why not use them here? Moreover, if, like a perfect vacuum, it is a mere heuristic device, why is it not all the same a heuristic device to which, through struggle, hard thinking, and the development of the productive forces, we might eventually get approximations? No one can be in an ideal speech situation, but some situations among the empirically possible do approximate it more than others, and they are the better—the more emancipatory—situations and indeed come closer to the ideals of the Enlightenment.

Perhaps it would be the case, given the depth and the cultural peculiarity of early socialization, that people would continue, even when fully and accurately presented with the same factual account of the world, to react to this factual account differently. They would agree about the facts but continue, because of this quite different conditioning, to respond to the same set of facts quite differently even when perspicaciously displayed. There would, that is, be agreement in factual belief but disagreement in attitude. That is surely a logical possibility, but whether it is a factual probability is another thing. My Danish grandfather who fought in the war over the Kiel Canal thought Germans were pigs. It is very doubtful today that a tolerably informed contemporary Dane living adjacent to Flensburg would so respond or think that for even a moment. Certain attitudes are very difficult to sustain given an accurate, factual understanding of the world. Some contemporary Portuguese immigrants to Canada have said, resisting my challenge, that Spanish people are dirty and dishonest. This is on a par with my grandfather's judgements. There are all sorts of such irrational ethnic slurs among almost all peoples—perhaps all peoples—but it is very difficult for such stereotyping to survive in a situation where people get even a moderately accurate picture of the world.

One might respond that while in these obvious cases there will under favorable circumstances be such a psychological extinguishment, there are more subtle cases where the original socialization is so powerfully embedded that later factual information, even when dwelled upon reflectively and carefully, will make little difference. People socialized with very pervasive and strong bonds of kinship, like those in the Icelandic sagas or in many primitive societies, will react very differently than will statistically normal members of our society to the killing, even if inadvertent, of their cousin by people not their kin. If an individual, say a drunk driver, inadvertently killed someone's cousin, that person would not feel an obligation to kill the drunk driver, even if he or she could, much less to kill some of the drunk driver's kin where the drunk driver him/herself was not available. In the normal case the drunk driver's relatives would not be considered to have had anything to do with the incident, to be responsible, or to be obliged to pay compensation, much less deserving of death. Such thoughts would not even enter into the moral or intellectual horizon. The reaction of a tenth-century Icelander or present-day Tauadean of the Papuan Mountains, though, would be very different indeed.[14]

How can we be so confident that if they only knew what we know and if we could come to know what they know, then after a time, say enough to let the impact of that knowledge sink in, typical members of both peoples would come to have the same or very similar moral responses, and that we would achieve a consensus about how to live? Well, we do not know, but we do have the facts concerning a greater consensus that goes with modernity.

To this one might respond, not unreasonably, that modernity itself is a particular kind of culture. That is indeed so, but why is it that it so extensively wins out where belief systems clash? And is it not also true that people who are part of the culture of modernity have a firmer and more extensive factual knowledge than others and, generally speaking, a sounder methodology for fixing belief (to use Peirce's phrase) than do more primitive peoples, and does this not both explain and give a sound rationale for the repeated victories of modernity?

IV

Something has been said about the possiblilites of an Enlightenment style of emancipation. There is a counter-Enlightenment response that comes trippingly on the tongue. We should not, even if we could become such rootless creatures, be without the distinctive and very particular glories of our varied and often incommensurable traditions. What distinguishes us is at least as precious as that which unites us. Any genuine self-definition must as well be a cultural identification. We cannot be, and should not strive to be, universal men and women. What makes us something, what gives our lives meaning, are our distinctive cultural identities. If we lose them we lose ourselves.

This thesis of both the unavoidability and desirability of a culturally determinate conception of self-definition has been powerfully argued by G. A. Cohen.[15] This is surprising because it comes from an avowedly Marxist philosopher (albeit an analytical Marxist) whose Marxism, though highly critical, is more in the tradition of Marxist theory than Habermas's quasi-Marxism. (I am inclined to think of Habermas as far more a progressive liberal than a Marxist. But Habermas sees himself as, in some sense, a part of the Marxist tradition.)

In the context of raising questions about the adequacy of Marx's anthropology, historical materialism, and the compatibility of Marx's anthropology and historical materialism, Cohen makes some acute points about the centrality of cultural self-definition. We should explore that claim for its own sake and to determine (a) whether it undermines the Habermasian Enlightenment project and (b) whether it undermines historical materialism. The latter (perhaps surprisingly), as well as the former, are important for the argument here. If historical materialism, in the careful, rational reconstruction that we see in Cohen as well as in William Shaw and Allen Wood, provides a good explanation of epochal social change, then we can use that reconstructed historical materialism to plug the lacunae in Habermas's account of emancipation.[16] Habermas has given us a model of what human emancipation would look like, a model of what it would be like to be free of ideological entrapment. But, as we have seen, he gave us none of the mechanics for getting from our state of distorted communication to a state of undistorted communication. If there is a sound version of historical materialism, it would supply an account of those mechanisms. However, if local attachments and cultural self-identity have the centrality Cohen thinks they have, they may undermine that Enlightenment project at both ends: They would perhaps show the inadequacy of Habermas's model, or at least raise questions about it, and they would raise serious questions about the truth of historical materialism. So looking at Cohen's argument here has a very strategic importance indeed.

To get at this, it is helpful to have Cohen's rational reconstruction of historical materialism before us. Cohen succinctly states the core of his rational reconstruction in the following terms:

> In Marx's theory, as I present it, history is the growth of human productive power, and economic structures (sets of production relations) rise and fall according as they enable or impede that growth. Alongside a society's economic structure there exists a superstructure, of non-production relations, notably legal and political ones. The superstructure typically consolidates and maintains the existing economic structure, and has the character it does because of the functions it fulfills.
>
> Historical materialism's central claims are that (1) the level of development of the productive forces in a society explains the nature of its economic structure, and (2) its economic structure explains the nature of its superstructure. I take (1) and (2) to be *functional* explanations, because I cannot otherwise reconcile them with two further Marxian theses, namely that (3) the economic structure of a society is responsible for the development of its productive forces, and (4) the superstructure of a society is responsible for the stability of its economic structure.
>
> (3) and (4) entail that the economic structure has the function of developing the productive forces, and the superstructure the function of stabilizing the economic structure. These claims ... do not *by themselves* entail that economic structures and superstructures are *explained* by the stated functions: x may be functional for y even though it is false that x exists *because* it is functional for y. But (3) and (4), *in conjunction with* (1) *and* (2), do force us to treat historical materialist explanations as functional. No other treatment preserves consistency between the explanatory primacy of the productive forces over the economic structure and the massive control of the latter over the former, or between the explanatory primacy of the economic structure over the substructure and the latter's regulation of the former.[17]

Cohen elegantly defends this rational reconstruction as being both Marxist and something that is a plausible candidate for being true. But subsequent to writing *Karl Marx's Theory of History: A Defense*, he has come to have his doubts not about whether it is Marxist, but about it being approximately true. One of the central causes of his having those doubts is the problem of cultural identity. In his "Reconsidering Historical Materialism," where he expresses those doubts, Cohen brings out clearly what is at issue, and in so doing effectively casts doubt on what has been described here as the Habermasian Enlightenment Project.

How the problem of cultural identity poses problems for historical materialism can be seen from examining a kind of relativizing difficulty that emerges from a moral Cohen draws from his favorite childhood book, *The Little Boy and His House*. People, the moral of that book has it, have a way, unless jolted very extensively, of going on doing what they always have been doing. One rather central reason for doing something for most people is that they and people around them have always done things that way. One of the ways, Cohen perceptively remarks, "a culture consolidates itself is by misrepresenting the feasible set of material possibilities as being smaller than it is in fact. Culturally disruptive material possibilities are screened out of thought and imagination: in certain contexts people prefer to think that they have no choice but to take a course to which, however, there are, in fact, alternatives."[18] A few paragraphs later Cohen continues:

> If, then, it all depends on where you live and what you have to build with, the importance of where you live is not purely materialist. The way of life where you live counts, as well as what you have to build with there. People live not by mud and bricks alone, but also by the traditions from which they draw their identity, the traditions that tell them who they are.[19]

We have here a form of cultural relativity and, particularly when this ties in with what Cohen takes to be a mistake in what he calls Marx's philosophical anthropology, this makes, Cohen believes, a special problem for historical materialism. Marx's anthropology, like his theory of epochal social change, was concerned very centrally with the activity of production. But what is being talked about here in Marx's anthropology and his historical materialism are importantly different. Human beings, as Marx stressed in his anthropology, are essentially creative beings. We are persons who are most at home with ourselves when we are developing and exercising our talents and powers.[20] This, Cohen believes, is true, but it is only part of the truth about us. There is another truth about human nature, a truth that Hegel stressed, to

which Marx did not sufficiently advert. That has been called the need
for self-definition. Cohen puts it thus:

> I claim, then, that there is a human need to which Marxist obser-
> vation is commonly blind, one different from and as deep as the
> need to cultivate one's talents. It is the need to be able to say not
> what I can do but who I am, satisfaction of which has historically
> been found in identification with others in a shared culture based
> on nationality, or race, or religion, or some slice or amalgam
> thereof. The identifications take benign, harmless, and cata-
> strophically malignant forms. They generate, or at least sustain,
> ethnic and other bonds whose strength Marxists systematically
> undervalue, because they neglect the need for self identity under-
> lying them.[21]

Marx, with his "anti-Hegelian Feuerbachian affirmation of the radical objectivity of matter," neglected that we as persons have a need to
see ourselves in a certain way, have a need to understand who we are
and who we were. He failed to give due weight to our need to form self-
images and to have some sense that we are a *we*. It is not that we should
come up with some idealist nonsense that all reality is ultimately an
expression of self, but Marx "overreacted . . . and . . . failed to do justice
to the self's irreducible interest."[22] *What is essential here is the self's
need to be defined, not its need to do the defining.* We need to discover who
we are and who we were; indeed one cannot have one without the other.
As the cliché goes, we have a need for roots.[23]

Marx, of course, did emphasize, and rightly, the development of
human powers, human capacities, as an end in itself. But that is not the
same thing as self-definition. We could develop our human powers
without gaining self-understanding. The latter, plainly, is much more a
reflexive activity. "A person does not only need to develop and enjoy
his powers. He needs to know who he is, and how his identity connects
him with particular others."[24]

Cohen contends that Hegel was of particular importance here in
teaching that a human being must "find something outside himself
that he did not create, and to which something inside himself corre-
sponds, because of the social process that created him, or because of a
remaking of self wrought by later experience. He must be able to identify himself with some part of objective social reality."[25] We must not
forget that typically the attaining of an identity is a very passive process indeed. People, as Cohen puts it, do not supervise their "own social
formation."[26] This does not mean that within limits we cannot, by our
own initiatives, enrich or alter our identities. We can, within limits,
alter our identities somewhat, but we cannot forge our identities *de
novo* for "on the whole one's identity must be experienced as not a matter for choice."[27] Marx, of course, realized that one's identity comes

within a community, but being part of that community, having a sense of a tradition that is one's tradition, having a sense of identity that is a particular identity, such as being a Canadian, a Jew, an intellectual, a farmer, a painter or an athlete, is something which for Marx was *only* instrumentally valuable. That, Cohen argues, was a mistake. Having a particular identity is also intrinsically valuable.[28]

Marx's ideal of the total development of the individual was also a mistaken ideal.[29] We have certain roles in life, and this is essential for our sense of identity. "[T]he very constraints of role"—say being a doctor or a lawyer—"can help link a person with others in a satisfying community."[30] Marx, who was also an Enlightenment figure, wanted us to shed such roles in the future communist society. There would be no philosophers nor musicians nor (presumably) doctors, though everyone would do a bit of all these things from time to time. But when we thus translate this into concrete terms, we can see that it is an absurd and dangerous ideal. Cohen explains his rejection of this ideal:

> I now wonder why roles should be abolished, and even why, ideally, people should engage in richly various activities. Why should a man or woman *not* find fulfillment in his or her work as a painter, conceived as his contribution to the society to which he belongs, and located within a nexus of expectations connecting him to other people? And what is so bad about a person dedicating himself to one or a small number of lines of activity only? Nothing is wrong with a division of labour in which each type of work has value, even though no one performs more than, say, two types of work, so that many talents in each individual perforce lie underdeveloped. Marx wanted the full gamut of each person's capacity to be realized: " 'free activity,' " he said, "is for the communists the creative manifestation of life arising from the free development of *all* abilities." But that ideal is too materialist. It is neither realizable nor desirable. You will see that it is unrealizable if you imagine someone trying to realize it, in a single lifetime. But it is not even *in general* desirable to realize it as much as possible. There is often a choice between modest development of each of quite a few abilities and virtuoso development of one or very few, and there is no basis for asserting the superiority of either of these choices in the general case. What constitutes the free development of the individual in a given case depends on many things, and his *free* development is never his *full* development, for that is possible only for beings which are sub- or superhuman. A society in which everyone is free to develop in any direction is not the same as a society in which anyone is able to develop in every direction: that kind of society will never be, because there will never be people with that order of ability.[31]

V

Suppose we agree with Cohen that there is this one-sidedness in Marx's anthropology. Still we need to ask what this has to do with historical materialism. Suppose it is the case that we have a need for identity not accounted for by Marx's anthropology, and that Marx's conception of the *full* development of the individual was an ill-considered notion. Why should this have any effect on the viability of Marx's theory of epochal social change? Or does it have any effect on its viability?

The issue is more complex than it might seem at first. One might say that historical materialist accounts have always underestimated the import of phenomena such as religion and nationalism as causes of social change. That historical materialists would do so is intelligible (though, of course, not justified) in the light of their acceptance of a mistaken anthropology. But we need to ask whether the connection between Marx's anthropology and his historical materialism is anything more than a purely accidental historical one. Why should we take Marx's theory to be a seamless web? Why should historical material- ism be attached to Marx's anthropology, or why should his anthropol- ogy be attached to his historical materialism? In addition, we need to ask if it really is the case that historical materialism underestimates the causal import of phenomena such as religion and nationalism.

Cohen remarks that the anti-Marxist cliché that Marx "misjudged the significance of religion and nationalism" is probably true.[32] Marx did not see their importance as causes of social change, and this impor- tantly affects his theory. Let us consider here only what Cohen has to say about nationalism. As we move from capitalism, Marx saw the workers losing all sense of national identity and having only a class identity as workers of the world. Recall his remark that working men have no country. All local attachments would lose their hold on work- ers as the working class developed in struggle. Marx's hope was not only that we would learn to throw off ethnocentrism, racism, and na- tional chauvinism, but also "that men and women [would] relate to other men and women as fellow human beings, and on a world scale, *not in addition to but instead of finding special fellowship in particular cul- tures.*"[33] That we can or even should so completely discount local at- tachments seems to Cohen both an unrealistic and undesirable concep- tion, the espousal of which mistakenly skews our theory of social change and makes our search for self-definition anomalous.

Cohen claims that Marx's view here is unrealistic. We do not relate to each other just as people. A Finn may come to love American jazz but he remains a Finn, someone distinct from the Americans. A Cana- dian might come to identify very much with the nomadic life of the

Lapps, but in an important respect he remains a different person. No matter how much a field anthropologist tries to go native, he cannot go the whole way. The idea that we can relate to each other *just as people* ignores the particularization needed for human formation and human relationships. People may and indeed should marry across cultural lines, but they would still, even after years of intimacy, sense their differences, differences that people living in the same intimacy from the same culture would not experience. We may come to love Russian literature. We may come to feel that the greatest Russian novelists surpass any of our own, but we still realize that to us it is a foreign literature. "Marxist universalism," Cohen remarks, "suffers from the abstractness of the Enlightenment universalism criticized by Hegel. The Enlightenment was wrong because the universal can exist only in a determinate embodiment: there is no way of being human which is not *a* way of being human."[34] We cannot, and still be human, cast off these identities, these local attachments. We can and should learn to understand and appreciate other people's distinct identities and learn not to be ethnocentric about our own, but those are distinct matters from the necessity and indeed the desirability of being a particular kind of human being with a particular set of local attachments. Since it is not possible to do so, the question of whether we should throw off these local attachments can hardly arise sensibly. Moreover, since so much of our sense of what makes a life meaningful is tied up with some particular identity or another, it is hardly desirable that we even try to escape such local attachements. This need not imply that we become or remain nationalistic, finding our identity, in part, through the state. We also need not, though we prize our own way, regard it as superior to the ways of others, or demand that it take precedence over these other ways. It is, as Cohen puts it, "a good thing that in our own time people are developing identifications of more local kinds, and also international ones, identifications which cut within and across the boundaries of states."[35] We can and should have internationalism along with particularism. Where this is so the particularism can be non-ethnocentric. But the central point here is that the erosion of all particularism is neither possible nor, even if possible, desirable.

Still, how does the fact—or indeed does the fact—that Marx did not see this muck up his theory of epochal social change? Cohen puts the question this way: "[H]ow much damage to historical materialism is caused by the fact that the phenomenon of attachment to ways of life that give meaning to life is materialistically unexplainable?" We do not explain it through talk about how the productive forces developed. "Is the force of that attachment great enough to block or direct the development of the productive forces, or influence the character of economic structures, in ways and degrees that embarrass the theory of history?"[36]

Cohen's answer here is that this question, at present at least, cannot be answered because the confirmation conditions of historical materialism remain unclear. He remarks:

> It may seem obvious that the human interest I have emphasized makes historical materialism unbelievable, but it is not obvious in fact. That people have goals that are as important, or even more important, to them than development of the productive forces need not contradict historical materialism, since even if "people have other goals which are always preferred to productive development whenever they conflict with it," the conflict might never determine the direction of events at critical junctures and might therefore never assume epochal significance.[37]

This is surely an empirical possibiltiy, and only detailed empirical research would determine whether in fact that preference ever determines the direction of events at critical junctures. If historical materialism is true, it is not *a priori* true. Still, it would be very valuable indeed to know a little more exactly about what we would have to observe or fail to observe in order to make that claim more or less likely.

We also need to ask, Cohen points out, whether Marxism's one-sided anthropology was the source of historical materialism's lack of focus on the role of nationalism and religion as causes of epochal social change. Yet, aside from the fact that each has the activity of production at its center, the anthropology and historical materialism have little to do with one another. Cohen thinks that the falsity of historical materialism does not follow from the falsity of anthropological theory, though, in fact, "historcial materialism *may* be false because it neglects what the anthropology cannot explain. . . . "[38]

Cohen then proceeds to explain, in what does not seem to answer that question plainly, how Marx's historical materialism and anthropology need not contradict one another.[39] In seeing that, it is vital to see that production "in the philosophical anthropology is not identical with production in the theory of history."[40] In the anthropology, Marx spoke of how people are productive, that is creative, by nature. Only under conditions of material plenty, in the condition of freedom conferred by that material plenty, would they be able to cultivate and exercise their manifold powers fully. And it is in such conditions that human beings are especially productive (i.e., creative) and realize their human powers. By contrast,

> . . . in the theory of history people produce not freely but because they have to, because nature does not otherwise supply their wants; and the development in history of the productive power of

man (as such, as a species) occurs at the expense of the creative capacity of the *men* who are the agents and victims of that development. They are forced to perform repugnant labor that is a denial, not an expression, of their natures: it is not "the free play of [their] own physical and mental powers." The historically necessitated production is transformation of the world into an habitable place by arduous labor, but the human essence of the anthropology is expressed in production performed as an end in itself, and such production is different, in form and content, from production that has a merely instrumental rationale.[41]

For Marx there was no development of the productive forces when nature was too generous. It was when there were scarcities so that people had to produce for reasons of survival and comfort that the productive forces developed. People produced here not because, as the anthropology said, it was their nature to produce; they produced against their inclinations in order to survive or to be able to live a less spartan life. The explanations for the fact that over time there is a tendency for the productive force to develop are, Cohen claims, scarcity, intelligence, and rationality. No mention is made in that context of the thesis of the anthropology that humanity by nature is productive.[42] This surely seems at least to indicate that the anthropology has no bearing on the theory of history.[43] However, the two, though distinct, are compatible, for the very development of the productive forces, driven by scarcity and human interests in overcoming scarcity, will if historical materialism is true, lead to communism, where, for the first time in history, man's human nature can be realized because people will be able finally to exercise to the full their creative powers. This is what Cohen means by saying that "an essence-frustrating cause could have essence-congenial effects."[44]

Some might still persist in saying that there is a contradiction between Marx's anthropology and Marx's historical materialism. They could do this by arguing that "according to historical materialism people produce because of scarcity, because they have to, while the thesis that humanity is by nature creative entails that people would produce even when they do not have to produce, when, indeed, they do not have to do anything."[45] And, indeed, that anthropology fits badly with Marx's historical materialist thesis that people would not produce in the Arcadian conditions of abundance that stimulate no historical development.

However, why not reply, as both Marx and Cohen do, by limiting the scope of historical materialism to pre-communist societies—that is to societies where conditions of scarcity obtain. Indeed, its scope might as well even be taken to exclude those societies in New Guinea and the Amazon which have not developed beyond a "Stone Age" culture where people (I speak now in the anthropological present) live in conditions of abundance. (This is not to suggest that all or most Stone Age cultures are like that but only that some may be. Furthermore, "abundance" means here that the enviroment is relatively benign and there is plenty to eat. That, of course, is not the only thing that can and should be meant by abundance.) Again, in such circumstances, if they really do exist, there would be no motive to develop the productive forces; yet people in these conditions remain creative—that is productive in the sense of Marx's anthropology—as can be seen from their elaborate sculpture, body painting, and hair dressing. So why not say that, where scarcity obtains, the nature of the production relations of a society is explained by the level of development of the productive forces, and where scarcity does not obtain, the production relations are not so explained? There seems to be nothing ad hoc about this, and we can go on to say, if we wish, that human beings are always productive, in the very wide sense of "productive" used in anthropology, though when they are in a subordinate class under conditions of scarcity, that productivity (creativity) tends to be severely circumscribed. Hence the phenomenon of alienated labor. In saying that creative work is essential to persons, we should be understood as saying that human beings do not *flourish* without it. They can and indeed do exist without it or with it being severely limited, as the long history of class oppression in class societies clearly attests.

VI

The above argument, if sound, shows that Marx's anthropology and historical materialism can be made compatible without unreasonable maneuvers. It also shows how a historical materialist can accommodate attaching more causal significance to this superstructure than is usually done by Marxists, and how in particular a Marxist could shed an Enlightenment picture of self-identity and accept the belief that self-identity must be culturally mediated. But it leaves serious questions about historical materialism's confirmation conditions. That aside, we still have Cohen's argument for the proposition that self-identity must be culturally defined. Does that argument give us sufficiently good reason to abandon the Habermasian Enlightenment picture of emancipation under conditions of undistorted discourse?

There is room for ambivalence here. On the one hand, the counter-Enlightenment has in various ways hammered home the importance in our very humanization of cultural particularities. The abstractness of Enlightenment universalism obscures from us the fact that some of these particularities are important to us. It deflects our attention from a recognition of the ways in which we are passive recipients, before the period of rational discernment, of much that constitutes our identity. We do not and cannot, as Cohen well puts it, supervise our own social formation. As stated earlier, there is no way of being human which is not *a* way of being human and, again as Cohen well puts it, we cannot relate to each other *just* as people. Part of what makes us human is that we are each a particular kind of human being, a member of a distinct community with its own sense of how it is appropriate to live, and its own distinctive conceptual categories for interpreting and responding to the world. On the other hand, there is such a thing as cultural borrowing. There is the possibility for people to forge new tablets and to come to understand an alien culture well, to see that the ways that culture has of viewing and responding to things may be superior to one's own inherited ways of doing and viewing things. We human beings do not always uncritically go on doing the things previously done.

Habermas's picture of undistorted discourse gives us an abstract model for making intercultural comparisons and critical assessments. From whatever culture or subculture in which we come of age, we inherit various legitimating beliefs. If we live in the conditions of modernity, we also come to know various quite different and sometimes conflicting legitimating beliefs. We are social animals with a sense of community (which means the sense of a distinct particular community), but we are also individuals, each with his/her own sense of life and with brains and desire that enable us to change things and to come to see things differently than our ancestors. To so stress the need for *gemeinschaft* that we leave out this point is also to miss something that is distinctively and importantly human. To not stress it for fear of falling into bourgeois individualism is to say something which is false about human nature. We human beings are neither conceptually nor morally imprisoned such that we, starting with a certain enculturation (which we all do), cannot rebuild the ship at sea—and indeed rebuild it timber by timber.

There are certain ways in which our differences are things we can simply welcome and in which no invidious comparisons are in order, though this is not true of all things. For those things of which it is not true, we do indeed need, without falling into cultural chauvinism, to forge criteria for intercultural comparison. The Enlightenment from Condorcet to Marx to Habermas and Rawls has sought to articulate such criteria. Habermas's conception of the ideal speech situation and of undistorted discourse is, in accordance with our current overfascination with language, a variant of such an Enlightenment project. It gives us some of the criteria we need for intercultural assessments. There is nothing in it that needs to deny the validity of some local attachments. The counter-Enlightenment can plainly recognize, though indeed some counter-Enlightenment figures did not, that particularism need not lead to nationalism where one treats one's own way of life as both dominant and supreme. Also, the Enlightenment need not be an insensitive, abstract universalism blind to the distinctive values of particular ethnic groups. It can acknowledge their sometime validity and inescapability, while still arguing that there are universal values and general viewpoints valid across cultures. These perspectives can be held in addition to, and not instead of, some of the distinctive values of a particular culture. Such values are essential for us to make sense of our lives, but human history has so evolved and our productive forces have so developed that more universalistic conceptions also demand our loyalty.

NOTES

¹Herbert Read, *The High Valley* (New York: Charles Scribner's Sons, 1965).

²Elinor Ochs and Bambi B. Schieffelin, "Language Acquisition and Socialization," in Richard A. Schweder and Robert A. Levine, eds., *Culture Theory* (Cambridge, England: Cambridge University Press, 1984), pp. 276-320. Note the bibliography at the end of the essay.

³Ibid., p. 279.

⁴On brute facts and the simple truth, see John Leslie Mackin, *Truth, Probability and Paradox: Studies in Philosophical Logic* (Oxford: Clarendon Press, 1973).

⁵Jürgen Habermas, *Communication and the Evolution of Society*, Thomas McCarthy, trans. (Boston: Beacon Press, 1976), pp. 1-68.

⁶Quentin Skinner, "Habermas's Reformation," *The New York Review of Books* XXIX: 13 (October 7, 1982): 36.

⁷Thomas Nagel, *Mortal Questions* (Cambridge, England: Cambridge University Press, 1978), pp. 106-127, 196-213.

⁸John Rawls, *A Theory of Justice* (Cambridge, MA: Harvard University Press, 1970); Nagel, op. cit.

⁹Skinner, op. cit., p. 38.

¹⁰Raymond Geuss, *The Idea of A Critical Theory: Habermas and the Frankfort School* (Cambridge, England: Cambridge University Press, 1981); Skinner, op. cit., pp. 35-38.

¹¹Skinner, op. cit., p. 38.

[12]Hans Magnus Enzensberger, *The Consciousness Industry* (New York: The Seabury Press, 1974).

[13]Edward Westermarck, *The Origin and Development of Moral Ideas*, Vol. 1 (London: MacMillan, 1908). See, as well, Timothy Stroup, "Edward Westermarck: A Reappraisal," *Man* 19 (1985): 575-592. Note the bibliography in Stroup.

[14]Christopher R. Hallpike, *Bloodshed and Vengeance in the Papuan Mountains: The Generation of Conflict in Taude Society* (Oxford: Clarendon Press, 1977).

[15]G. A. Cohen, "Reconsidering Historical Materialism," in James R. Pennock and John W. Chapman, *Marxism: Nomos XXVI* (New York: New York University Press, 1983), pp. 227-251.

[16]G. A. Cohen, *Karl Marx's Theory of History: A Defense* (Princeton: Princeton University Press, 1978); William H. Shaw, *Marx's Theory of History* (Stanford, CA: Stanford University Press, 1978); Allen W. Wood, *Karl Marx* (London: Routledge and Kegan Paul, 1981), pp. 63-122.

[17]G. A. Cohen, "Functional Explanation," *Political Studies* 28: 1 (March 1980): 129-130.

[18]Cohen, "Reconsidering Historical Materialism," op. cit., p. 231.

[19]Ibid., p. 232.

[20]Ibid.

[21]Ibid., p. 235. Isaiah Berlin has brilliantly brought out the importance of such issues in *Against the Current* (New York: Viking Press, 1980), pp. 333-355, and in *Vico and Herder* (London: Hogarth Press, 1976).

[22]Cohen, "Reconsidering Historical Materialism," op. cit., p. 233.

[23]Ibid., p. 234.

[24]Ibid.

[25]Ibid.

[26]Ibid., p. 235.

[27]Ibid.

[28]Ibid., p. 237.

[29]Ibid.

[30]Ibid., p. 236.

[31]Ibid., pp. 236-237 (Footnotes omitted).

[32]Ibid., p. 238.

[33]Ibid., p. 239. Author's italics.

[34]Ibid., p. 240.

[35]Ibid.

[36] Ibid., p. 241.

[37] Ibid.

[38] Ibid.

[39] Ibid., p. 243.

[40] Ibid., p. 242.

[41] Ibid. (Footnotes omitted).

[42] Ibid.

[43] Ibid.

[44] Ibid., p. 243.

[45] Ibid., p. 244.

DOES LINGUISTIC HETEROGENEITY ERODE NATIONAL UNITY?

Donald W. Larmouth

University of Wisconsin-Green Bay

In the popular press and elsewhere, we frequently find the argument that support of ethnic languages, especially through bilingual education, threatens national unity in the United States. Usually the same argument cites examples of other nations where linguistic and cultural minorities are asserting themselves and acting in opposition to the national government, even to the point of violence. For example, former Senator S. I. Hayakawa's campaign to solicit funds to support a Constitutional amendment includes a "national opinion survey" which says in part, "In order to avoid the political upheavals over language that have torn apart Canada, Belgium, Sri Lanka, India, and other nations, would you favor legislation making English the official language of the United States?" (The next question asks for financial support.) There can be no doubt that language is a powerful and pervasive symbol of ethnocultural unity, and it follows intuitively that linguistic homogeneity would support or enhance national unity. However, while this may be true in some instances (though not actually in very many), it is not self-evident that linguistic heterogeneity inevitably erodes national unity. Although there are clear instances where language has served as a rallying point for political separatism, there are other instances where national unity appears to have been sustained despite great internal linguistic and cultural differences, and there are still others where the situation is more ambiguous. In this chapter, we shall examine some of the social and political conditions which support nationalism and determine the extent to which language is related to these factors. By doing so, we may establish a more systemic basis for discussing the extent to which linguistic differences influence national unity.

Factors in Nationalism and Ethnocultural Unity

It seems appropriate to begin by trying to define the elements of nationalism. In doing so, we can identify not only what establishes and sustains a sense of national unity, but also what factors might give rise to disaffection, erosion of national unity, and even separatism. Joshua Fishman provides a convenient and useful framework for such a discussion, suggesting that nationalism is built from broadly shared perceptions of historicity, autonomy, and authenticity promulgated by urban elites in a context of urbanization and substantial economic and social change.[1]

It should be clear at the outset that these factors are collective perceptions rather than "facts"—they are part of the mythology of the people and have the same pervasive power. A sense of ethnocultural unity depends on a shared perception of a glorious past which represents the "authenticity, purity, and nobility of the beliefs, values, and behaviors that typify the community of reference."[2] Nationalism must establish a sense of rational continuity with the past, and national leaders selectively identify those elements of the past which best authenticate and support present designs. The great murals in Mexico City which depict the Indians as heroes, the Spaniards as syphilitic monsters, and bathe the modern mestizo in light are but one of many examples of efforts to establish a sense of historicity which helps to authenticate the nationalist concept.

Continuity with a noble past contributes to a perception of autonomy, a sense of uniqueness which accentuates a broad feeling of contrast with other ethnocultural groups. It also implies internal control of the collective destiny of the group, as opposed to control by another group. This sense of "control" is not meant to refer to actual economic, military, or political conditions. Indeed, control imposed from the "outside" can heighten the group's collective perception of contrast and autonomy and enhance support for its efforts to assert autonomy in more tangible ways, to take real control of its destiny.

Along the same lines, a sense of territoriality is a contributing factor in nationalism. Regardless of the fact that national boundaries may change out of all recognition, even to the point of disappearance, identification with an idealized or traditionally significant territory or homeland can be important in establishing a sense of ethnocultural unity. Many Americans who have never stood astride their national boundaries with Canada or Mexico can still sketch an outline of our national territory (often excluding Alaska and Hawaii, not to mention Puerto Rico), while Lithuanian expatriates in Chicago continue to teach their children about a national territory that no longer exists.

However, while ethnocultural unity is not absolutely dependent on a sense of territoriality in geopolitical terms (the Basques in Spain do not have a national territory, but they certainly have a strong tradition of place), it seems clear that territoriality is an additional way to authenticate a nationalist concept.

Historicity, autonomy, and territoriality all help to authenticate a sense of ethnocultural unity, but other factors are also necessary before such a sense is likely to manifest itself in nationalistic terms. Fishman points out that economic development can dislocate or destroy traditional identities and redefine groups in fundamental ways.[3] If, as often happens, economic opportunities favor one group and not another, those on the outside may either try to identify themselves in some way with the advantaged group (thereby possibly subordinating their original ethnocultural identity in favor of a broader unity) or, conversely, assert their own distinctive identity (through a new nationalist or separatist movement) as a way of gaining access to the same advantages. Historically, nationalist movements "initially spread as newly favored populations . . . sought to protect themselves from the claims and controls of concurrently less preferred sociopolitical units," while disadvantaged groups became "similarly conscious only as a result of partial changes in ther circumstances which . . . serve[d] to heighten their sense of relative deprivation."[4] This sense of contrast is basic to the concept of nationalism.

Along with economic development and its changes in the social order, there must be an urban elite which effectively communicates a nationalist identity to the lower classes. The latter may have only local identification or may otherwise be disenfranchised and excluded from the important social and economic decisions of the larger polity. The elite articulates the ennobling ideals of the legendary past, asserts the group's autonomy and territoriality, and attempts to authenticate the new order. As Fishman notes, "The spread of nationalism is, therefore, marked not by its existence in the upper reaches of society, but by its successful communication to and activation of the urban (and ultimately also the rural) lower middle and lower classes."[5] The urban elite forms a cohesive intellectual community which plants and nurtures the idea of broader unity and establishes its authenicity in the minds of the people, not merely through public proclamations and pamphlets, but through scholarship and artistic expression which bring forward the myths and symbols and "rediscover" past leaders, heroes, poets, and founding fathers.

Finally, another major factor in the establishment of an active nationalism is urbanization. Dislocation from the rural countryside to the

urban center because of increased industrialization and economic development opens the possibility of extensive redefinition of ethno-cul-
tural identity, moving toward a broader supraidentification and away
from localism.[6] To put it another way, nationalist movements do not
usually develop in rural areas where local groups identify primarily
with villages and small localities, but nationalist ideas can spread from
urban areas to the surrounding countryside. The city populations are
also the primary audience for the efforts of the nationalist elite; indeed,
the development of such an elite is itself a product of urbanization.

In general terms, then, we can see that a sense of nationalism is dependent upon the establishment of a broader unity (an ethnocultural
identification beyond one's immediate group or location), which comes
about through common recognition of rational continuity with an illus-
trious past (historicity), a common sense of autonomy or contrast from
other ethnocultural groups, and a sense of territorial definition (even in
the absence of an actual geopolitical territory). All of these combine to
heighten a general perception of authenticity for the nationalist concept. These perceptions do not develop, though, unless there is a significant level of economic development and social change which acts to
dislocate or reorient significant numbers of people away from outlying
rural communities and toward urban centers. Nor will they develop
without the active promotion of urban elites who perceive the need for
a national identity and articulate the authenticity of the nationalist
design. To conclude this section, it is appropriate to note that Fishman
did not intend to confuse "nationalism" with the establishment of a
separate nation-state, although that is one of the possible consequences
of nationalism. Division within a national polity is at least as likely, if
the urban elites are successful in their efforts to establish a broader
unity within the population.

Language and National Unity

Language is a powerful instrument for national policy precisely because it is such a pervasive symbol of ethnocultural unity. In this section, the ways in which language supports the elements of broader
unity and authenticates the nationalist concept will be outlined.

It is almost self-evident that language can support a sense of historicity when there are documents (religious works, historical records, a
recognized and revered literature, significant tracts or public declara-
tions, etc.) in the language. Less obvious, perhaps, is that a substantial
oral tradition can work the same way if it is widely known in a vernacular language, thereby directly linking a glorious past to the thoughts of

the present.[7] Either way (or both ways), language establishes a rational basis for a sense of continuity with the past.

Beyond a sense of historical continuity, language also can directly authenticate a nationalist viewpoint because it is the most powerful and pervasive mechanism for cultural transmission: "[T]he mother tongue expressed a nationality's soul or spirit [because] it was a collective achievement par excellence . . . the surest way for individuals to safeguard (or recover) the authenticity they had inherited from their ancestors as well as to hand it on to generations yet unborn."[8] Language also powerfully contrasts one ethnocultural group to another, reinforcing a sense of autonomy. In addition, language also supports a sense of territoriality and helps to legitimate territorial claims (or serve as a way to brush aside demographic shifts of the intervening past), as it does in the modern state of Israel.

However, a language can do none of these things unless it has sufficient status—unless it is itself recognized as a legitimate symbol of nationalism. To achieve such status, a language must have a writing system that is broadly recognized and accepted, even if the bulk of the population is not literate. Nonwritten languages may be very important in a locality (witness the very large number of languages within many African states), but will not move beyond their immediate region without a writing system. Charles Ferguson has identified "graphization" as the first step in the establishment of an indigenous language as a national language, noting that "the use of writing leads to the folk belief that the written language is the 'real' language and speech is a corruption of it."[9]

A national language is also codified or standardized, a process which follows closely behind the establishment of a writing system. A great deal of passion and conflict may arise as a group seeks to standardize the language, as standardization is part of the process of authenticating the language as the most legitimate symbol of ethnocultural unity. While it is the province of scholars (members of the urban elite) to argue the details of what is and is not standard, the process is typically recognized and supported by the general public, whether or not they can follow the arguments per se.

Nurturing, developing, and supporting the language as a group symbol can become a vital objective in a national movement, although such development can take very different shapes in different national contexts. In the United States, various self-anointed guardians of the purity of the English language routinely complain about the alleged deterioration of English grammar and vocabulary, and their complaints are echoed by many opinion leaders in the popular press. In contrast, in Sweden the national language is systematically updated through careful planning and dissemination.[10] When the members of the larger group are directly involved in the process, as in the recovery of American Indian languages, their participation is typically vigorous and enthusiastic. It may also be combative, given the diversity of oral varieties and the efforts of various groups to see their particular variety established as the standard. Whatever shape it takes, the language standardization process is inevitably a part of the establishment of a language as a symbol of nationalism.

Beyond a recognized writing system and a standardized form, a language must be elaborated or "modernized";[11] it must have sufficient range in styles and lexicon to be a viable instrument for nationalist discourse. Lexical expansion is required to reflect "the more abstract subtleties of imported or recently innovated higher learning and fashionable society,"[12] but equally the necessities of health care, technological development, exploitation of natural resources, military operations, parliamentary discourse, literary expression, and so on. The elaboration of vocabulary, though, must develop within a legitimate context; wholesale borrowing of words from another language may be seen as undermining the purity of the language and diminishing its authenticity, thereby lessening its status as a symbol of broader national unity. This is reflected in the frequently apologetic attitude expressed by speakers of immigrant languages in the United States, who recognize intuitively that the legitimacy of their language is diminished by large numbers of English loanwords, although they retain their sense of ethnicity through other means.[13] Thus, even though there may be no functional difference between loanwords and words coined from native material, there can be a significant difference in their perceived legitimacy in the lexicon of a national language.

The upshot of this brief overview is that language can be and usually is extremely powerful in the development and support of a nationalist point of view because it so vividly authenticates a people's ties to a revered past, their automomy from other groups, and even their territorial claims. But to do so, a language must have a recognized writing system and a standardized form. Moreover, it must have the lexical and stylistic range to serve a wide variety of topics and contexts, including those which have emerged as a result of urbanization and economic development. Most of all, it must be recognized as the embodiment of the vernacular tradition—the rootstock of a broader ethnocultural unity.

Linguistic Diversity and National Unity

We have seen that national unity is borne of several broadly-based perceptions and socioeconomic conditions, and that language can be directly related to the development and support of these perceptions. If there is widespread recognition and acceptance of a particular language as the national language, it can greatly enhance the feeling of broader unity so essential to the establishment and survival of a new nation.

A good example of such broad acceptance is Swahili in Tanzania. While Swahili had existed as a standard language only since the 1930s and had served as a significant second language in that region only since the mid-nineteenth century,[14] it achieved broad acceptance after Tanzania gained its independence in 1961 and is now well established as the national language. To be sure, the selection of the southern dialect of Swahili instead of the Mombasa dialect did produce some ill will, but the southern dialect was already widely spoken as a second language in large inland areas. Considering the fact that there were over one hundred other languages spoken natively within Tanzania, its unifying capacity has been very important. Swahili did not belong to any one group and was therefore an ideal choice through which to organize the resources of the newly independent country.[15] Before and after independence, knowledge of Swahili was a way to participate in affairs beyond the local community, even as English remained the most important language for interaction with the outside world (as well as for advanced education). Poems and letters in praise of Swahili regularly appear in magazines and newspapers, but its role in a national cultural revival is rather more obscure since it is spoken as a mother tongue only by a coastal Islamic group which is not in the cultural mainstream. However, through the efforts of the Ministry of Community Development and National Culture, the language has been cultivated and expanded ("modernized," in Ferguson's terms) to serve an increasingly wider range of topics and circumstances, and this effort has been supported by several private organizations. Overall, then, it is clear that Swahili, despite its short official history, has been very successful in embodying the nationalist idea and establishing a broader unity among a very diverse population.

In Tanzania, Swahili was the only second language (other than English) which had wide acceptance. In Nigeria, with three major regional languages and a long history of local hostilities, the situation is rather more complicated. Statistically, the majority of the people in Nigeria speak Hausa as a second language, but they are primarily of the northern region, which is predominantly Muslim and far less developed than the western region, where Yoruba predominates, or the eastern region, where Igbo is widely spoken. Just prior to independence, the Northern Elements Progressive Union proposed to require instruction in Nigeria's three main languages in all schools, but the Northern Peoples Conference argued that Hausa should be selected as the only national language.[16] The divisons following independence obscured the language issue for a time, while English continued as the most important language of wider communciation, though unrecognized as the national language.[17] In the northern region, Muslim tradition and extensive use of Hausa consolidated the leadership in opposition to the largely Christian southern regions, and political factions also emerged along ethnocultural and regional lines.[18] The political maneuvering among the regional factions is too complex to summarize here, but the conflicts clearly emerged along linguistic and religious lines, with rumblings of secession, a series of military coups, and widespread corruption.[19] General Gowon's decision in 1967 to divide Nigeria into twelve states broke up the unity of the northern region, but it also triggered the secession of the eastern (Igbo) region under Colonel Ojukwu[20] and the Biafran war, which ended in 1970 with the victory of the federal government. Although the major regions had ceased to exist as official political entities under Colonel Aguyi-Ironsi in 1966,[21] regionalism continued. Meanwhile, the central government tried to defuse some of the linguistic problems by encouraging bilingualism among students in the National Youth Service Corps by stationing them in regions other than their own. Nevertheless, national unity is still precarious, and the government is obliged to continue recognition of regional languages.

What are the essential differences between these two examples? In both countries, linguistic heterogeneity is extensive: Tanzania has over 100 indigenous languages, Nigeria over 160. Is the greater degree of unity in Tanzania simply a function of the fact that Swahili is widely spoken as a second language, while three languages compete in Nigeria? In the framework that has been established in this chapter, it seems appropriate to look at matters of social change and economic development to answer this question.

At the time of Nigerian independence, the Yoruba region was more modern, more urbanized, had a generally higher level of education (in Western terms, anyway), was more oriented to Western culture, and enjoyed a higher standard of living than the Hausa region. Since the civil war, much of the national power has been centered in the Yoruba region as well. These conditions enhance the sense of contrast which was earlier identified as an essential ingredient in a nationalist perspective—a sense which is underscored by linguistic differences. The speakers of Hausa see their language as an embodiment of a distinctive tradition which has spread across many other ethnocultural groups in the northern region. There were eleven times as many Koranic schools in the northern region as in the rest of Nigeria.[22] Prior to the federal elections in 1964, political parties used Hausa in most of their literature. As political power centralized in Kaduna, Hausa became a significant broadcasting language; meanwhile, the power of local tribal units was diminishing.[23] Overall, the use of Hausa helped to unify the northern region, along with consolidation of its economic and political power, and its extensive incorporation of Arabic further symbolized a cultural and religious tradition quite apart from the eastern or western regions. In Tanzania, in contrast, no other indigenous language was so widely spoken as Swahili, and no other language symbolized a particular region or definable group within the larger national context. But it is also true that economic development in Tanzania had not created a large "have not" group or a significant disenfranchised group, nor were there other bases for a feeling of autonomy from other significant polities in the country. (It might be more accurate to say the "have not" status is not limited to distinct groups, but is widespread across ethnocultural lines.) While local languages continue to be spoken and taught, there appears to have been no systematic discrimination against particular groups such that they might find cause to seek their own destiny. Meanwhile, Swahili has been vigorously promoted as a national language, carrying with it the important ideas of a noble past and authenticating the "Tanzanian idea" in the minds of the people.

These examples demonstrate that linguistic diversity per se does not imply national disunity; it is hard to imagine situations that could be more diverse. Obviously, what is important is the relative status of the languages involved, and whether each language authenticates a distinct group with other reasons to feel separate from other groups in the country. In Nigeria, the three regional languages have high status, overriding many local languages; in Tanzania, only one indigenous language, Swahili, has sufficient status to be considered as an instrument of national policy.

Turning our attention to the United States, we can immediately note the fact that, at one level, we are linguistically a heterogenous nation, with many different immigrant languages as well as American Indian languages. Working again within the general frame of reference established previously, we can see very quickly that nationalist groups did not emerge around German or Italian or Swedish or any of the other European immigrant languages, despite the fact that they saw extensive use in the United States. Certainly there was no lack of ethnic feeling or identification: German in particular was well established in schools, in German language newspapers, etc., and there were many German settlements of substantial size. In Wisconsin, for example, there were over two hundred German language newspapers published at one time or another, reflecting the fact that there were three major waves of German settlement in the nineteenth century which replenished the readership.

There seem to be two major reasons for the fact that nationalist groups did not emerge from European immigration. One is what Heinz Kloss calls "tolerance-oriented rights,"[24] a term which he uses to refer to more or less passive tolerance of the right of the individual to use his mother tongue at home and in public; the freedom to assemble and organize, to establish social, cultural, and economic organizations, publish newspapers, etc., in one's mother tongue; and, most narrowly, to cultivate one's mother tongue in private schools. Until the anti-foreign hysteria that peaked immediately after World War I, all of these rights were honored, with few exceptions, for a considerable period, and Kloss cites several court cases which successfully challenged local or state efforts to abrogate them. Tolerance-oriented rights meant that immigrant groups were not placed (at least officially) on the defensive and had little reason to mount an organized effort which might have heightened a sense of nationalism, as happened when the Franco government attempted to ban the use of Basque in Spain after the Spanish Civil War (much to its later regret).

Tolerance-oriented rights continued in the broad sense without serious challenge; that is, the freedom to use one's mother tongue at home or in cultural or economic organizations. However, in 1918, Iowa Governor W. S. Harding banned non-English languages from schools, churches, telephone conversations, and public discourse in a state that was 60 percent German, and fifteen other states had banned the use of languages other than English in schools by 1919.[25] By 1923, the number had risen to thirty-four states.[26] Thus the narrowest (and most important) level of tolerance for languages other than English was severely diminished in the early part of this century, and it continued until the passage of the Bilingual Education Act in 1968. By 1981, twelve states (including Iowa) had mandated bilingual education under specific conditions.[27]

But even by 1918, a large majority of European immigrants had already lost their mother tongue or had seen its status diminish through extensive loanwords, pidginization, and loss of literacy. Much of the support for a "nativist" (English only) point of view came from people who were only a generation or two removed from immigrant status themselves.

This is an indication of the second major reason for the failure of nationalist groups to develop from immigrant populations. There were significant social and economic pressures to assimilate the dominant, English-speaking culture, and the opportunity to participate in the process was not denied (again, in official terms, discounting local prejudices) to any of the major European immigrant groups, even those who came late and settled in urban ghettos. Even though the United States went through a major dislocation of its population from rural areas to the industrializing cities, the opportunity to make such a move was not contingent on ethnic background or language. While speakers of English characteristically enjoyed more economic and social advantages than non-English speakers, the non-English speakers moved quickly to acquire English and were actively encouraged to do so by a growing public school system. Immigrants, therefore, given the choice of asserting a distinctive identity or identifying themselves with the economically advantaged group, chose the latter, subordinating their original ethnocultural identity. As a result, ethnically homogenous communities are hard to find in the United States and, where they do continue, are located in rural areas as relic communities, often widely separated from other similar ethnic communities, or as remnants of the "ethnic wards" which grew up in many American cities.[28] Examples of such relic communities in the upper midwestern region include some of the Finnish communities in the Upper Peninsula in Michigan, some Czech communities such as Stangelville or Tisch Mills, Wisconsin, and some instances of "professional" ethnic communities like the Swiss German community in New Glarus, Wisconsin, which make a vigorous appeal to tourists. Whatever individual instances of prejudice or limited opportunities might be cited (my mother remembers signs saying "No Irish Need Apply"), the general pattern for European immigrant groups has been one of rapid assimilation into the dominant culture, with corresponding reduction and loss of immigrant languages.

In terms of the framework within which this discussion began, then, none of the characteristics of nationalism (historicity, autonomy, territoriality, or authenticity) were established for any of the European immigrant groups in the United States, despite urbanization, major social changes, and economic development. The immigrant groups were not put on the defensive by official assaults against their cultures or their languages until most of them were well on the way to assimilation, thus they did not form an aggrieved minority and agitate for autonomy. Moreover, there were significant opportunities for immigrant groups to participate in the general economic growth of the country, and these groups chose, through learning English, to identify with the larger "American" national concept rather than nurturing a contrastive ethnic identity. Thus, despite the isolated exceptions that can always be mentioned, the general pattern was one of rapid assimilation, even though ethnic identity might still be felt strongly within the individual families, ethnic neighborhoods, and relic communities.

Given this history, it seems strange that anyone in the United States could even begin to argue that support of non-English languages through bilingual education would undermine national unity. But the languages currently of greatest interest are not the "traditional" European immigrant languages. Typically, the language most at issue is Spanish, and Spanish does not have the same sort of history as German, Swedish, Polish, Dutch, or other immigrant languages. Since the history of Spanish in the United States is different, we might expect its present circumstances to differ too. However, as will be pointed out, Spanish turns out not to be very different after all.

Many Spanish speakers in the United States can rightly claim a longer history in North America than most European immigrants. Moreover, they have a much clearer regional identification than the speakers of traditional European immigrant languages, which could lead to a sense of territoriality. Nancy Conklin and Margaret Lourie cite 1978 data from the National Center for Education Statistics which show very substantial concentrations of Hispanics who claim Spanish as their mother tongue: over 6,500,000 in the Southwest, just over 2,000,000 in the Northeast, over 750,000 in the Midwest, and over 900,000 in the Southeast.[29] Conklin and Lourie estimate that there are close to 20,000,000 Hispanics in the United States, or roughly 9 percent of the total population.[30] It is important to note, however, that this is a very diverse population—Cubans emigrating after Castro overthrew Batista were mostly upper class, very different from the people entering the continental United States from Puerto Rico, and even in the Southwest there were historically at least three different Hispanic populations.[31] Still, one might argue that there is a sufficient concentration of Hispanics in the Southwest to form the basis for a feeling of territoriality.

There would also have been a basis for a feeling of cultural autonomy. Mexican-American families for whom the concept of *La Raza* is significant perceive important differences between their culture and the dominant culture. William Madsen claims that Mexican Americans in South Texas perceive the Hispanic culture to be morally superior to the dominant culture, with its value on the extended family and its lack of emphasis on competition,[32] that would seem to support a sense of contrast and autonomy. They have also suffered a long history of economic and social discrimination which has given them plenty of reason to perceive contrasts between their opportunities and those enjoyed by members of the dominant culture. Such perceptions have already been exploited, perhaps most visibly in Cesar Chavez's efforts to organize agricultural workers. In many respects, the history of Mexican Americans in the United States can be seen as similar to the history of French-speaking people in Canada, among whom separatist movements have surfaced which have been very visible in the American press. Admittedly, then, some of the ingredients for a nationalist movement are present in the Hispanic community, and with the large number of Hispanics in the United States and the expectation that they will soon be the largest minority population,[33] it is perhaps not surprising that many people feel that support for Spanish in the public schools would only nurture further nationalist identification and sow the seeds of future discord.

But a nationalist movement has not developed within the Hispanic community (excluding Puerto Rico, which is a very different situation from the continental United States). One reason is that there has been a significant degree of assimilation of Hispanics. Earlier studies which suggested a high level of Spanish language retention in the United States were based on census data, but Calvin Veltman has shown that these data did not reveal the high degree of anglicization that has actually occurred.[34] Veltman used data from the 1977 Survey of Income and Education involving over 150,000 households and the High School and Beyond survey of more than 1,000 public schools to show that U.S.-born Hispanics are rapidly anglicizing, and that Spanish is retained largely because of the continuing in-migration of monolingual Spanish speakers. Veltman says that foreign-born Hispanics are highly motivated to learn English, and that their children are very likely to become English monolinguals or to use Spanish only rarely. Thus, the higher retention of Spanish is really a function of continuing immigration—the same situation that extended the life of German in Wisconsin and other midwestern states in the nineteenth century. Moreover, the status of Spanish is somewhat diminished by its extensive adoption of English loanwords, such as the very long list described by Roberto Fernandez in Miami-Cuban Spanish.[35] In this sense, Spanish is not very different from the European immigrant languages. Rapid anglicization is clearly motivated by economic concerns, and to the extent that economic opportunities have continued for Hispanics (or are perceived to be greater than are available in Mexico or Latin America), the rate of assimilation is likely to continue to be high. Jack Levy notes that as economic opportunities have increased for ethnic language minorities, more and more Hispanics have entered the middle class.[36] With this in mind, it hardly seems likely that support for Spanish through bilingual education will somehow result in the erosion of national unity.

It is appropriate to point out that there is still some potential for problems involving Spanish. Reynaldo Macias and others have argued that the Bilingual Education Act of 1968 and subsequent legislation have not actually been supportive of Spanish or other languages in any substantive way; they have encouraged states to repeal laws which prohibited the use of non-English languages or mandated exclusive use of English, and they have focused national attention on the needs of non-English speaking people.[37] In effect these laws have reestablished tolerance-oriented rights, and the bilingual education programs mandated by state legislatures have retained a clear sense of assimilation as the primary goal, even while permitting bilingual/bicultural education; in effect, they are anglicization statutes, not bilingual statutes.[38] Consider the language of the 1975 bilingual education statute in Wisconsin:

> It is the policy of this state that a limited-English speaking pupil participate in a bilingual-bicultural education program only until such time as the pupil is able to perform ordinary classwork in English.

> It is the policy of this state that fundamental courses may be taught in the pupil's non-English language to support the understanding of concepts, while the ultimate objective shall be to provide a proficiency in those courses in the English language *in order that the pupil will be able to participate fully in a society whose language is English.*[39]

Readers familiar with the concept of "bilingual-bicultural education" will recognize that the Wisconsin statute's language misuses the term, as the statute is clearly assimilative, not pluralistic, in intent. However, it makes further provision for an "optional expanded program" which is more genuinely pluralistic. Here is the relevant language:

> "Optional expanded program" means a program which provides the following:
> (a) Instruction in reading, writing, and speaking the English language; and
> (b) Instruction at all grade levels, through the use of the native language of the limited-English speaking pupil, in the subjects necessary to permit the pupil to progress effectively through the educational system.[40]

Obviously the intent is "effective progress," not maintenance of another culture, but this statement has been the warrant for pluralistic bilingual-bicultural programs in the Milwaukee Public Schools, and there would seem to be some basis for suggesting that enhancement of educational opportunity for Hispanic children is at least possible under this statute. It might be further argued that Spanish-speaking populations have fulfilled Heinz Kloss' conditions for "promotion-oriented rights," in which the government actively supports and nurtures minority languages:

> Only when the immigrant generation has succeeded in giving its native languages firm roots among the grandchildren . . . , made the sacrifices for a private cultivation of the language . . . , [and] taken root in the new country while retaining their native language, can they demand that the state come to their aid and promote their language.[41]

However, if Veltman is correct,[42] the degree of anglicization is much greater than the language claims represented in the U.S. Census data. Moreover, Kloss distinguishes between original Hispanic settlers and those who arrived in the United States much later,[43] suggesting that the later immigrants do not fulfill his conditions for promotive rights, although Macias dismisses this as a specious distinction,[44] arguing that Mexican Americans and Puerto Ricans were integrated into the United States by military conquest and have a 350-year-old historical continuity in North America. Indeed, much of Macias' argument fits well within the nationalist framework from which this chapter has been working. But while there seems to be substantial support for enhancing educational opportunities for linguistic minorities—although evidence of educational improvement through bilingual education is sparse and ambiguous[45]—requests for instruction in their ethnic language seem to be mainly a demand for greater participation in the educational system and a way to prevent further attrition of these languages, not a strategy for gaining greater autonomy or to authenticate a separatist effort.

It would seem that conditions surrounding the Hispanic minority are such that, with the exception of Puerto Rico (where a separatist/ independence party is still active), there is little prospect for a sense of nationalism to emerge. But the situation is quite different with some American Indian groups; indeed, a strong nationalist sense has emerged in several instances, and it seems to be clearly linked to the conditions for nationalism that have been used here as a framework for discussion, although the populations are generally so small or so isolated that the larger national unity hardly seems to be threatened. Still, these instances are worth exploring because they have had great regional significance, including some important disputes in the Midwest, and because the recovery of American Indian languages seems to be an important part of the process of reasserting their sense of nationalism.

American Indians in Wisconsin, Minnesota, and parts of Michigan have been very active in asserting treaty rights, and these efforts are a way to revive a sense of historicity as well as territoriality. In northern Wisconsin, Ojibwe and other bands have recently reached agreement with the Department of Natural Resources which will enable them to spear fish and hunt game in areas outside their reservations. Ojibwe in Wisconsin and Michigan have also won the right to fish commercially in the Great Lakes for species (especially lake trout) which are protected from white commercial fishermen, an event which has caused some outbreaks of violence near Whitefish Bay in Michigan. In the Green Bay area, the Oneida are currently negotiating historical land claims with the county government (not without acrimony), and there seems to be some agreement that efforts to subdivide traditional Menominee lands for sale to whites for summer homes triggered a movement to restore tribal status to the Menominee.

Historicity and autonomy are also enhanced through the revival of traditional ceremonies. A good example of this is the naming ceremony among the Oneida, where families travel to Canada to join other Oneida, who are perhaps seen as maintaining more authentic traditional religious ceremonies since the Wisconsin Oneida are a Christian sect. Both the Oneida and the Menominee asserted their autonomy from Wisconsin by establishing tribal schools when local public schools continued to be unresponsive to their needs, and Ojibwe bands in Minnesota have done much the same thing. The Ojibwe, Oneida, and Menominee have also established vigorous tribal governments and have actively developed tribal businesses as a strategy for greater economic autonomy, as they have been bypassed in large measure by the urbanization and economic development of the dominant culture in the region. Finally, each group is led by elites who are well educated and have persuasively articulated nationalist values, even though they may not necessarily be speakers of the tribal languages themselves.

The Ojibwe, Oneida, and Menominee have also been very active in efforts to recover their languages as another strategy to assert and authenticate their autonomy and maintain continuity with a glorious past. The Ojibwe have been very successful in this work, with a project at the University of Minnesota going back more than a decade. A similar, though much smaller, language recovery project has been conducted in the Oneida community for ten years, and Oneida is taught as a regular part of the tribal school curriculum as well as in a special program for adults. Efforts to establish a curriculum for the Menominee language proceeded more sporadically in the early to mid-1970s, but they now also have an active instruction program in the elementary grades. These examples of language recovery are appropriately considered as part of a general strategy to reassert a broader ethnocultural unity which would include the majority of tribal members (virtually all of whom had lost most of the traditional culture as well as the language), because all three languages were in imminent danger of extinction. If the languages had been lost, it would have been extremely difficult for these groups to maintain a sense of authenticity and reestablish a broader unity among the tribal members.

The circumstances surrounding the Ojibwe, Oneida, and Menominee are quite distinct from those American Indians who have vigorously maintained a tribal identity such as the Navajo, the Hopi, and the Lakota. Indeed, the languages of the upper midwestern tribes were in a far more precarious state than Cherokee, which, though seriously threatened in the first half of this century, has recovered with some vigor.[46] Even if the languages are maintained in only a few ceremonial or official settings, they are still likely to support what seems clearly to be a nationalist movement. Furthermore, retention of American Indian languages not only authenticates a broader unity within particular tribes and bands; it is also significant as various American Indian groups act in concert, as in the Great Lakes Intertribal Council, to assert traditional land claims, treaty obligations, and so on. An American Indian group which no longer maintained its language would probably not be accorded the same status within the council. Indeed, as the Menominee can directly attest, their very status as a tribe might be called into question, as it was during Menominee termination proceedings.

The extensive research and development process that has characterized these and other American Indian language recovery efforts also reflects the same nationalist concerns for authenticity and historicity that were mentioned earlier in connection with Swahili. They are typical of efforts to elevate indigenous languages to national status. Native speakers who serve as resource persons as well as teachers in these programs are very concerned with historical accuracy, as well as with structural precision in pronunciation, grammar, and vocabulary. Also, since the languages are being reconstructed largely from the oral repertoire of living speakers, the variability inherent in oral languages is a source of continual debate as a standardized and codified form of the language is established for use in the schools, especially in instances such as the Menominee where there is considerable linguistic mixture from other languages such as Ojibwe and Potawatomi. Efforts to elaborate the linguistic system to reflect contemporary needs are a further source of disagreement, much as they have been in the establishment of other national languages.

Overall, it would seem that a persuasive case for the importance of language as a symbol of national unity can be made from the experiences of American Indian groups, even though they are too small or too scattered to cause much concern for unity at the national level. As efforts have continued to standardize and elaborate American Indian languages, there is a strongly felt need to authenticate them as proper carriers of ethnocultural identity—a need which has been characteristic of efforts to establish national languages in other countries. At least for those American Indian groups for whom assimilative efforts have not succeeded in obliterating traditional languages and tribal identities, it seems reasonable to suppose that they will continue to feel a heightened sense of authenticity and assert a broader ethnocultural unity which, over the near term at least, are likely to continue to produce conflicts at local and regional levels. At the same time it would also seem that the collective health of American Indian communities can be greatly enhanced by the reassertion of a clear ethnocultural identity, even as it was threatened by the anomie that accompanied the linguistic and cultural alienation of the recent past, and this seems to be more than sufficient justification for the continued support of efforts to recover American Indian languages.

Conclusion

We have seen that national unity has several dimensions based upon the collective perceptions of the people: historicity, the sense of continuity with an ennobling past; territoriality, the sense of homeland or national territory beyond the immediate experience of individuals; autonomy, the sense of uniqueness or contrast with other peoples—all of which combine to authenticate a broader unity, extending beyond small localities and regions and encompassing a large number of distinct ethnocultural groups. National unity is also dependent upon urbanization and the social changes and economic development that attend it, plus an urban elite which articulates and rationalizes the nationalist concept. Language, as an instrument of national policy, can support these nationalist perceptions; indeed, when it is successfully promoted, the national language embodies the national spirit, symbolizing the "soul" of the nation.

We have also seen that the very concepts which unify a nation can divide it, if they are perceived by a disenfranchised minority who have not enjoyed the fruits of economic development, who feel themselves to be apart from the dominant population, perhaps suppressed by it, and who see themselves excluded from any realistic opportunity for advancement. Many developing nations are confronted with such disenfranchised (and disenchanted) ethnocultural minorites, and there are numerous instances in which they genuinely threaten national unity—even assuming that such unity has been previously established. This is why the recurrent objections to bilingual education are wrong—fundamentally wrong. If we were to follow former Senator S. I. Hayakawa's lead and adopt a Constitutional amendment to establish English as the national language in the United States (and exclude other languages in the process, as he and others have argued), we would increase a risk which is presently minimal—a risk of disenfranchising a significant number of people, perhaps sufficiently to give rise to the very disunity that we fear. Though it may seem paradoxical, the best strategy would seem to be to continue to support a full range of opportunities for participation in the social and economic opportunities of the dominant culture, including opportunities to learn English, without disenfranchising or threatening ethnocultural minorities and their languages. Furthermore, since it seems clear that minority languages pose no threat to national unity in the United States, there is little basis for opposition to efforts to recover or maintain them. Such a policy would be consistent with other, broader statements of human rights (such as the Universal Declaration of Human Rights adopted by the United Nations) which, though they do not mention language rights explicitly, entail other dimensions of nationality or ethnocultural identity which, as we have seen, are intimately bound up with language.

NOTES

[1] Joshua Fishman, *Language and Nationalism: Two Integrative Essays* (Rowley, MA.: Newbury House, 1972).

[2] Ibid., p. 8.

[3] Ibid., p. 10.

[4] Ibid., p. 12.

[5] Ibid., p. 15-16.

[6] Ibid., p. 19-20.

[7] Ibid., p. 45.

[8] Ibid., p. 46.

[9] Charles A. Ferguson, "Language Development," in Joshua Fishman, Charles A. Ferguson, and Jyotirindra Das Gupta, eds., *Language Problems of Developing Nations* (New York: John Wiley, 1968), p. 29.

[10]Charles A. Ferguson, "National Attitudes Toward Language Planning," in James E. Alatis and G. Richard Tucker, eds., *Language in Public Life: Georgetown University Round Table on Languages and Linguistics* (Washington, D.C.: Georgetown University Press, 1979), pp. 52-53, 56.

[11]Ferguson, "Language Development," op. cit., pp. 32-33.

[12]Fishman, *Language and Nationalism*, op. cit., p. 61.

[13]Nancy Faires Conklin and Margaret A. Lourie, *A Host of Tongues: Language Communities in the United States* (New York: Free Press, 1983), p. 173.

[14]W. H. Whiteley, "Ideal and Reality in National Language Policy: A Case Study From Tanzania," in Fishman, Ferguson, and Gupta, eds., op. cit., p. 327.

[15]Ibid., p. 331.

[16]John N. Paden, "Language Problems of National Intergration in Nigeria: The Special Position of the Hausa," in Fishman, Ferguson, and Gupta, eds., op. cit., p. 204.

[17]Ayo Bamgbose, "The English Language in Nigeria," in John Spencer, ed., *The English Language in West Africa* (London: Longmans, 1971), p. 35.

[18]Guy Arnold, *Modern Nigeria* (London: Longmans, 1977), pp. x-xi.

[19]Michael Crowder, *The Story of Nigeria*, 4th ed. (London: Faber & Faber, 1978), pp. 266-271.

[20]Ibid., p. 272.

[21]Arnold, op. cit., p. xiii.

[22]Paden, op. cit , p. 206.

[23]Ibid.

[24]Heinz Kloss, *The American Bilingual Tradition* (Rowley, MA: Newbury House, 1977), pp. 22-23.

[25]Conklin and Lourie, op. cit., pp. 70-71.

[26]Ibid., p. 229.

[27]Ibid., p. 230.

[28]See ibid., p. 57.

[29]Ibid., p. 56.

[30]Ibid., pp. 17-18.

[31]Ibid., p. 17.

[32]William Madsen, *The Mexican-Americans of South Texas* (New York: Holt, Rinehart & Winston, 1964), pp. 15-17.

[33]Jack Levy, "Policy Implications/Complications Arising from Native Language Attrition in U.S. Ethnolinguistic Minority Groups," in Richard D.

Lambert and Barbara F. Freed, eds., *The Loss of Language Skills* (Rowley, MA: Newbury House, 1982), p. 195.

[34]Calvin J. Veltman, *Language Shift in the United States* (Berlin: Mouton, 1983).

[35]Roberto G. Fernandez, "English Loanwords in Miami Cuban Spanish," *American Speech: A Quarterly of Linguistic Usage* 58: 1 (Spring 1983): 13-19.

[36]Levy, op. cit., p. 196.

[37]Reynaldo Macias, "Language Choice and Human Rights in the United States," in Alatis and Tucker, eds., op. cit., p. 93.

[38]Joshua Fishman, "Language Policy: Past, Present, and Future," in Charles A. Ferguson and Shirley Brice Heath, eds., *Language in the USA* (New York: Cambridge University Press, 1981), pp. 517-518.

[39]Sec. 115.95(4) and (5), Wis. Stats. Author's italics.

[40]Sec. 115.955(8), Wis. Stats.

[41]Kloss, op. cit., p. 289.

[42]See Veltman, op. cit.

[43]Kloss, op. cit., p. 20.

[44]Macias, op. cit., pp. 97-98.

[45]Levy, op. cit., pp. 192-194.

[46]Conklin and Lourie, op. cit., pp. 199-202.

LANGUAGE MINORITIES IN THE UNITED STATES: CONFLICTS AROUND ASSIMILATION AND PROPOSED MODES OF ACCOMMODATION*

Wallace E. Lambert
and Donald M. Taylor

McGill University

A foreign observer once described the American character in terms of three major preoccupations; namely, concerns with war and peace, with bread and butter, and with black and white. Fetching as this set is, it neglects another persistent preoccupation that is, perhaps, even more important and distinctive—a concern with what is and what is not "American." In fact, this chapter will use this last concern as a background theme to organize our thoughts about ethnolinguistic minority groups in North America, and how far these groups want to or can go in their attempts to keep heritage cultures and languages alive while simultaneously becoming as American (or Canadian or Mexican) as they want to be, or as they must be. Thus, Hispanic Americans and Navajo Americans are like French Canadians or Inuit Canadians and Nahuatl Mexicans in the sense that each group confronts social demands to juggle a heritage culture and language with a national culture and language, and each has to decide whether it can keep both in motion and whether it is worthwhile.

A current example of this basic American concern is discernible in the United States in the debate on the virtues and drawbacks of providing schooling in languages other than English for language minority children. The Reagan administration has questioned publicly whether it is American to have language minority children taught even parttime in Spanish, Chinese, Navajo, or whatever other home language may be involved. Underlying the administration's skeptical attitude on the language of instruction in public schools is a deeper concern about the likelihood of newcomers to the United States ultimately adjusting to the new land through assimilation, rather than simply living in ethnic enclaves and not assimilating. The worry is that immigrants or refugees may come to the United States to make a living, but leave their hearts elsewhere. Deeper still is a general concern about ethnically and linguistically pluralistic societies. Can they ever be cohesive, or are they intrinsically divisive? Perhaps pluralistic societies can manage diversity of national origin and religion, and may have to live with differences of skin color, but can they also support language diversity? Can any society put enough heat under the melting pot to dissolve languages?

This chapter attempts to specify a process and a policy for addressing the issue of culture and language diversity in North America. It begins with an examination of the attitudes held by language minority and majority groups toward culture and language diversity. It then summarizes a wealth of data now available on effective strategies for the development of bilingual skills. Finally, it presents a general blueprint for maximizing the effectiveness of public education in the context of cultural and language diversity, a blueprint that is meant to accommodate the perspectives and wishes of all ethnic subgroups in the society.

Attitudes Toward Language and Cultural Diversity

Reliance on the melting pot or any other form of social pressure to confine or eliminate heritage customs and heritage languages is essentially a manifestation of a concern to keep America "American" and a desire to monitor carefully what is not American. As we shall see, one trouble with trying to keep the nation American is that the demographic characteristics shift in ways that make it unclear as to what America actually is, since minorities are fast becoming as numerous as majorities.

The history of the United States began with colonies that were ethnically and linguistically diverse, and although accommodations to the English language were negotiated, languages other than English were and apparently still are tolerated in communities and in schools outside the public school system. Our personal experiences are a case in point. In a New England community where one of us grew up in the 1930s and 1940s, various ethnic groups had their own community or parish centers and it was a commonplace to be a member of one of the many uniformed baseball teams representing, for example, the Portuguese-American Civic Club, the Polish-American Civic Club, the Italian-American Civic Club, or the House of David Center. These teams would compete in schedules that also included Irish and old-line Yankee groups. Recent visits to the same community show that the same ethnic subgroupings exist and, what is more, religious services conducted in Portuguese, French or Polish, and public school programs offering elementary grade instruction conducted partly in languages other than English, are at least tolerated by the community at large and fully appreciated by the minority group members involved. In that New England community today, one can attend a wedding reception or a party where Portuguese or Polish will be the nearly exclusive language of interaction among guests ranging in age across three generations.

One can get the impression from such examples that, at least in some parts of the United States, there has been, and still is, a good deal of freedom extended to minority groups to regulate how far they wish to go in becoming American. Some tacit rules exist, however; for example, English has to function as the "market language," that is, the main language to be used around the city "commons," in the business district, and in the public schools. Still, members of each ethnic group apparently had, and still have, the full right to return to their own subcommunity and be as ethnic there as they so choose. There is, though, certainly a threshold of tolerance on the part of the older residents, and minority groups have to be skilled and tactful in their displays of ethnicity. If no one even noticed or cared about minority groups' ethnic displays, they might have reason to worry, just as they might be worried if others overly encouraged them to be ethnic. Thus, the concerns about what is or is not American are felt by newcomers as well as by the more established citizenry.

In an important study conducted in 1963, Nathan Glazer and Daniel Moynihan[1] found that ethnic minorities in America had maintained, to a surprising extent, their ethnic identification through successive generations. Looking back in 1983, Glazer and Moynihan congratulated themselves on the accuracy of their 1963 forecast that no basic change in the trend toward ethnic maintenance would transpire in the succeeding twenty-year period.[2] There is, however, a very lively, ongoing debate about the actual depth of ethnic maintenance in the United States. For instance, Richard Alba,[3] working with 1980 census data, sees clear signs of progressive assimilation. Focusing on intermarriage statistics, he finds progressively larger proportions of Americans with European heritages marrying outside their ethnic groups, although the choices are clearly bounded by social class and color lines. Thus, Americans of Italian, Portuguese, Anglo-Saxon, and Jewish background tend to be intermarrying if they are of comparable socioeconomic standing, whereas blacks, whites, and most Asians overwhelmingly marry within racial boundaries, and presumably within socioeconomic ones as well.

The counterarguments in the debate can take many forms.[4] Does it necessarily follow that mixed ethnic marriages eradicate each of the contributing ethnic heritages? One study of the children of such unions found, in fact, that the adolescent offspring of mixed ethnic parents appreciated both sources of their own dual ethnicity, respected both parents and their backgrounds, and showed strong signs of bilinguality in the languages involved.[5] Thus, it could be that intermarriage permits family members to be "double-breeds" rather than "half-breeds" or "no-breeds." Moynihan[6] takes a different tack working with the same 1980 census data. He noted that 83 percent of the American people in the census defined themselves in terms of their ethnic backgrounds; only 6 percent referred to themselves as "Americans" or "from the U.S.A." Moynihan also suggests that there are twice as many ethnic parades in New York now than there were twenty years ago, and many more ethnic language storefront signs in public view.[7] This important debate among researchers is lively and will certainly continue.

Aware that we may be reading more into it than what is called for, we think we see something else going on in the minds of both Americans and minority ethnic groups with regard to what being American means. There seem to be many debates underway. There are certainly changes in what newcomers to North America (immigrants or refugees) are ready to do regarding assimilation. Put somewhat harshly, newcomers seem less interested in becoming American or Canadian than they are in being *in* America or *in* Canada. For instance, in interviews with Arab-American and Albanian-American parents in Hamtramck—an inner-city Detroit community—one father explained: "There is no way my children can be anything else but Arab first and Arabic-speaking first. Like good Jews who are Jewish first, my son wouldn't be a son if he were not Arab first." An Albanian adult explained: "I'm grateful to be here, but I'm here to give my family a chance, not to become American." A Vietnamese adult in Montreal told us: "I'm grateful to be here, but this is not my place of choice. I will not become less Vietnamese by living here."

These are not extreme sentiments. In fact, part of our ongoing study in the greater Detroit area involves presenting parents from various ethnolinguistic minority groups with a statement of the major debate about assimilation versus the maintenance of heritage cultures and languages. They are asked to take a stand. Some of the parental groups involved are recent immigrants, while others are from families who have resided in the United States for two or more generations. We find, though, that length of residence does not make much difference in their

replies. In the city of Hamtramck, we were able to draw sizeable samples of lower working-class Polish-American, Arab-American, Albanian-American, and black parents in their homes and conduct structured interviews, using social-psychological scaling techniques, in the
appropriate home language of each group. Then we conducted the
same survey in nearby Pontiac, Michigan, where we collected data
from Mexican, Puerto Rican, working-class whites (part of a large, stable group who split their lives of work, family, and retirement between
the Detroit area and various Southern communities), a white middle-
class group, and a second black group residing in Pontiac. Again, all
but one white group were from lower working-class backgrounds. They
were instructed in advance on how to use a seven-point answering
scale. One question relevant to this chapter was worded as follows:

> There is an important debate in America about cultural and ra-
> cial minority groups. Some people believe that cultural and racial
> minority groups should give up their traditional ways of life and
> take on the American way of life, while others believe that cul-
> tural and racial minority groups should maintain their tradi-
> tional ways of life as much as possible when they come to
> America. Where do you stand in this debate?

Should *give up* traditional ways of life.	1	2	3	4	5	6	7	Should *maintain* traditional ways of life.

The results, summarized in Figure 1 (see p. 63), are consistent and
unmistakable, revealing a very strong endorsement of a policy of ethnic heritage maintenance and a clear rejection of assimilation. This endorsement appeared in the responses of all immigrant groups, even the
Polish parental group, the majority of whom were second- or third-
generation residents of the United States. In fact, even the three American parental groups—the white working-class and white middle-class
groups and the black parents from Pontiac—although closer to the
neutral point on the scale, took a stand on the side of cultural maintenance rather than assimilation. This suggests that the more established
American groups might well understand the sentiments of newcomers
on the assimilation issue. The main conclusion, however, is that various immigrant groups in the United States endorse heritage maintenance to an unexpected extent. These, of course, are parents' viewpoints, and not necessarily those of their children, but as parents there
is no question about them sending a clear message about cultural and
heritage maintenance to their children.

FIGURE 1
GROUP COMPARISONS OF MEAN RESPONSES ON THE DEBATE OVER ASSIMILATION VERSUS MULTICULTURALISM

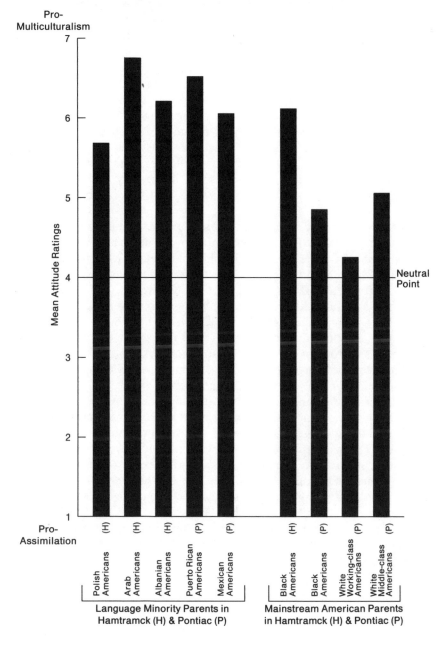

Yet these same parents send a second, equally important message to their children; namely, that they must become fluently bilingual and learn to handle English as well as the native speakers with whom they will interact and compete for jobs. To overlook this second message would be to miss the whole ideal plan these parents seem to have for their children. It would also misrepresent and distort the real challenge these children have to face. For parents, the plan is not to have children stay ethnic in America, but to make them comfortably *bi*cultural and *bi*lingual. For children, the challenge is much more manageable because two separate environments encourage them, on the one hand, to become as American as everyone else, and on the other, to keep ties with one's heritage culture and language. This does not mean, however, that all children will be up to the challenge or that none will fail in the juggling act. Also, some may reason, incorrectly we believe, that striving for biculturality will make them neither one thing nor the other.

Be that as it may, the second message parents send is very clear in our Michigan data. The same parental groups were asked to imagine three possible alternatives for their child or children: a) That they were fluently bilingual in their heritage language (or dialect in the case of black parents) and English; b) That their children spoke English only; and c) That their children spoke only their heritage language. Then they were asked such questions as: Would your child(ren) be more or less sympathetic to different cultural and racial groups? Would they be more or less proud of him/herself in one case or the other? Would they feel more or less accepted in America? Would they have more or less of a chance for certain jobs others cannot get?

Samples of the parents' reactions are plotted in Figure 2 (see pp. 65-67). They reveal a surprisingly widespread belief in the benefits of mastering a heritage language or dialect as well as the national language, English. Our parental groups are of the opinion that people feel more accepted and less like second-class citizens in America if they are bilingual rather than skilled only in English. Furthermore, it is believed that people have a greater sense of pride about their identity, and, what is especially interesting, that being bilingual is a sign of intelligence, an aid in earning good grades in school, and a decided advantage in the concrete economic domain of getting better and more difficult-to-find jobs.

FIGURE 2

VIEWS ON THE VALUE OF BILINGUALISM: A SAMPLE
OF SCALES FOR LANGUAGE MINORITY PARENTS

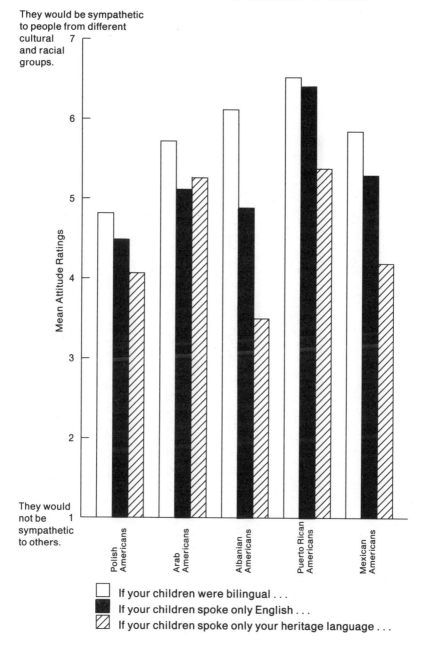

They would be sympathetic
to people from different
cultural
and racial
groups.

Mean Attitude Ratings

They would
not be
sympathetic
to others.

Polish Americans
Arab Americans
Albanian Americans
Puerto Rican Americans
Mexican Americans

□ If your children were bilingual . . .
■ If your children spoke only English . . .
▨ If your children spoke only your heritage language . . .

FIGURE 2 (cont.)

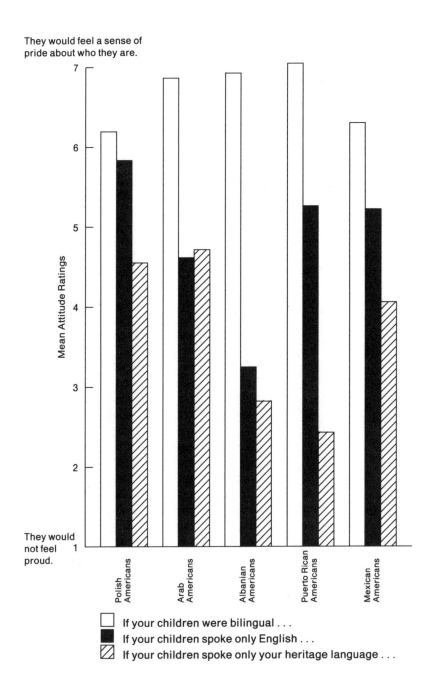

They would feel a sense of
pride about who they are.

☐ If your children were bilingual . . .
■ If your children spoke only English . . .
▨ If your children spoke only your heritage language . . .

FIGURE 2 (cont.)

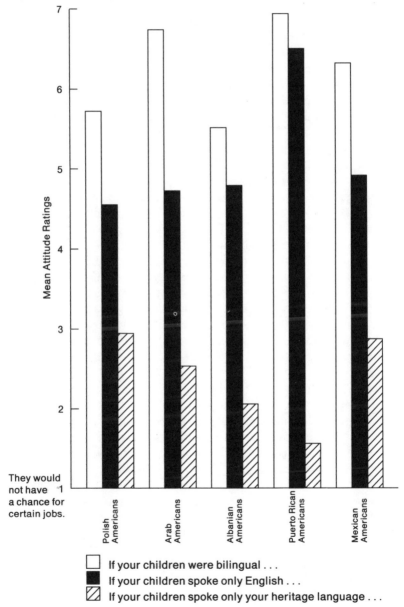

They would have a chance
for jobs others cannot get.

Mean Attitude Ratings

They would
not have
a chance for
certain jobs.

Polish Americans · Arab Americans · Albanian Americans · Puerto Rican Americans · Mexican Americans

☐ If your children were bilingual . . .

■ If your children spoke only English . . .

▨ If your children spoke only your heritage language . . .

There are some interesting differences of opinion among ethno-linguistic groups. For instance the Puerto Rican parents, in contrast to Mexican Americans, are not so sure that bilinguality helps school grades, but the general support for a bilingualism which includes strong skills in the home or heritage language is unmistakable even in the case of Puerto Ricans. In fact, the white working-class and white middle-class parents, although less emphatic, also share the very favorable outlook on the benefits associated with bilingualism. For these groups, bilingualism means English and a foreign language like Spanish, French, or German.

Overall these outcomes support our main argument, namely, that parental beliefs and expectations help shape children's motivation, provide them with a clear manageable goal—to become fully bilingual—and as a consequence, supply their children with a cultural and a practical rationale for becoming bilingual and bicultural.

How do these parents think they can make this plan work? Can the family and ethnic community retain the heritage culture and languages on their own and leave Americanization and English language development to the public schools? The Detroit parent groups were questioned about this issue and were given a range of possibilities, starting with the alternative of never using any other language but English and progressing as follows: (a) Use the heritage language (or the black dialect of English) with older family members only; (b) use it as the main family language; (c) study the language/dialect in religious or community-run classes; (d) study and use the language part-time in public schools; and finally, to the alternative that we felt was somewhat extreme, (e) give equal time to home language or dialect and English in the public school system.

Parents' responses were illuminating. First, parental groups in general rejected the "never use" alternative and most not only wanted to make a heritage language or dialect a major home language (not just one restricted to interactions with the older generation), but also a language used for learning in the public schools either on a part-time or an equal-time basis with English. There are interesting group-to-group differences in perspective on the issue. For example, the white working-class sample of parents who were asked to think in terms of their own special style of English were generally neutral in their reactions to each step of this scale. The white middle-class samples were generally supportive of other ethnolinguistic groups' use of their heritage languages, but relative to most other groups, they favored the idea of having community-based language training centers rather than using heritage languages in the public schools. They did not support the idea of giving equal school time to such languages. The Puerto Rican parents tended to reject the alternative of community-based language classes and emphasized the use of Spanish on an equal-time basis in public schools. This makes the Puerto Rican parents stand out as similar to the Arab-American parents and quite different from the Mexican-American parents. But again, the general theme is clear: Sizeable proportions of parents representing minority language groups in the United States want a broad spectrum of alternatives for the use of heritage languages or dialects, and they want public schools to play a substantial part in the maintenance of their languages.

What can we conclude from these parental responses? We see two lines of thought here. First, immigrant newcomers to the United States seem more prone than we anticipated to express publicly how they feel as immigrants. In particular, they are not ready to reject their Puerto Rican, Mexican, Arab, Albanian, Polish, or whatever way of life, but are more likely to focus on the unfair politico-economic situations in their home countries as the main motive for packing up and heading for a new nation that promises better chances to get ahead and a fairer outcome for effort expended. The clearly pluralistic nature of the United States that they would have encountered as immigrants during the past twenty to thirty years would encourage them to remain as ethnic as they might have wanted.

Second, they may have come with fewer stars in their eyes about the United States than their predecessors had. Since the 1960s and 1970s, the merits of the American way of life have been brought into question and challenged, especially by American college students who have become more internationally oriented and experienced and who wondered if the United States had any right to impose the American system of values on other societies or on newcomers. The question is whether the American way is special or better in any fundamental sense. It is likely that members of other societies also had similar questions in mind, even though they may have seen North America as a preferred place to live and raise a family. For recent immigrants, then, old country ways—politics and poverty aside—may not have seemed all that bad in comparison to the ways of the new country.

If there is any truth in this diagnosis of the newcomers' state of mind, it certainly will not sit well with those in the host nation who worry about what is and is not American. Some can see an implied insult embedded in such thinking; namely, that newcomers are happy to make their lives here, but rather than have their children become Americanized, would just as soon preserve as much as possible of their own style of life. But who is it that might be insulted in this instance? In demographic terms, who are the Americans? What is most surprising when one looks for a first-level answer to this question is to find out how ethnically diversified America has become, and how small the dominant ethnic clusters actually are. For instance, only approximately 14 percent of Americans have an Anglo-Saxon heritage, putting them on an equal numerical footing with those with a Germanic heritage and only slightly ahead of black and Hispanic-American subgroups, with the prospect that the Hispanic group may become number one within the century.[8] It is therefore quite a different America than the image one might have formed on the basis of the composition of dominant elite groups in the United States. The irony in all this is that in striving to preserve ethnic heritages while escaping Americanization, immigrant groups may be contributing more to what America seems now to be than they might realize. They can, it seems, be themselves and in so doing be as American as anyone else. This, of course, would make the process of not becoming too American much easier for them because, in one sense, *not being* American gets progressively closer to *being* American. Furthermore, the hard-line Anglo-Saxons who are prone to worry about all this may soom become too few in number to be worried about!

The Development of Bilinguality: Social-Psychological Considerations

The whole topic of ethnic and ethnolinguistic minority groups—the attitudes they hold toward Americanization, the dreams they have for their children, and the host society's reactions toward them—concern us. As social psychologists, we see possible ways that our professional training and research experiences might throw one small beam of light on what is actually occurring in pluralistic societies like the United States and Canada, and, we hope to suggest particular plans of action that might have a positive effect for all people concerned. It may be presumptuous to even make the topic our concern, but there are too many sad, unfair, un-American things going on in the lives of these groups, starting with the lives of their children, to not examine every possible point of view.

A recent overview sponsored by the Carnegie Corporation of some of the issues involved points out the sad effects on "the children of stress,"[9] but it also illustrates that those who are given the responsibility of dealing directly with minority parents and their children need new perspectives because they are neither professionally trained to diagnose the underlying social-psychological processes nor to devise general plans of action to ameliorate the situation. It is unreasonable to leave teachers and educators—even those specializing in bilingual/bicultural education or Hispanic Studies or Afro-American Studies—to their own resources to deal with the daily, front-line contacts with minority groups, and also to expect them to deal with the sociology and psychology of ethnicity in modern pluralistic societies. What follows, then, is an analysis of the underlying social-psychological issues involved, and several plans of action that have the prospect of success. It should be clear in advance that we do not perceive language minority groups as willfully or insensitively insulting the more established ethnic groups in America with their apparently intense desire to keep their cultures and languages alive in their new land. Rather, these desires are interpreted as signs of a new internationalism that incorporates a perception of a world shrinking in size, a new forced interdependency among people who cohabit the world, and a new conception of people's attachment not only to their "own" particular corners of the world, but to the world as a whole. This analysis will start with language issues and move to these broader psychological and social issues.

When policy decisions are made about education for language minority children, it would be inappropriate to let language considerations play the dominant role, even in the case where the immigrant youngster has a home language different from that of the school and of the host nation. Rather than emphasizing language, the educational offerings themselves should be kept clearly in the center of focus. These should be deep and comprehensive because the children and families involved have enough problems in coping, belonging, and succeeding in a new land without being shortchanged with a superficial or nonrelevant program of education. With attention focused squarely on providing ethnic-minority students a comprehensive, even better than average, education, policymakers can only then broaden their perspective to include language issues: a) The psychological realities of language—a realization that languages are always intimately linked with peoples' identities and social skills, and with their feelings of security and confidence; and b) The social realities of language—that language programs have serious implications not only for a particular target group, like language minority children, but also for all other groups who share the same social environment and who interact with those in the target group. Educational policymakers can then ask themselves a set of critical questions about the language competencies of immigrant ethnic pupils. In the United States, the questions would likely take this form: Are there grounds for hope for immigrant ethnic children who are essentially monolingual in a language other than English? Do children who are nearly bilingual in that language and English suffer confusion and divided loyalties? Can anything be done for those who have only a rudimentary mix of parts of the two languages, to the extent that they are actually hampered in their verbal potential across the board?

In each instance policy decisions are complex. There are no simple answers. Take the case of essentially monolingual, non-English-speaking children. Should one try to help by immersing them in English so that they can catch up? At first glance, the obvious answer would be "Proceed with full speed!," but such an apparently constructive decision is not without its costs. Immersion or submersion in English in this instance represents an abrupt turning off of a linguistic system that is simultaneously the child's "home" language (with all that that implies) and "conceptual" language—the linguistic code that has functioned from infancy to form, maintain, and elaborate thoughts and ideas. It is also a culturally significant language, be it Albanian, Basque, or Chinese, and to wash it out of the child's mind, whether it be through disuse, through swamping by English, or through social disrespect in any form, is to reduce by one an American adult-to-be who could have linguistic and cultural command of a significant foreign language. Washing it out also produces culturally frustrated and disappointed adults who might well feel that, in becoming Americanized, they were induced to eradicate an extremely central part of themselves.

How about the subgroup of children who are either already close to being bilingual or potentially so in the home language and English? How much should English language training be emphasized in this instance? The same considerations mentioned previously hold again, and perhaps with even more force, because in this case real opportunities could be missed to help children become comfortable with *two* precious languages—just what parents seem to want.

What typically happens in such decisionmaking, just when the argument for the value of bilingualism starts to make some sense, is that policymakers are prone to shift to another related issue: They begin to worry about divided allegiances and about bilinguality itself, which is too easily seen as a clear sign of mixed-up allegiances. The important question, then, is whether such worries and suspicions are justified in light of what is now known about bilinguals and bilingualism.

Consider next the subgroup of ethnic immigrant children who become trapped between the language of home and the language of the new nation, trapped in the sense that they are grossly handicapped in dealing with any form of written or spoken language. This subgroup, which is sometimes referred to as "semilingual"[10] or as "in a psycholinguistic limbo,"[11] must be treated with special care because its members are less likely to respond to any form of remedial language programs, even those that immerse or submerge them in English. Protracted language rehabilitation or catch-up programs can also put such children hopelessly behind in the academic subjects that are appropriate for their age. These basic academic subjects are just what these frustrated children want and need most, and they are also just what they would grasp best if language did not get in the way.

While attempting to answer such questions, policymakers have to broaden their perspective one step further to include the host-nation peers of the immigrant youngsters. The English-speaking white and black mainstream students are not passive onlookers to the struggles of ethnic immigrants. Indeed, their reactions determine the ultimate success or failure of the struggles. They function as representatives of the host nation's major reference groups, and they are taken as positive or negative models by language minority children. Should these mainstream models become suspicious or negative, or should they feel relatively neglected because of the attention shown to immigrants, no educational program for ethnic immigrants will work. How to involve the mainstream children—black as well as white—and to solicit their support in any program for immigrants becomes the critical question. And since the mainstream students most likely to be negative, the blacks, are those who have not been given the opportunity to be fully integrated or adequately educated themselves—like those in most urban areas of the United States—these already neglected mainstream minority groups become the most critical element of all in the puzzle of policy decisions concerning language minority groups.

Ironically, the complex issue of helping language minority children become educated, regardless of the language problems involved, ends up being the least of our worries. This is so because there is some cogent and persuasive research information to present that can help language minority children become both well educated and comfortably Americanized. Similarly, research-based suggestions exist for the simultaneous education of English-speaking American mainstreamers. However, were these suggestions to be put into practice in various communities, and were they to become promising and exciting educational alternatives for language minority groups and for the established mainstreamer, they could at the same time be seen as threatening and disheartening by a neglected mainstream minority group such as blacks in the United States. This most important issue of all will be discussed later.

For the present, the aim is to offer suggestions for a new and different form of bilingual education for ethnolinguistic minority children, one that puts the main emphasis on education while it broadens the scope of bilingual education to include majority or mainstream young people as well as ethnolinguistic minority groups. Bilingual education,

however, cannot be divorced from its psychological and social consequences. We offer first an overview of our thoughts on bilingual education, paying attention to the psychology and the sociology of such an
education. The suggestions are certainly not meant for policymakers
alone—they are also meant for educators, teachers, parents, and especially for the children involved.

A Canadian Model

Our arguments will be illustrated with examples from Canada as well
as the United States. This may help American readers gain some perspective on their own problems since Canada, like the United States, is
struggling to make its society fairer not only for Canada's two "founding peoples," French-speaking and English-speaking Canadians, but
also for members of numerous other language groups who have immi-
grated to Canada. Although Canadian in content, these examples are
pertinent to American society because similar social processes are
clearly at work in both settings. They are more visible in Canada because of sociopolitical movements toward independence or separation
on the part of the French Canadians. Although there are numerous Ca-
nadian/American parallels, there are still important differences. For instance, Canada's Constitution has clear provisions for the protection of
the language and culture of both French- and English-speaking subgroups, and although the government has a policy favoring multiculturalism, it does not provide extended financial support for education
conducted in any of the numerous other home languages spoken in
Canada. Since World War II, non-English-speaking immigrants have
made up a sizeable proportion of Canada's population. To its great
credit, the United States has federal laws requiring educational help—
including instruction through various languages other than English—
for all non-English-speaking ethnic groups who, it is recognized, are
placed at a disadvantage in schools and in occupations that presume
native competence in English. However, the United States shows no
signs of recognizing or appreciating the de facto bilingual character of
its contemporary society, which has nearly as many families with
Spanish as the home language as there are people in the total population of Canada. And the English/Spanish bilingual character of contemporary America is only one strain; there are various other, equally
vital ethnolinguistic groups, each contributing to a fascinating multicultural American society. There is, then, much more to be done to
capitalize on this ethnolinguistic richness in both the United States and
Canada.

French-speaking Canadians have had a long history of finding themselves second-class citizens in a social world which has reinforced Anglo-American values and the English language. The second-class status manifested itself in the form of French-speaking Canadians playing subordinate roles to English Canadians, the dominant subgroup in Canadian society, comparable to the English-speaking white mainstreamers in the United States. Not only have French Canadians been grossly underrepresented in the upper levels of nationwide status hierarchies, but even in the Province of Quebec, where they constitute some 80 percent of the population, French Canadians have not, relative to English Canadians, made it occupationally or economically. Their style of life has been ignored, ridiculed, and blamed as the cause of their social and economic position. The trouble is that this type of thinking becomes contagious and, over time, even members of the marked minority group begin to believe that they are inferior in some sense and blame themselves for it.[12] It takes much reflection in frustrating situations of this sort to see through the sophistry and realize that one's ethnic or social-class group is in no way inherently inferior, but simply that those with the power advantages have learned well how to keep the advantages and that their social-class cushion makes keeping power relatively easy for them. Stereotyping or otherwise marking minority groups—people they really know very little about—becomes an effective way for the majority group to keep others out of the power sphere.

As social psychologists, we began to study this state of affairs in Canada some twenty-five years ago, just as two extreme solutions to the "French Canadian problem" were coming into vogue: 1) French Canadians should pull up their socks and compete—meaning they should master English and Anglo-American ways—while toning down their French Canadian-ness; and 2) French Canadians should pull apart or separate—meaning they should form a new independent nation where they could be masters of their own fate and where the French-Canadian language and culture could be protected. Both alternatives were worrisome because one meant giving up a style of life that was precious, and the other meant closing a society through separation, "closing" in the sense that Karl Popper[13] uses the term in describing sociopolitical attempts to create a conflict-free subworld where the "good old ways" will be protected. Instead, we viewed the French-Canadian way of life as something valuable for Canada as a whole—a nation whose potential and fascination rest in its multicultural/multilingual makeup—whether or not it was appreciated as such by the majority of English or French Canadians.

The interest was in reducing, if possible, the ignorance of French Canadian-ness and in enhancing an appreciation for it among Anglo-Canadian children. This then became the guiding purpose for the research initiated at McGill University on "early immersion" schooling[14] wherein English-speaking children, with no French language experience in their homes and little if any in their communities, entered public school kindergarten or grade one classes conducted by a monolingual French-speaking teacher. This early immersion or "home-to-school language switch" program is kept exclusively French through grade two, and only at grade two or three is English introducted in the form of a language arts program for one period a day. By grade four particular subject matters are taught in English (by a separate English-speaking teacher), and by grades five and six some 60 percent of instruction is in English.[15]

The concept of immersion schooling was based on a very important and fundamental premise: That people learn a second or third language in much the same way as they learn their first, and that languages are best learned in contexts where the person is socially stimulated to acquire the language and is exposed to it in its natural form.

The consistent findings from nearly twenty years of longitudinal research on children in immersion programs permit several conclusions which bear not only on the linguistic consequences of the programs, but the psychological and social consequences as well: Immersion pupils are taken along by *monolingual* teachers to a level of functional bilingualism that could not be duplicated in any other fashion short of living and being schooled in a foreign setting. Furthermore, pupils arrive at that level of competence: without detriment to home-language skill development; without falling behind in the all-important content areas of the curriculum (indicating that the incidental acquisition of French does not distract the students from learning new and complex ideas through French); without any form of mental confusion or loss of normal cognitive growth; and without a loss of identity or appreciation for their own ethnicity. Most important of all in the present context, the immersion pupils also become informed about and develop a deeper appreciation for French Canadians by learning about them and their culture through their teachers and through their developing skill with the language of French Canadians.

What is exciting about this program, over and above its educational and cognitive impact, is that it opens children's minds to an otherwise foreign and possibly threatening outgroup. It also provides them with certain sociopolitical insights that monolingual mainstreamers would likely never have attained. For example, the immersion children come to the realization that peaceful democratic coexistence among members of distinctive ethnolinguistic groups calls for something more than simply learning one another's languages.[16] Having learned the other language well and having learned to appreciate the other cultural group, children with immersion experience realize that effective and peaceful coexistence requires something even more important—opportunities for the young people of both ethnic groups to interact socially on an equitable basis. This is a very sophisticated insight that most adults either lose or never attain.

Thus, a new approach to the development of bilingual skills is now available, and since it works as well in other parts of Canada where few if any French Canadians are encountered in social life,[17] it, or some variation of it, can be expected to work equally well in the United States.

By focusing on subject matter mastery and making language learning incidental, immersion programs differ substantively from second language teaching programs (e.g., French-as-a-second-language programs) where subject matter mastery is not a main goal, where the new language is the focus, and where only small amounts of time are devoted to the second language component. That component also becomes the responsibility of a specialist rather than the classroom teacher. Thus, immersion programs are much more intense and comprehensive than second language programs; since no specialists are involved, the cost of immersion programs is hardly any different from usual (since the classroom teacher is also the language specialist), and the class size (i.e., thirty to thirty-two pupils to a teacher in Canada) is usually kept to the average. There are no paid native-speaker teacher aides in immersion classes.

Immersion education differs from typical bilingual education programs as these are conducted in North America. No bilingual skills are required of the teacher, who plays the role of a monolingual in the target language (if he or she is not in fact monolingual), and who never switches languages, reviews materials in the other language, or otherwise uses the second language. Rather, bilingualism is developed through two separate monolingual instructional routes.

There are currently some ten or more communities in the United States where comparable early immersion programs for mainstream English-speaking children are underway (in Spanish, French, and German, so far), and from all available accounts they are working splendidly.[18] Part of the reason for their success is that school administrators and principals, after an initial period of skepticism and wariness, have become extremely pleased and proud of the outcomes. Furthermore, the costs of the programs are surprisingly low compared to second language teaching programs, because the regular teachers' salaries simply go to the new "foreign speaking" teachers.

What really counts as success, though, is the pride of progress reflected by teachers, parents and pupils. For example, Frank Grittner, the supervisor of second language education for the State of Wisconsin, has collected data on third-grade English-speaking children (few with German ethnic backgrounds) in a German immersion program where they were taught through German for three years.[19] That particular immersion program was part of a plan for desegregation in the Milwaukee Public Schools, and thus some 40 percent of the pupils involved were black. At the end of third grade, all of the German immersion pupils scored in the average to above average range on the Metropolitan Achievement Test for Reading (in English), compared to 70 percent for the Milwaukee schools in general, and 77 percent for American norm groups. Likewise for the mathematics test scores (also tested through English), the respective numbers were 92, 71, and 77 percent. Similar outcomes are available for English-speaking American children in a French immersion program in Holliston, Massachusetts, as of the end of grade two.[20] In New York City, where an interesting program of partial immersion in Spanish for English-speaking pupils has been tried out, the end-of-year parental responses and evaluations are extremely favorable. What characterizes the parents' reaction is the delight they show that their children are learning about Spanish-speaking people and developing an appreciation for them, while simultaneously acquiring the basics of the language. They are pleased not for "instrumental" reasons but for "integrative" ones, i.e., because intergroup harmony is initiated, not because their children can profit in the business world by knowing Spanish.[21]

Furthermore, there is strong evidence to show that monolingual Anglo-Canadian children can handle easily a "double immersion" program wherein French and Hebrew, for example, are used in separate streams, as the languages of instruction for Jewish youngsters in Montreal.[22] The striking success of double immersion programs, incidentally, gives second thoughts to Canadian policymakers who promote multiculturalism but stop short of providing at least some instruction via a heritage language. The point is that ethnic minorities in Canada might easily handle and enjoy education that is trilingual—French, English, and heritage language—just as these Jewish children handle and enjoy education that is French, Hebrew, and English.

The variants of the immersion program that might be particularly relevant when applied in the United States are limited only by one's imagination. For instance, the New York City variant is a partial immersion program that can be increased in time devoted and in scope to satisfy large numbers of pupils with a variety of language options.[23] Then there is an extremely interesting "Language to Share" program[24] wherein ethnic-minority adolescents are trained to be junior teachers of their home language to pupils two or three years younger than themselves. Similarly, there are possibilities for "language exchange" programs[25] wherein anglophone pupils who are interested in learning a particular foreign language are paired up by a master teacher with a pupil who has that foreign language as his/her home language, and who exchanges two or so hours per week in teaching it informally while receiving English instruction in return.

Psychological Implications of Two-Language Programs

What this all means is that there is now available an effective means of developing a functionally bilingual citizenry. The evidence, both scientific and anecdotal, is so consistent that our concern is not that such programs will not be implemented, but rather that they will be instigated without careful consideration to the psychological and social consequences.

Note first that it was the *English-speaking* Canadian and the English-speaking American mainstreamers—the segments that are most secure in their ethnic and linguistic identity, yet the ones most in need of knowledge and sensitivity regarding other ethnic and linguistic groups—that were involved in the immersion experiments. The more that mainstream children are sensitized to and educated in another language and culture, the better the chances of developing a fairer, more equitable society. The better, too, are the chances of improving the self-concepts of ethnolinguistic minority children, who are heartened and complimented when they realize that mainstream children are making sincere gestures to learn about them, their language, and ways of life.

We have referred to this process of developing bilingual and bicultural skills among English-speaking Canadians or American children as an "additive" form of bilingualism, implying that these children, with no fear of ethnic/linguistic erosion, can add one or more foreign languages to their accumulating skills while profiting immensely from the experience cognitively, socially, and even economically.[26] Most mainstream parents are aware of these advantages and are surprisingly eager and anxious to have their children enroll in immersion programs or variants thereof. They want something more for their children than the traditional foreign language programs that they followed a genera-tion ago, most of which failed to develop either language competence or cultural sensitivity.

However, we draw a very sharp contrast between the additive form of bilingualism just described and the "subtractive" form which con-stitutes a totally different psychological and social reality, having dif-ferent outcomes, different potential hazards, and different means-to-ends demands. Hyphenated American children, like their French-Ca-nadian counterparts, embark on a subtractive bilingual route as soon as they enter a school where a high prestige, socially powerful, domi-nant language like English is introduced as the exclusive language of instruction. Perceptive members of ethnolinguistic minority groups have good grounds for worry and concern about the steamroller effect of a powerful dominant language; it can make foreign home languages and cultures seem "homely" in contrast, ghosts in the closet to be erad-icated and suppressed. The effects of this subtractive aspect of bilin-gualism among francophone university students in Quebec has been carefully studied by Taylor, Roch Meynard, and Elisabeth Rheault.[27] Two findings from that research help illustrate our main point. First, it was found that feelings of threat to one's ethnic identity function as a *negative* motivation in the second language learning process. Second, it turned out that those francophones who were least fluent in English were the ones who felt their cultural identity to be most threatened.

Just as French is too precious to be subtracted out of Canadian soci-ety, so too are the multitude of "foreign" languages and cultures ex-tant in the United States too precious to be eradicated from that soci-ety. Even more devastating is the cognitive risk children run when their basic conceptual language—the linguistic system that has been used to form and express thoughts and ideas from infancy—is abruptly put aside and suppressed so as not to interfere with the new school language.

A major responsibility of educational policymakers then becomes one of transforming subtractive forms of bilingualism into additive ones, for the benefit of both the ethnolinguistic minority groups as well as the mainstreamers. Community experiments that attempt to imple-ment such transformations, although few in number so far, are now underway.[28] Basically these experimental programs call for schooling to be conducted in the likely-to-be neglected home language of the ethnolinguistic minority child, beginning at kindergarten or grade one. The programs continue until it is certain that that language is strongly rooted and able to flourish on its own, and that the children themselves get grounded and oriented as to their ethnic identity. The programs do provide a concurrent strand of English language instruction (in the form of ESL or English immersion, with a separate teacher) for part of the day, but the dual-track program involving home language instruction is kept up for the first three or four years of primary education. It is only then that a switch to a primarily English language program can safely take place.

In practice, it is no simple matter to get these programs started or to maintain them, because language minority parents are often led to believe that there are dangers in having home-language instruction in the primary grades. With patience and tact the basic advantages can be presented, and once the originally skeptical parents and the local school authorities see the outcomes, they become the best future salespersons for other parents.

Richard Tucker recently evaluated a number of such community-based studies and concluded that there is "a cumulative and positive impact of bilingual education on all youngsters when they are allowed to remain in bilingual programs for a period of time greater than two or three or even five years and when there is an active attempt to provide nurturance and sustenance of their mother tongue in addition to introducing teaching via the language of wider communication."[29] This is the best way for the American society to help salvage minority languages and cultures and to help develop a new generation of children who could be happy to be *both* American *and* Hispanic, Haitian, Polish, Navajo, Arabic, or whatever. But note the two essential ingredients of the suggested plan: 1) At the same time as the needs of the ethnic-minority child are being catered to, the mainstream child is simultaneously developing skills in and an appreciation for at least one of these other languages and its associated culture; and 2) No time is taken from the all-important task of developing competence in the critical content subjects that make up a solid and demanding educational curriculum. The incidental learning of language and learning about another culture need not, and should not, be an obstacle to providing a thorough education in science, math, creative language arts, etc. Immigrant ethnic groups need such education as much as anyone else. Educational policymakers must not be distracted by the current confusion in the United States about bilingual education from their responsibility to produce a valuable curriculum that permits both minority and mainstream children to actualize their full potentials while contributing to a new, ethnically rich society.

Social Implications of Two-Language Programs

It would be naive to assume that members of different ethnolinguistic groups would be interested in learning a second language for the same reasons. The distinction between additive and subtractive bilingualism points to particular motivational differences that can have important consequences. It would be equally naive to assume that educational programs targeted for one group affect only that group. Any attention given one group will have both direct and indirect implications for all other social groups in the same setting and for the intergroup relations that develop. Thus, when a second language program is implemented for English-speaking white students, the effects will most certainly be felt by members of the immigrant and black communities. If the second language introduced in such a program is one spoken by immigrants, it can easily appear that English-speaking white students are being given preferential "access" to that community, and more generally that they are in a position to "add" a skill that could make them an even more powerful group. Similarly, giving immigrant children special educational attention, like providing them with instruction in their home language as well as in English, will have an impact on other groups. The immigrant group can be perceived as being given advantages that allow them to become rapidly competetive, thus threatening strategic and well-established power relations.

The Neglected Group: Black Americans

If the intergroup implications of language programs are important for the English-speaking white and ethnic immigrant groups, they are critical for the English-speaking black community. Blacks already have many deep reasons for feeling neglected and exploited in American society, and these feelings can be exacerbated very easily by the educational solutions suggested so far. Whether the setting is Chicago, Detroit, Boston, New York, Dade County in Florida, or elsewhere, one can easily imagine that black families will be upset because special attention is being directed toward language minority as well as white establishment children, giving them, in the long run, more advantages over black children. We cannot expect black children in Dade County, for example, to learn Spanish, Haitian, Creole, and/or French with necessarily the same aims in mind as the white English-speaking American child. Accommodating an immigrant group by learning its language could be seen by blacks as a new type of humiliation. American blacks have difficulty identifying themselves as American if they have to rely on the white American's definition of "American," and the personal and social advantages of becoming bilingual that are so attractive to English-speaking white Americans may be unimportant and irrelevant for blacks. For them, becoming bilingual in Spanish might mean that a new Spanish-speaking immigrant elite group could use blacks as their "hewers of wood" just as white elites have traditionally done. Blacks can be humiliated further if their children are surpassed in educational and occupational competitions by total newcomers to America who succeed because of the special educational attention they receive.

Blacks in the United States have much experience with various national and local attempts to improve the educational and occupational achievement of their children. Desegregated schooling and Head Start programs are notorious examples. Some research evidence on desegregated schooling shows that black children suffer badly from low self-esteem and inferiority, and that their self-esteem is lowered, not raised, by desegregated school contacts with whites.[30] Such psychological damage should not be surprising given that school environments have been largely defined by white habits and values. Similarly, there are data that suggest desegregation makes white children's attitudes toward blacks less, not more, positive.[31] Thus, the prospects of wider desegregation that includes ethnic immigrants are not promising for blacks because their self-esteem could be further debased by any signs of relative success on the part of language minority children, and they—the blacks—might become the target of negative attitudes from a new source, namely, language minority groups.

Bleak as the prospects of desegregated schooling are for black pupils' self-esteem and the prejudice directed against them, integrated schooling nonetheless does improve the academic achievement of blacks.[32] This important fact is a hopeful one to build on in any new suggestions for America's multiethnic educational system. What suggestions, then, can be made for the education of black American children that can be effectively integrated with the plans suggested previously for language minorities and white English-speaking mainstream Americans? Our suggested solution presupposes, again, that language issues are kept secondary to the main interest of providing comprehensive educational preparation for all pupils to ensure that they are given equal chances to cope in the highly technical society they all are to enter. (An illustration of this type of educational preparation is given in a paper written for the World Bank by Lambert and Nelly Sidoti.[33]) It is also presupposed that all participating social groups desire a solution, that is, that all groups want a resolution of social conflict (even though conflict itself is required for the solution), and that no one group will impose a one-way resolution on all participants.

A Multi-Group Plan

In the post-1980s period, integrated schools in the United States will be mixed three ways, with white English-speaking mainstreamers, black mainstreamers, and language minorities. Meeting the educational needs of any one particular group through innovative programs is itself a major challenge; it is more problematic to implement programs in such a way that no one group is, or feels, unjustly treated in the process. Here attention must be shifted from meeting the individual needs of particular communities to meeting simultaneously the needs of various groups in an effective but fair manner for all concerned.

The English-speaking white, black, and language minority groups are socially separate collectivities in important respects, and each has contributed to the rich, multiethnic social system that the United States has become. At the same time, however, these separate social groups share membership in a common social environment and are all essential members of a particular state and a common nation. As a consequence, the unique needs of each group are formulated within the context of this shared social system. There are, therefore, certain fundamental needs, values, and aspirations that all individuals share as citizens of their community, their state, and their nation. The central concern is with the education of children from diversified ethnic and linguistic backgrounds, and with the task of preparing them for full participation in the social, economic, and political life of American communities. The concrete question we arrive at then is: What are the agreed-upon aims of education that all members of all three groups share? Presumably, a facility in English for their children would constitute one aim shared by all parents, as would an adequate academic preparation to cope successfully in a highly technical society (no matter how that idea would be expressed). But how should a "facility in English" or an "adequate academic preparation" be defined concretely, and who should define it? Usually such pervasive, shared aims are defined by the most powerful group in the society, and this makes most shared aims impositions on the less powerful group or groups. To be left out of the definition process leaves members of these other groups, at best, only provisionally committed to such aims. A facility in English and an adequate academic preparation then must become shared aims in another sense. Sharing requires that members of all groups involved agree through collaboration on what the realities of American life are today, and through free participation of all groups—conflictual as this may be—on what in concrete terms is meant by a facility in English and an adequate academic preparation.

Beyond the shared aims, each community also has a set of unique needs which are equally relevant and important for them. The responsibility of each community then is to describe what its particular needs are, and how these are related to their perspective of the shared needs. For the English-speaking white community in the United States, this may require no special attention to the shared aim of facility in English, but that community may well want to safeguard adequate academic preparation and also place special emphasis on the development of bilingual skills for their children. The language minority communities may place great stress on the need for help in attaining excellence in the shared aim of English language skill and its relation to adequate academic preparation, while at the same time they explore for themselves the importance, or not, of keeping the heritage language and culture alive. The black community may also perceive the need to direct resource attention to the shared aim of English language skills and particularly to adequate academic preparation which, they may argue, has not been provided in the past. Thus, they might bargain for a greater share of resources to make up for past shortcomings. The particular aims of the black community might include special attention to Black English as a formal element in the general curriculum, coupled with a share in second language learning for their own children.

It should be made clear that these illustrative examples might not be the actual shared or unique aims or needs of any of the three communities. Decisions and choices would have to be made by the three (or more) communities in concert in the case of defining shared aims, and by each community on its own in the case of defining unique needs. The essential feature of the proposal is that each community's special needs be considered, and that no group be slighted in terms of resource allocation. What differs is the nature of the resource allocations, each of these determined by the communities themselves.

Who is to take the initiative so that all parties to this community-based problem will want to congregate in order to compete equitably and ultimately collaborate on a program of shared and unique educational goals? Policymakers in responsible positions who do not facilitate such a congregation are signalling their disagreement with the proposals offered in this chapter. They can no longer maintain that white or black English-speaking mainstreamers are irrelevant to the central issue of educating language minority children. That position is no longer tenable.

In conclusion, it is argued that quality education for children need not be jeopardized because it is made bilingual and bicultural. Instead, we are persuaded by an accumulation of recent psycholinguistic and social psychological research that all children—mainstream English-speakers as well as language minority children—can be helped to develop high-level skills in two languages and two cultures at the same time as they achieve at or above normal standards in the educational demands made on them. The procedure suggested for two-language and two-culture training is fundamentally different from conventional bilingual/bicultural education as typically taught in American public schools over the past twenty years. It involves an immersion-type program that is sensitive to the additive, in contrast to the subtractive, consequences of attempts to develop bilingual skills. Thus, we suggest that English-speaking mainstreamers take a good part of their elementary education through the medium of a foreign or second language that is relevant to their social setting, while non-English-speaking language minority children be given a similar chance to develop a stable and deep level of competence in their heritage language at the same time as they develop full bilinguality through English. Children who become functionally bilingual and bicultural in this fashion would constitute a new breed of young Americans, particularly well equipped to cope with and contribute to the fascinating multicultural society that the United States is increasingly becoming. Our only concern is that in attempting to implement language-enriched educational programs, policymakers may be left to their own resources without the collaboration of behavioral scientists, and thus be insensitive to the psychological and the social realities of language for all groups in the society—the language minorities, the mainstream white English-speaking, and the mainstream black English-speaking. We are especially concerned that policymakers might be insensitive to language minority parents and the dreams and wishes they have for their children.

NOTES

*The research reported here was made possible by subventions from the Spencer Foundation and from the The Social Sciences and Humanities Research Council of Canada.

Portions of this chapter were published previously in Wallace E. Lambert and Donald M. Taylor, "Language in the Education of Ethnic Minority Immigrants," in Ronald J. Samuda and Sandra L. Woods, eds., *Perspectives in Immigrant and Minority Education* (Lanham, MD: University Press of America, Inc., 1983), pp. 267-280; and Wallace E. Lambert and Donald M. Taylor, "Language in the Education of Ethnic Minority Children in Canada," in Ronald J. Samuda, John W. Berry, and Michel Laferrière, eds., *Multiculturalism in Canada: Social and Educational Perspectives* (Toronto: Allyn and Bacon, Inc., 1984), pp. 201-215, and are reprinted with permission.

[1]Nathan Glazer and Daniel P. Moynihan, *Beyond the Melting Pot* (Cambridge, MA: MIT and Harvard University Press, 1963).

[2]Jane Perlez, "Beyond 'Beyond the Melting Pot,' Moynihan and Glazer Feel Vindicated," *The New York Times* (December 3, 1983): 27.

[3]Quoted in Glenn Collins, "A New Look at Intermarriage In the U.S.," *The New York Times* (February 11, 1985): C13.

[4]Ibid.

[5]Carol Aellen and Wallace E. Lambert, "Ethnic Identification and Personality Adjustments of Canadian Adolescents of Mixed English-French Parentage," *Canadian Journal of Behavioral Science* 1 (April 1969): 69-86.

[6]Collins, op. cit.

[7]Lisa Wolfe, "Moynihan, As A Fellow At Columbia, Revels In A Return to Campus Life," *The New York Times* (February 26, 1985): B1.

[8]Thomas Sowell, *The Economics and Politics of Race* (New York: Morrow & Co., 1983).

[9]Bernard Lefkowitz, "Renegotiating Society's Contract With the Public Schools: The National Commission on Secondary Education for Hispanics and the National Board of Inquiry Into Schools," *Carnegie Quarterly* 29: 4 (Fall 1984/Winter 1985).

[10]Tove Skutnabb-Kangas and Pertti Toukomaa, *Teaching Migrant Children's Mother Tongue and Learning the Language of the Host Country in the Context of the Socio-cultural Situation of the Migrant Family* (Helsinski, Finland: The Finnish National Commission for UNESCO, 1976).

[11]Wallace E. Lambert, "Bilingualism and Language Acquisition," in Harris Winitz, ed., *Native Language and Foreign Language Acquisition*, Vol. 379, Annals of the New York Academy of Sciences (New York: The New York Academy of Sciences, 1981), pp. 9-22.

[12]Wallace E. Lambert, "A Social Psychology of Bilingualism," *Journal of Social Issues* 23: 2 (April 1967): 91-109.

[13]Karl R. Popper, *The Open Society and Its Enemies*, Vols. 1 and 2 (London: Routledge and Kegan Paul, 1966).

[14]See Wallace E. Lambert and G. Richard Tucker, *Bilingual Education of Children* (Rowley, MA: Newbury House, 1972); Merrill Swain, "French Immersion Programs Across Canada," *The Canadian Modern Language Review* 31: 2 (November 1974): 117-129; and Fred Genesee, "Scholastic Effects of French Immersion: An Overview After Ten Years," *Interchange* 9: 4 (1979): 20-29.

[15]Wallace E. Lambert, "A Canadian Experiment in the Development of Bilingual Competence: The Home-to-School Language Switch Program," Mimeograph (Montreal: McGill University, Psychology Department, 1979).

[16]See Larry Blake, Wallace E. Lambert, Nelly Sidoti, and David Wolfe, "Students' Views of Intergroup Tensions in Quebec: The Effects of Language

Immersion Experience," *Canadian Journal of Behavioral Science* 13 (April 1981): 144-160; and Gary A. Cziko, Wallace E. Lambert, Nelly Sidoti, and G. Richard Tucker, "Graduates of Early Immersion: Retrospective Views of Grade 11 Students and Their Parents," in Robert St. Clair and Howard Giles, eds., *The Social and Psychological Contexts of Language* (Hillsdale, NJ: Lawrence Erlbaum Associates, Inc., 1980).

[17]See Swain, op. cit.

[18]See written reports by Andrew D. Cohen, "The Case for Partial or Total Immersion," in Antonio Simoes, Jr., ed., *The Bilingual Child: Research and Analysis of Existing Educational Themes* (New York: Academic Press, 1976), pp. 65-89; Douglas D. Samuels and Robert J. Griffore, "The Plattsburgh French Language Immersion Program: Its Influence on Intelligence and Self-Esteem," *Language Learning* 29: 1 (March 1979): 45-52; and Montgomery County Public Schools, *End of the Second Year Report on the French Language Immersion Program at Four Corners* (Montgomery County, MD: 1976). The authors have also received accounts of early immersion programs in personal communications with William J. Derrick (1980), Frank Grittner (1981), James O'Connell (1981), and Nelly Sidoti (1981).

[19]Grittner, personal communication, op. cit.

[20]O'Connell, personal communication, op. cit.

[21]Sidoti, personal communication, op. cit.

[22]Fred Genesee and Wallace E. Lambert, "Trilingual Education for Majority Language Children," *Child Development* 54: 1 (February 1983): 105-114.

[23]Sidoti, op. cit.

[24]See Susan C. Thomas, *A Language to Share* (Newton, MA: Educational Development Center, Inc., 1980).

[25]Wallace E. Lambert, "An Alternative to the Foreign Language Teaching Profession," *Interchange* 9: 4 (1978): 95-108.

[26]Wallace E. Lambert, "Some Cognitive and Sociocultural Consequences of Being Bilingual," in James E. Alatis, ed., *International Dimensions of Bilingual Education: Georgetown University Round Table on Languages and Linguistics* (Washington, D.C.: Georgetown University Press, 1978), pp. 214-229.

[27]Donald M. Taylor, Roch Meynard, and Elisabeth Rheault, "Threat to Ethnic Identity and Second-Language Learning," in Howard Giles, ed., *Language, Ethnicity, and Intergroup Relations* (London: Academic Press, 1977).

[28]See discussions of these experiments in Lambert, "Bilingualism and Language Acquisition," op. cit.; Lambert, "An Alternative to the Foreign Language Teaching Profession," op. cit.; Carolyn Kessler and Mary Ellen Quinn, "Bilingualism and Science Problem-Solving Ability," Unpublished paper presented at the 14th Annual Convention of Teachers of English to Speakers of Other Languages (San Francisco: 1980); and Rudolph C. Troike, "Research Evidence for the Effectiveness of Bilingual Education," *NABE Journal* 3: 1 (Fall 1978): 13-24.

[29]G. Richard Tucker, *Comments on Proposed Rules for Nondiscrimination Under Programs Receiving Federal Financial Assistance Through the Education Department* (Washington, D.C.: Center for Applied Linguistics, 1980).

[30]Walter G. Stephan, "School Desegregation: An Evaluation of Predictions Made in *Brown v. Board of Education*," *Psychological Bulletin* 85: 2 (March 1978): 217-238.

[31]Ibid.

[32]Ibid.

[33]Wallace E. Lambert and Nelly Sidoti, "The Selection of Appropriate Languages of Instruction and the Use of Radio for Education in Less Developed Countries," Unpublished Manuscript (Washington, D.C.: The World Bank, Department of Education, 1981).

LEGISLATION, REGULATION, AND LITIGATION: THE ORIGINS AND EVOLUTION OF PUBLIC POLICY ON BILINGUAL EDUCATION IN THE UNITED STATES

Ricardo R. Fernández

University of Wisconsin-Milwaukee

Since the late 1960s, bilingual education has been promoted by the federal and state governments, and by many community groups, as the principal means of attempting to provide equal educational opportunities for national origin minority group (NOM) children who are limited in their English language proficiency (LEP). The vast majority of LEP students in this country are Hispanic. Much discussion and, at times, heated debates have taken place regarding the need for bilingual education in the nation's public schools. Questions abound concerning the effectiveness of this particular pedagogical approach, its goals and objectives, its cost, and its impact on the larger society.

This chapter will trace the origins and development of federal and state policy related to bilingual education in U.S. public schools over the last twenty years. It will focus on bilingual education legislation, regulation and enforcement efforts, and judicial precedents. It will also attempt to describe how the interplay among the various competing interests in the political process and in the society at large has helped to shape the bilingual education policies which have evolved since the enactment of the Elementary and Secondary Education Act of 1965.[1]

Legislation

Federal Legislation (1968-1984)

The passage of the Elementary and Secondary Education Act (ESEA) by Congress in 1965 represented a major step in federal involvement in the nation's schools. The large infusion of monies into compensatory education and other programs to address the needs of poor children marked the beginning of a new relationship between the federal government and the public (and private) schools, which has evolved over the past two decades into efforts to promote equality of opportunity for disadvantaged students, school desegregation, bilingual education, gender equity, education for handicapped children, and most recently, a push for excellence.[2]

When Senator Ralph Yarborough, Democrat of Texas, introduced a bilingual education bill in Congress early in 1967, his primary intent was to address the long-neglected needs of Mexican-American children in the Southwest. His proposed bill would have authorized "bilingual-bicultural" programs, including teaching English as a second language (ESL) as well as teaching Spanish in programs to instill in Spanish-speaking students a knowledge about and pride in their home language and culture.[3] After much debate in the Senate and in the House, the legislation was broadened to serve *all* children of limited English-speaking ability. In January 1968, Public Law 90-247, which added Title VII ("Bilingual Education Programs") to the ESEA, was signed into law by President Lyndon Johnson.[4]

A brief review of the salient features of this new "Bilingual Education Act" is in order. The findings of Congress pointed to "one of the most acute educational problems in the United States . . . which involves millions of children of limited English-speaking ability." The act provided financial assistance to school districts "to develop and carry out new and imaginative elementary and secondary school programs designed to meet these special educational needs."[5] A focus on children from low-income families ($3,000 per year or less) made Title VII consistent with Title I (Compensatory Education) of the same act. A list of authorized activities summarizes the various types of programs envisioned by lawmakers:

(1) bilingual education programs;

(2) programs designed to impart to students a knowledge of the history and culture associated with their languages;

(3) efforts to establish closer cooperation between the school and the home;

(4) early childhood educational programs related to the purposes of this title and designed to improve the potential for profitable learning activities by children;

(5) adult education programs related to the purposes of this title, particularly for parents of children participating in bilingual programs;

(6) programs designed for dropouts or potential dropouts having need of bilingual programs;

(7) programs conducted by accredited trade, vocational, or technical schools; and

(8) other activities which meet the purposes of this title.[6]

As an innovative approach to addressing the needs of limited English-speaking ability (LESA) children, the law emphasized the need for experimentation. The testimony presented at hearings on the bill, which emphasized various indices of the level of dysfunction of LESA children such as very high dropout rates, contained very little data about the types of educational approaches that could be used. This dearth of objective evidence was recognized in the Senate Committee Report on the Bilingual Education Act, which stated:

> Because of the need for extensive research, pilot projects and demonstration, the proposed legislation does not intend to prescribe the types of programs or projects that are needed. Such matters are left to the discretion or judgments of the local school districts to encourage both varied approaches to the problem and also special solutions for a particular problem of a given school. The legislation enumerates types of programs as being illustrative of possible solutions.[7]

Nevertheless, a "bilingual-bicultural" approach was recommended when LESA children experienced difficulty in school. Against the backdrop of massive failure of Hispanic and other LESA children in the nation's schools, the urgency to move ahead with a new policy, a fresh, albeit untested, approach, seemed quite sensible. Funding was set at a modest $7.5 million, and the federal bilingual education experiment began.

It is easy, almost a generation later, to overlook the significance of the Bilingual Education Act of 1968. In passing this legislation, Congress was charting a new course in educational policy for the country, one which involved "a fundamental policy shift from monolingualism to permissive use of bilingual instruction."[8] Opposition to bilingual education of any type was intense, yet the need for action overcame this resistance at the federal level.

The implementation of Title VII in the early years (1969 to 1973) was fraught with difficulties. John Molina attributes this to "the inexperience of educators in this country" with bilingual education, as well as to "the vagueness inherent in the Act itself." In his words, "[B]ilingual education was too new and philosophically threatening to be accepted by many school districts which often favored remedial and English language programs instead. The lack of appropriate materials in non-English languages, and the need for trained bilingual teachers, made difficult the starting of new programs with appropriate emphasis on native languages."[9] A concrete example of vagueness in the act is the definition of LESA children as "children who come from environments where the dominant language is other than English."[10] No distinction is made between English monolingual children and children with varying degrees of skill in English and in their native language.

An attempt to clarify the goals of the programs to be funded by issuing guidelines on the use of two languages for instruction brought about controversy over the goals of bilingual education. Molina points out that "[T]he 1971 guidelines and the philosophical position of Title VII suggested a maintenance approach to bilingual education," and programs were envisioned that would help students to "develop greater competence in English and [also to] become more proficient in their dominant language...."[11] Indeed, a 1973 position paper developed by the Division of Bilingual Education in the then U.S. Office of Education defined bilingual education as "an approach which would effectively manifest itself in a well-planned, concrete educational program beginning at the pre-school level and continuing through a child's elementary school career, being maintained through language arts courses in the students' dominant language at the secondary level."[12] However, the 1971 guidelines were nullified by a legal opinion requiring that regulations be based on actual language from the law. The ambiguity over the objectives of bilingual education remained under discussion until 1974, when the first major revision of the act took place. Nevertheless, from 1969 through 1973, appropriations increased from $7.5 million to $45 million, and from 76 programs serving 26,521 children to 209 programs serving 129,380 students. Bilingual education was no longer a fledgling program, and its strength would increase significantly as a result of events which took place in 1974.

The year 1974 was a key one in the continuing development of policy regarding bilingual education. In January, a unanimous U.S. Supreme Court ruled in *Lau* v. *Nichols* that federal civil rights statutes prohibited discrimination based on language in the nation's schools.[13] Although it is difficult to assess its total impact, the *Lau* decision was significant in shaping educational policy toward LESA children, not only in Congress but across the country, where it paved the way for swift legislative action in several states with large NOM/LEP student populations. The decision did not endorse bilingual education or any other method of instruction; that was left to the discretion of educators and policymakers. Nevertheless, still operating under the axiom that, absent contrary evidence, understandable instruction was a sensible policy, and supported by early research studies, Congress proceeded to reauthorize Title VII.[14]

The outcome of the reauthorization, however, was a much changed piece of legislation which differed significantly from its earlier version.

Raymond Padilla argues that the 1974 Amendments "[c]onstituted a fundamental rethinking of federal support for bilingual education."[15] A new push for equity expanded the resources and the implementation of bilingual education by eliminating the poverty criterion, thus expanding the potential pool of students who could be served. It also sharpened the focus of the legislation on the acquisition of English language skills by tightening the language used in the policy and in the definitions sections to describe the purpose of bilingual education, which then was "designed to enable them [LESA children], while using their native language, to achieve competence in English."[16] The transitional thrust intended by Congress can best be captured by the definition of a program:

> The term "program of bilingual education" means a program of instruction, designed for children of limited English-speaking ability in elementary or secondary schools, in which, with respect to the years of study to which such program is applicable—
>
> (i) there is instruction given in, and study of, English and, to the extent necessary to allow a child to progress effectively through the educational system, [in] the native language of the children of limited English-speaking ability. . . .[17]

The law expressly forbade programs "designed for the purpose of teaching a foreign language to English-speaking children,"[18] although it did allow such children to participate in bilingual programs on a limited basis so that language and cultural exchanges could take place among students. Any previous ambiguity was removed, and the legislative intent of Congress clearly pointed to a transitional policy which had the learning of English as its fundamental goal. The amendments also recognized the importance of training to prepare teachers and other personnel associated with bilingual programs, and allocated funds to undertake much needed research studies in the field of bilingual education.

Between 1975 and 1978, Title VII appropriations registered impressive growth, and its budget rose from $85 million to $135 million. A total of 379 programs served 268,497 students in 1975; by 1978 the number of programs had increased to more than 500, and some 300,000 children were receiving services. In these same years, parallel to the implementation of federally-funded bilingual education programs in hundreds of school districts, a number of states approved legislation that mandated bilingual instruction for LESA children and provided funding for such programs. In 1975 the U.S. Commission on Civil Rights issued a major report on bilingual-bicultural education. Enforcement efforts by the executive branch through the Office for Civil

Rights (OCR) of the then Department of Health, Education, and Welfare resulted in the adoption of educational plans by several hundred school districts across the country. These plans had to comply with suggested federal guidelines that were weighted in favor of transitional bilingual education. Much controversy was generated by the actions of OCR. In addition, the stir caused by a major research study conducted by the American Institutes of Research[19] (A.I.R.) under the auspices of the then U.S. Office of Education, which reached mostly inconclusive findings about the effectiveness of bilingual programs in various sites across the country, set the tone for the debate on bilingual education during the second reauthorization of Title VII in 1978.

Once again, the debate over the goals of the program surfaced at the hearings and in the exchanges among legislators. Teachers' unions, such as the American Federation of Teachers, opposed bilingual education, not on its merits but mainly because of the political implications for displacement of nonbilingual staff with bilingual teachers. Concern about the effectiveness of bilingual instruction as a pedagogical method to teach English to language minority children had been heightened by the A.I.R. report and by a highly-publicized monograph written by *Washington Post* journalist Noel Epstein.[20] Epstein criticized the "bicultural" aspect of bilingual education ("affirmative ethnicity" in his words) as an improper role for the federal government to play, and questioned why transitional bilingual education was promoted as the only acceptable (i.e., fundable) method of instruction allowed under Title VII. Even though it already existed in large measure, Epstein argued in his polemical style for even more "flexibilty" in the methodologies that should be tried in attempting to learn what approach would work best.

An analysis of the Education Amendments of 1978[21] reveals several noteworthy changes. While the main focus was still on equal educational opportunity, for the first time the research agenda was expanded greatly to require that studies be conducted on various aspects of bilingual education, such as language acquisition, methods of English and reading instruction, identification of students, teacher training, and cultural characteristics of students served. An important change was made in the definitions, which referred to "limited English proficiency" rather than "limited English-speaking ability," reflecting a growing awareness that, in addition to speaking, language skills which encompass understanding, reading, and writing were needed for students to achieve academically.[22]

Growing concern about segregation, which was a major equity issue at the federal level in the 1970s, prompted lawmakers to allow the participation in the program of children whose language was English (up to a maximum of 40 percent of all children). The provision emphasized, however, that "the objective of the program shall be to assist children of limited English proficiency to improve their English language skills. . . ."[23] Title VII funds were also authorized to assist school districts in implementing Title VI (Civil Rights Act of 1964) compliance plans, pursuant to OCR's guidelines developed after *Lau v. Nichols.*[24] In addition, monies were set aside in the Emergency School Aid Act (ESAA) to assist school districts in addressing the racial isolation and other educational needs of NOM/LEP students and their families.[25]

Parent participation was expanded by a requirement that advisory councils made up of a majority of parents had to be consulted in the development of applications for Title VII funding.[26] Pertinent to this chapter were the requirements that Title VII programs serve those children most in need (i.e., LEP children first), and that "if any child is enrolled for two years, that child shall have an individual evaluation establishing the need for continued services."[27] The intent was to reinforce the transitional nature of the program by placing an affirmative burden on the district to justify the participation of *every* LEP student in the program after a limited and arbitrary period of time.

Faulty implementation of bilingual programs, exacerbated by a dearth of qualified personnel, continued to be highlighted by the press and electronic media, and the public controversy over bilingual education policy continued in the years following the 1978 amendments. A new administration in Washington made it a priority to rescind proposed regulations promulgated by OCR in 1980 which would have required transitional bilingual education as *the* minimally acceptable method of teaching LEP students. Title VII funding was reduced in 1981, but Congress refused to merge the program into block grants to the states under the Education Consolidation and Improvement Act (ECIA) of 1981.[28] President Ronald Reagan himself went on record as supporting a limited role for the federal government in transitional bilingual education, but his opposition in a spring 1981 speech to anything that resembled language preservation and other alleged misdirected efforts was strong and unequivocal: "[I]t is absolutely wrong and against American concepts to have a bilingual education program that is now openly, admittedly dedicated to preserving their [LEPs'] native language and never getting them adequate in English so they can go out into the job market and participate."[29]

By the time that the most recent process of reauthorization for Title VII began in 1984, various efforts were underway in Congress to curtail drastically the federal role in bilingual education. Bills were introduced in 1983 which would have sharply reduced funding and would have limited participation in the programs.[30] These attempts, although unsuccessful, brought to the fore vocal opponents of bilingual education who raised arguments against transitional bilingual education being the only acceptable approach to the education of LEP children under current legislative policy, and pushed for alternative methods to be promoted on an experimental basis by the federal government. It was as if legislation had come full circle, and the thrust of the original 1968 legislation toward innovation and experimentation was being adopted again by Congress.

The proposed reauthorization bill began as H.R. 5231, the "Academic Equity and Excellence through Bilingual Education Act," and was sponsored by Representatives Kildee, Democrat from Michigan, and Corrada, Democrat from Puerto Rico, both strong supporters of transitional bilingual education.[31] The title reflected a blending of objectives which tried to capture in the bill's policy section[32] the old equal educational opportunity commitment, together with the current national push toward excellence in education. The notion that the inconclusiveness of the research on the effectiveness of bilingual education required more flexibility was acknowledged by opponents and, reluctantly, by some advocates. Under the proposed legislation, school districts were to be allowed a measure of freedom in order to examine which curricular approaches were most suitable to meet locally identified needs. Many of the provisions of the 1978 amendments were retained, e.g., allowing up to 40 percent of English-speaking children to participate in bilingual programs so as to prevent the segregation of NOM/LEP students; greater parental involvement; an emphasis on serving LEP children most in need; and a clear, unambiguous purpose: "to help children enter an all-English class as soon as possible."[33]

Perhaps the most significant feature of the 1984 amendments was that the law specifically authorized a variety of "Programs of Academic Excellence."[34] This aspect was very much in line with national public debate on the quality of public education and effective schools research. In addition to transitional bilingual education, "programs of developmental bilingual education," "special alternative instructional programs for students of limited English proficiency," and "programs of academic excellence" were authorized. Services extended beyond the school to the families of LEP students, who were entitled to take part in English literacy programs as well as to programs for preschool, special education, and gifted and talented students.[35] The bill represented a political compromise with bipartisan support to allow for experimentation in alternatives to transitional bilingual education, such as ESL and structured immersion, as well as maintenance programs (with up to 50 percent English-speaking students in the classroom) that included expanded foreign language instruction. Funding levels, although still inadequate to serve all children in need, were negotiated to preserve the integrity of bilingual education programs (the essential intent of the original Bilingual Education Act), while simultaneously setting aside additional funds for the various alternative approaches.

Thus at the federal level, the "transitional" versus "maintenance" debate was set aside temporarily during the four-year period (1984 to 1988) for which the bill is authorized. As new documentation of the effectiveness of the range of approaches becomes available, it will be possible to have a better picture of what is (or is not) working. Undoubtedly, data will be subject to interpretation and much conjecture, and one should not expect a final resolution of the debate at the end of this period. Rather, it is much more likely that a continuation of the present compromise, with increased appropriations to allow for additional experimentation with alternative approaches, will emerge in the next reauthorization. However, the debate over program goals related to native language development will continue because, fundamentally, it is based on deeply held values and attitudes by opponents and advocates which transcend research evidence and established policy.

State Legislation (1971-1985)

The passage of the Bilingual Education Act in 1968 did not go unnoticed in state legislatures. In 1971, Massachusetts became the first state to enact a law—the Transitional Bilingual Education Act— which required school districts to develop and implement programs for children of limited English-speaking ability and provide funds for this purpose.[36] By 1973, Texas, Illinois, and California had enacted similar mandates, followed by Michigan (1974), New Jersey (1975), and Wisconsin (1976).[37] Presently, there are twelve states that require bilingual instruction.[38] The *transitional* emphasis of all state legislation can be said to be modeled after the Massachusetts law. The primary differences among state bilingual education statutes are based on the types of programs required by grade levels (elementary and/or secondary), the duration of services provided to LEP students, and funding formulae.

Colorado presents an interesting case study of changing legislation. In 1975 the legislature approved a comprehensive bilingual education bill which was hailed by advocates as a major victory in a state that historically had not been supportive of issues like bilingual education. Yet the Colorado legislation, born out of intense political pressure by Hispanic lawmakers supported by community activists and other lobbying groups, was quickly targeted for changes by conservative legislators. In 1980, after heated debate and several attempts at compromise, the law was repealed and in its place the "English Language Proficiency Act" was approved by the legislature and signed into law.[39] The law called for services to be provided by school districts to LEP students, but was completely silent as to the method(s) of instruction, leaving that decision to local school boards and administrators. At the urging of Hispanic lawmakers, a clause was added to emphasize that the bill did not prohibit school districts from using funds provided under this act for bilingual educational programs.[40] The new law's potentially negative impact on bilingual programs did not materialize, as had been predicted, and many districts opted to continue to offer the same programs which were in place before repeal of the Colorado Bilingual Education Act.

Although it is impossible to predict whether other states will follow Colorado's lead, there does not appear to be any urgency in other state legislatures to follow suit at this time. Bilingual education mandates will probably continue in place, especially in those states with significant numbers of NOM/LEP students. The cost to a school district of any expansion of services as a result of repealing bilingual education and allowing any method selected to address the educational needs of LEP students would be quite high, since the numbers of students served would increase, and this is likely to prevent any sudden, major overhaul of state bilingual laws. But it is probable that the impact of the 1984 amendments to Title VII will be felt in state legislatures in the coming years.[41]   Pleas for flexibility in alternative approaches to transitional bilingual education will no doubt be made by superintendents in districts hard pressed to deal with a growing linguistic diversity in their student body. Bilingual instruction is not always feasible when small numbers of children from diverse backgrounds are present in a classroom, and some districts will ask for help to fund ESL and remedial approaches. However, districts with high concentrations of Hispanics and other major language minority groups are likely to continue to deliver bilingual services, regardless of what other (usually smaller) districts may choose to do.

Regulation and Enforcement

The federal government's initial efforts to issue regulations regarding LEP children can be traced back to 1970. In May of that year, the Office for Civil Rights of the then Department of Health, Education, and Welfare issued a memorandum pursuant to its authority under the Civil Rights Act of 1964.[42] The May 25th Memorandum, as it came to be known, was sent to several hundred districts with more than 5 percent national origin minority group children. The document attempted to clarify the obligation of districts toward NOM children deficient in English language skills. Districts were ordered to "take affirmative steps to rectify the language deficiency in order to open its instructional program to these [LEP] students."[43] No specific approach, e.g., bilingual education, ESL, etc., was required or even suggested. Prohibitions were issued against discriminatory tracking or ability grouping, which often keeps NOM/LEP students out of college preparatory courses, as well as against assigning NOM students to special education classes on the basis of tests given in English. Finally, adequate notification to parents was required, in their own language if necessary, so that the information sent home from the school would be understandable to them. School districts were asked to review current practices and modify them in light of these requirements. Technical assistance in program development and implementation was offered by OCR, but there were relatively few districts which asked for it. Enforcement was limited by this method of self-identification of potential violations of civil rights statutes by the transgressing districts.

This situation changed radically after the *Lau v. Nichols* decision. The Office for Civil Rights established an advisory group of experts from a variety of disciplines to recommend suggested approaches that could be urged on school districts to help bring them into compliance with the Supreme Court's decision. In 1975 this group prepared a document entitled "Task Force Findings Specifying Practices Ruled Unlawful under *Lau v. Nichols*," which immediately became known as the "*Lau* Remedies."[44] This document outlined specific steps to be followed to achieve compliance, including identification of the student's primary or home language, program selection, curriculum and personnel requirements, prohibition of racial/ethnic isolation, parental notification, and evaluation. A review of the *Lau* Remedies shows that transitional bilingual education was the *minimal* requirement recommended for elementary and intermediate programs for the non- or limited-English speakers. A blanket disapproval of the use of other methods at these levels was also included:

Because an ESL program does not consider the affective nor cognitive development of students in this category and time and maturation variables are different here than for students at the secondary level, an ESL program is *not* appropriate.[45]

At the secondary level, ESL was allowed, along with other options such as High Intensive Language Training, transitional bilingual education, bilingual/bicultural, or multilingual/multicultural. However, districts were admonished that "if the necessary prerequisite skills in the native language(s) have not been taught to these students [enrolled in transitional bilingual education or another form of bilingual education], some form of compensatory education in the native language must be provided."[46] The guidelines were very clear, though, on the intent of this recommendation:

[S]tudents . . . must receive such instruction in a manner that is expeditiously carried out so that the student in question will be able to participate to the greatest extent possible in the regular school program as soon as possible.[47]

Transition into an all-English program was the goal, along with avoidance of segregation. Exit requirements from the program called for evidence of academic achievement as well as acquisition of language skills.

A cursory look at the *Lau* Remedies makes it obvious that they favored bilingual instruction.[48] After *Lau*, it became almost axiomatic that understandable (i.e., bilingual) instruction was preferable to other approaches such as ESL. Therefore, it is easy to see how in 1975 a group of experts, based on knowledge then available to them, could have shown a preference toward bilingual education, whether of the transitional or maintenance type.

Since the *Lau* Remedies were never published as official regulations, opposition to them was somewhat diffuse, although some districts objected strenuously to their use. Indeed, in 1976 "OCR reminded its regional offices that the *Lau* Remedies were only guidelines and that it could not prohibit ESL instruction and require school districts to provide bilingual-bicultural instruction."[49] Nevertheless, compliance agreements were negotiated by OCR with more than four hundred districts between 1975 and 1980, many of which contained provisions for bilingual education, since they were guided by the *Lau* Remedies.

In 1978, as part of a settlement of a case in Alaska,[50] OCR agreed to publish official regulations which would finally spell out the obligations of school districts to LEP students. For more than two years, OCR worked on the new rules and, after much internal discussion, a "Notice of Proposed Rule Making" appeared in the Federal Register in August 1980.[51] The stated purpose of the proposed regulations was:

(a) To ensure that students will not be excluded from participation in, be denied the benefits of, or be subjected to discrimination in education programs and activities because they have a primary language other than English; and

(b) To ensure that a student's limited proficiency in the English language will not bar the student from equal and effective opportunities to participate in Federally assisted education programs and activities.[52]

Under these rules, students who were more proficient in their native language than in English had to be taught bilingually and also had to receive intensive English instruction. Students whose proficiency in English was superior to their native language proficiency could receive instruction in English. However, for students who were equally limited in both languages, the rules allowed two options: English-only instruction or bilingual instruction.[53] Once again, research evidence was inconclusive as to which approach would work best for these children, so the rules allowed some flexibility in this area. But the preferred method—the only allowable method—under the rules for LEP children was transitional bilingual education.

It could be argued that in developing the proposed rules, OCR was guided by current policy. After all, bilingual education was *the* method of instruction funded by federal law. It was consistent, therefore, to issue guidelines that followed the principles which governed the Bilingual Education Act. Notwithstanding this, congressional action in response to the flurry of protests by most of the major educational organizations against the proposed rules was swift. In late August the House adopted an amendment prohibiting the Department of Education from using any money to enforce the proposed regulations. In September the Senate approved a similar amendment, which was attached to the House Joint Continuing Resolution to keep programs operating in fiscal year 1981.[54]   The proposed *Lau* regulations were, in effect, dead in the water. By the time of their highly publicized official withdrawal in February 1981, any hopes of enacting strong, enforceable rules focusing on LEP students had vanished. The push for local control and decentralization meant that the federal government was relinquishing its more active pre-1981 role in favor of giving added responsibility for compliance to states and local districts. The Department of Education's policies related to NOM/LEP students reverted to the May 25th Memorandum, to the *Lau* decision (for a brief period, to the old *Lau* Remedies), and to recent court decisions such as *Castaneda*, as the bases for enforcement by OCR, a practice that continues to this day. Where bilingual education mandates exist, state laws and regulations are the guiding principles for school districts. In most states some flexibility has been built into the law through amendments passed over the years, so that districts now have a great deal of latitude in meeting requirements.[55] Whether transitional bilingual education gives way to no mandate at all, and complete discretion is given in some states to school districts as to the types of program which must be offered to LEP students, appears doubtful at this time and remains a matter for conjecture.

Litigation

The impact of litigation on policymaking in the area of bilingual education has been significant. The earliest litigation, which dates back to 1930,[56] centered on the permissibility of segregating Mexican-American children for the purpose of giving them understandable instruction, provided that a previously-administered objective linguistic assessment demonstrated such a need. Most of the early (pre-*Brown* v. *Board of Education*[57]) litigation involving Mexican Americans dealt with the segregation of students as a necessary means to afford them bilingual education.[58] However, it was not until the early 1970s that the federal courts addressed the issue of bilingual education as a remedy for past and present discrimination against Mexican Americans. In 1971 a federal district court ordered an extensive educational plan which included components of bilingual-bicultural education to be provided by bilingual teachers in all grades.[59] In *Serna* v. *Portales*,[60] a case involving a small district in eastern New Mexico, a comprehensive bilingual instructional plan was ordered by the district court, and the order was affirmed by the appellate court. In New York, a major case was filed in 1972 against the New York City Board of Education; it was settled in 1974 by the signing of a consent decree which required the district to offer bilingual programs to thousands of Hispanic children who were limited in their English language skills.[61] This case had a national impact, given the size of the population entitled to services. It was also cited extensively in subsequent litigation in many other cities.

The seminal case in bilingual education was *Lau* v. *Nichols*.[62] In reversing the judgment of the Ninth Circuit, which had affirmed the district court's decision, a unanimous U.S. Supreme Court used clear, direct language to strike down unfair practices:

There is no equality of treatment merely by providing students with the same facilities, textbooks, teachers and curriculum; for students who do not understand English are effectively foreclosed from any meaningful education.

Basic skills are at the very core of what these public schools teach. Imposition of a requirement that, before a child can effectively participate in the educational program, he must already have acquired those basic skills, is to make a mockery of public education. We know that those who do not understand English are certain to find their classroom experiences wholly incomprehensible and in no way meaningful.[63]

The Court did not endorse any specific method of instruction, although it did refer to bilingual instruction as one of the possible avenues to respond to the needs of LEP children. Yet, *Lau's* impact on school districts and state legislatures across the country was dramatic. It provided advocates for bilingual education with a legal tool to promote this method as the single most appropriate means to deal with the educational needs of language minority students. For the first time a clear signal had been sent from the nation's highest judicial authority, and the push for bilingual education received a much-needed shot in the arm.

Although there is much other relevant litigation,[64] including various desegregation cases in which Hispanics intervened to protect existing bilingual education programs,[65] it is appropriate given the scope of this discussion to focus on recent litigation that has had important policy implications for bilingual education.

The first case of significance is *Idaho Migrant Council* v. *Board of Education*,[66] in which the Ninth Circuit Court of Appeals found that the Equal Educational Opportunities Act of 1974[67] (which had codified the findings of *Lau* v. *Nichols*) and the Civil Rights Act of 1964 created obligations on the part of the state education agency "to ensure that the needs of students with limited English language proficiency are addressed."[68] No program of instruction was recommended, but the decision affirmed the applicability and validity of the EEO Act of 1974 to states as well as to local school districts.

The second case emerged from the latest round of litigation in *U.S.* v. *State of Texas*,[69] which began in 1970 as a desegregation case. United States District Judge William Wayne Justice found that Texas was guilty of pervasive de jure discrimination against the state's Hispanic children in violation of the Fourteenth Amendment of the U.S. Constitution, and also in violation of the Equal Educational Opportunities Act of 1974. As a remedy, the court ordered a comprehensive, statewide bilingual education program. The decision contained a detailed analysis of transitional bilingual education,[70] with particulars on how the Texas Education Agency had failed to carry out its responsibilities under state and federal law. This is significant because the court showed that it was convinced that nothing less than a comprehensive transitional bilingual program would constitute an adequate remedy. Although the decision was reversed by the court of appeals on the grounds that the district court had exceeded its authority, its impact stimulated the Texas legislature to expand the resources and the scope of its bilingual education mandate, and thus reinforced the validity of transitional bilingual education as an appropriate pedagogical approach.

Another important case is *Castaneda* v. *Pickard*,[71] in which the Fifth Circuit Court of Appeals found that the Raymondville, Texas Independent School District's bilingual program, because of its inadequacies, violated the EEO Act of 1974. The court's analysis is thorough and deserves to be quoted at length:

> We understand section 1703 (f) to impose on educational agencies not only an obligation to overcome the direct obstacle to learning which the language barrier itself imposes, but also a duty to provide limited English speaking ability students with assistance in other areas of the curriculum where their equal participation may be impaired because of deficits incurred during participation in an agency's language remediation program.[72]

The court recognized that districts have considerable latitude in setting up their language response programs:

> [Sec.] 1703 (f) leaves schools free to . . . discharge these obligations simultaneously, by implementing a program designed to keep limited English speaking students at grade level in other areas of the curriculum by providing instruction in their native language at the same time that an English language development effort is pursued, or to address these problems in sequence, by focusing first on the development of English language skills and then later providing students with compensatory and supplemental education to remedy deficiencies in other areas which they may develop during this period.[73]

The court did not entangle itself in trying to judge the merits of the various possible approaches. Rather, it avoided these matters, choosing to leave it to local school boards to decide what might work best in their circumstances.

In order to judge the adequacy of the program developed by a school district to address the needs of LEP students, the court developed a three-pronged test. First, the district had to show that its program was "informed by an educational theory recognized as sound by some experts in the field or, at least, deemed a legitimate experimental strategy."[74] Second, the programs and practices actually in use had to be reasonably calculated to implement effectively the educational theory previously adopted. The language of the court was explicit: "We do not believe that it may fairly be said that a school system is taking appropriate action to remedy language barriers if, despite the adoption of a promising theory, the system fails to follow through with practices, resources, and personnel necessary to transform the theory into reality."[75] Finally, the outcome of the implementation had to be analyzed and, if necessary, revised in order to achieve the desired results: "If a school's program, although premised on a legitimate educational theory and implemented through the use of adequate techniques, fails after being employed for a period of time sufficient to give the plan a legitimate trial, to produce results indicating that the language barriers confronting students are actually being overcome, that program may, at that point, no longer constitute appropriate action as far as that school is concerned."[76]

The significance of *Castaneda* becomes evident not only because it has become the cornerstone for legal analysis in subsequent litigation, but also because it allows districts more flexibility in choosing a method to instruct LEP pupils. It is clear that this case influenced the thinking of many in Congress on how to proceed with the reauthorization of Title VII in 1984. Until convincing evidence is brought forth proving the effectiveness of a particular method of instruction for LEP students, it is reasonable to expect that *Casteneda* will provide the guiding principles for bilingual program reviews.

Finally, the last significant decision came in December 1983 in the latest round of *Keyes* v. *School District No. 1, Denver, Colorado.*[77] After finding pervasive violations of the rights of language minority students because of the failure by the district to implement a transitional bilingual education program, the court ordered wide-ranging relief and affirmed the appropriateness of bilingual education as an educationally sound and promising approach to the educational needs of LEP pupils. In an interesting development, the court also found that in the context of desegregation, the district's failure to implement fully its transitional bilingual education program amounted to a failure to attain the unitary, non-racially and -ethnically discriminatory school system required by federal constitutional and statutory law.[78] As the first major decision which addresses language instructional and programmatic issues since *Castaneda, Keyes* represents an important application of the principles established by *Castaneda.* As a result of the decision, which was not appealed, the Denver Public Schools in 1984 entered into a consent decree which called for a major expansion and upgrading of its transitional bilingual program. Thus, it is an important precedent which no doubt will be cited in other jurisdictions when bilingual education litigation is undertaken and remedies are being proposed for alleged violations of the constitutional and civil rights of LEP children.

In summary, litigation related to bilingual education has been an essential component of the policymaking process at the local, state, and national levels. Although it is difficult to measure exactly the impact which any individual case has had (except *Lau*), there can be no doubt as to the cumulative influence of litigation on the process of policy formulation.

Context

The preceding historical analysis of legislation, regulations/enforcement efforts, and litigation details selected significant events that took place in each area related to the educational needs of LEP students. It cannot, however, capture the complex and dynamic interplay that occurred among these three areas, including the branches of government which they represent. Neither can it portray the political backdrop and the ideological currents which have always had a definite impact in shaping the outcome of the debate on bilingual education in the United States.

The bilingual education movement emerged in the late 1960s as part of the civil rights movement, with Hispanics following the aggressive leadership of the black community in asserting their rightful place in American society. As a product of the War on Poverty and the ESEA of 1965, bilingual education was a form of compensatory education. Language and cultural differences were viewed as "disadvantages" when compared to the appropriate norm (English and white, middle-class American values). A political constituency was created through this new equity push, one that did not go unnoticed by politicians, especially in the Southwest and California.

The 1970s were a time of ethnic pride, especially for white European ethnic groups who felt left out of the black, Hispanic, and other minority group revivals. Michael Novak wrote about the "rise of the unmeltable ethnics,"[79] and even Congress responded by passing the Ethnic Heritage Studies Act which supported research and related activities on topics like cultural pluralism and ethnicity in American society.[80] Alex Haley's *Roots*[81] became an instant success as an account of the author's search for his African ancestors and his own identity as an American. Rodolfo Gonzales' epic poem, *I Am Joaquin*, was perhaps the best known literary example of ethnic revival among Chicanos in this period.[82]

The Hispanic demographic explosion began to capture the eye of the American public in the late 1970s, and the 1980 census confirmed what the media had been reporting already—the so-called "decade of the

Hispanics" had arrived. Angry polemics about governmental policies in, for example, affirmative action and school desegregation, were a part of the debate during these years, and continue to attract attention today. Of particular interest here is the debate over immigration policy, which began to acquire momentum with the arrival of several hundred thousand refugees (the "boat people") from Vietnam, Laos, Cambodia, and Thailand in the period from 1975 to 1980, the Cuban exodus of 1980, the arrival of thousands of Haitians who claimed political asylum and, most recently, the displaced victims of civil strife in Central America.[83]

Language played an important role in the debates that ensued as a result of this massive immigration, which stimulated xenophobic fears in the hearts of many Americans, especially in those cities and states that bore the brunt of these new arrivals. Dade County (Miami), Florida became the focus of national attention when a referendum was passed prohibiting the use of public funds to promote any language other than English.[84] Although it was amended later and has not had the anticipated negative impact on social (and other) services to the county's Spanish-speaking population, the referendum was clearly anti-Hispanic, and it received considerable publicity in the national media. Language was also an issue, albeit indirectly, in *Plyler* v. *Doe*,[85] in which the Supreme Court ruled that the children of undocumented workers were entitled to free public education. Clearly, bilingual education and other language assistance programs would have to be provided to these children, which helped to make the issue a major one in Texas politics and in the national media.

The political strength of Hispanics, which had grown in the 1970s, was also felt in Congress and in some state legislatures. The electoral awakening of minorities following tha passage of the Voting Rights Act of 1975 and its reauthorization in 1982 made Hispanics, along with blacks, a force to be reckoned with, at least in certain states and cities. In California, bilingual ballots became the subject of a controversy that has not subsided. The role of advocacy groups on both sides of the bilingual education issue has been significant. On one side, favorable to bilingual education, one finds the National Association for Bilingual Education, the League of United Latin American Citizens, the National Council of La Raza, and the Mexican American Legal Defense and Education Fund, assisted by the National Education Association. On the other side, major groups such as the American Federation of Teachers and the National School Boards Association have opposed strongly the *Lau* regulations proposed in 1980 by the Department of Education. More recently, an organization called "U.S. English" has come on the scene. Its avowed purpose is to press for a Constitutional amendment declaring English to be the official language of the United States. The organization's leaders include former California Senator S. I. Hayakawa, who is an outspoken opponent of bilingual education, and Gerda Bikales,[86] the group's executive director. Although U.S. English's literature indicates that they are in favor of foreign language teaching in American schools, their position before Congress has been marked by an anti-bilingual education tone. As a result of the efforts of U.S. English, a number of states have passed legislation declaring English the official language.[87] It is difficult to assess what ultimate impact these laws will have on Hispanics and other language minority groups, but it is obvious that there is enough concern across the country about the impact of immigration and bilingualism to foster the passage of laws and referenda to proclaim what Americans never before felt a need to do: State officially that English has been, is, and will continue to be the language of the United States.

The danger, of course, is that policies may revert to those of the pre-1970s, with prohibitions and punishments being imposed on children for speaking a language other than English in school. It becomes difficult to draw the line on limitations to non-English language use (e.g., bilingual ballots, use of another language in emergency answering services or in the workplace, etc.). While it is true that efforts like U.S. English's well-financed campaign, with slick mailings and media spots, have been a major factor behind the passage of English-only resolutions in a number of state legislatures, county boards, and city councils throughout the United States, it is also true that most Americans have not heard of this organization. Whether a majority of Americans would agree with its goals is impossible to say, and would likely depend on the way the question was posed in a nationwide poll, or on whether immigration happened to be a hot issue when the question was asked. Multiple issues are always combined in any national poll or debate concerning bilingual education.

Related to language and, more broadly, to the process of acculturation of immigrants into American society, the splash in the media made by Richard Rodriguez's book, *Hunger of Memory*,[88] is worthy of note. An articulate and moving account of a Mexican-American's boyhood and transition into manhood, sprinkled with poignant vignettes of the pain and frustration of learning English and "fitting in," of becoming Americanized, and of his decision to cast aside his home language and traditions, the book was acclaimed and effectively promoted by opponents of bilingual education and affirmative action who liked Rodriguez's rejection of these two concepts.

Emotions aside, research has *not* played a significant role in the policymaking related to bilingual education to date. Early in the history of Title VII, studies conducted in the 1960s were often cited in congressional testimony as evidence of the effectiveness of bilingual instruction. The work of Lambert, Tucker, Fishman, Gaarder, Modiano, and Macnamara[89] was cited frequently, in spite of the fact that most of it focused on research conducted outside the United States. In 1975 the U.S. Commission on Civil Rights issued an influential report which, after a broad but superficial review of literature which hardly looked at research, enthusiastically endorsed bilingual education:

> The Commission's basic conclusion is that bilingual-bicultural education is the program of instruction which currently offers the best vehicle for large numbers of language minority students who experience language difficulty in our schools.[90]

This strong support was not absolute; the commission recognized that its endorsement did not preclude the use of the English as a second language (ESL) approach in those instances where there were small numbers of language minority children. Indeed, OCR's enforcement practices under the *Lau* Remedies, although requiring transitional bilingual education as a minimum when large numbers of LEP children from the same language group were involved, allowed districts to use ESL, especially after good faith efforts to find teachers and aides who spoke the language in question had proved unsuccessful.

Noel Epstein's polemical monograph, *Language, Ethnicity, and the Schools,*[91] raised various policy questions, and relied heavily on preliminary data from the longitudinal study conducted by the American Institutes for Research. The A.I.R. report was a major force in the debate about bilingual education across the country and in Congress because it cast a negative image by claiming that the evidence of its effectiveness was weak. Although there were several rebuttals of Epstein[92] and the A.I.R. report[93] objecting to their methodology, data collection techniques, selective analysis, and conclusions, the negative impact of these works on bilingual education was uncontestable. The grounds for greater flexibility and experimentation can be traced to both of these documents, which served to politicize even more an already politically sensitive issue. Other reports that showed the effectiveness of bilingual education, which had been conducted by state education agencies in Michigan, Colorado, and New Jersey,[94] did not receive the publicity that earlier, negative reports had received, and were dismissed as advocacy documents that were not grounded in solid research.

By 1981 the internal review of the effectiveness of bilingual education, which had been commissioned by the Department of Education prior to the issuance of the new proposed *Lau* regulations in August 1980, was leaked to the press, which quickly disseminated its findings. The authors, Keith Baker and Adriana de Kanter, who were federal employees with no background or training in the field of bilingual education, reviewed the extensive research literature and concluded, after rejecting most of the previous studies based on their own methodological or other objections, that there was no conclusive evidence concerning the effectiveness of bilingual education. Therefore, they argued, federal policy should not endorse it as the only approach to teach LEP children, and more flexibility was called for under Title VII. Baker and de Kanter continued to advocate for various approaches to be used which they had found to be effective, such as "structured immersion," a method in which a bilingual teacher speaks only English in class, but students are allowed to use their native language to ask questions and discuss subject content with the teacher.[95] Although it may appear somewhat anomalous that persons with no professional expertise in a research area became "experts" overnight, one must consider that the dearth of sound research on bilingual education in the United States was largely responsible for this sad state of affairs. No research money was appropriated through Title VII until the late 1970s, and most of the available evidence about bilingual education came from research conducted in other countries. Given the urgency to serve millions of LEP youngsters in response to pressure from civil rights groups, Congress did not feel it was necessary to fund basic research in this area since it would take years to yield results. Even though the Baker-de Kanter report was roundly criticized by many experts for its faults and limitations,[96] its impact on policymaking was felt in Congress. The 1984 Bilingual Education Act embodies some of the recommendations for experimentation and flexibility made earlier by Baker and de Kanter.

There are a number of major research projects currently underway, as per the directives of Congress in the latest reauthorization of Title VII. However, it will be years before results are known and any impact on policymaking is felt. The work of James Cummins, Stephen Krashen, Tove Skutnabb-Kangas, and Eduardo Hernandez-Chavez[97] has done much to clarify the issues surrounding the pedagogical goals and specific objectives of bilingual education and other methods of instructing language minority students. Their research suggests that English language proficiency, by itself, is not the only variable in predicting the minority student's academic success. Other factors, such as the sociocultural context in which learning takes place, may be as important as the language of instruction, be it in the first or second language. As research in bilingual education and related areas addresses, through ethnography, the sociocultural contexts as factors in the learning process, more data will become available which should cast additional light on these complex issues.

To be sure, it is highly improbable that the issue of effectiveness will ever be settled "beyond the shadow of a doubt" through research findings, or that research will serve as the primary means of guiding public policy development in this area. Available research will be subject to interpretation to prove or disprove whether bilingual education "works." Pedagogical issues (language assessment, curriculum and instruction of LEP students, etc.) are likely to be set aside and subsumed in the debate over social policy issues, such as bilingualism. Indeed, the political tone which is found in much educational research (e.g., testing) permeates bilingual education. As Edward Fiske of the *New York Times* put it, "With the possible exception of desegregation, no subject has aroused as much passion over schools as educating students with 'limited English proficiency.' "[98] Thus, the political nature of the debate over bilingual education is bound to continue, regardless of research findings, given the nature of the topic, its high visibility nationally, and its prominent place on the social, economic, and political agenda of language minority groups, especially Hispanics.

As can be seen from this brief overview of the context in which bilingual education exists in the United States, there are many elements involved in policymaking, and their interaction is affected by several factors, including racism and other ideologies, personal values and attitudes toward language, political orientation and agenda, and a myriad of other variables, all of which make up the environment in which this debate takes place.

Conclusions and Implications for the Future

The evolution of bilingual education as educational policy has been based on interaction among the three branches of federal and state governments in a context that has social, political, and ideological dimensions. Congressional action led the way in 1968 with the passage of Title VII of the ESEA of 1965, which was followed by legislative action in many states during the decade of the 1970s. Parallel to this came the enforcement efforts of the Office for Civil Rights, beginning with the May 25th Memorandum and, after 1975, the *Lau* Remedies. Court decisions in which bilingual education was an issue began to take place in the early 1970s, with *Lau* v. *Nichols* as the landmark case which stimulated a major push for bilingual education across the country. Actions by the judicial branch in the early 1980s, especially the *Castaneda* decision, have broken new ground for the assessment of what constitutes an adequate educational response to the identified needs of LEP students.

The debate over how best to address the needs of NOM/LEP students has been resolved in favor of transitional bilingual education, as evidenced by state laws and federal legislation over the years. There is great diversity in the types of programs, with variations based on local parent and community demands. In spite of this, the 1984 Bilingual Education Act recognizes the need for additional experimentation with various instructional methods, including different types of immersion approaches as well as developmental or maintenance programs, to determine what works best for which types of students under what specific circumstances. Interestingly, at the federal level, the simplistic "either/or" dichotomy—bilingual education or ESL—has yielded to a more comprehensive view of the problem.. Yet, in a broader sense, the debate has been simultaneously escalated into an English versus Spanish (and other languages) battle in various states.

To complicate matters even more, a growing public recognition of the "foreign language crisis" in America has come about in recent years. A presidential commission declared in 1979 that "America's gross inadequacy in foreign language skills is nothing short of scandalous, and it is becoming worse."[99] The report included specific recognition of bilingualism as a domestic issue, and language minorities were described as being "a largely untapped resource of talent . . . who . . . can be expected to make rapid, new, and valuable contributions to America's capacity to deal persuasively and effectively with the world outside its borders."[100] Senator Paul Simon's book, *The Tongue-Tied American*,[101] gives eloquent testimony that the language chauvinism resulting from Americanization has created a problem that has economic and security, as well as cultural dimensions. However, the promotion of language learning by all Americans, while viewed by the public as a desirable goal and a sound educational policy, has not received the acceptance that is demonstrated through budget support at federal, state, and local district levels. It may be that the push for excellence generated as a result of the report of yet another presidential commission[102] will cause foreign languages to be put back into the curriculum of the nation's public schools in a truly meaningful way. How this would affect the debate over bilingual education is unclear, but advocates for bilingual instruction and for individual bilingualism among Americans will surely link excellence to bilingual proficiency.

With regard to future developments, one can speculate about what may happen in a number of areas. First, the changing demographics of the nation's major school districts, as a reflection of the growing numbers of language minority students across the country, are likely to keep the debate on bilingual education and foreign language learning very much alive. Second, pressure may develop in the next decade and a half to make second language acquisition a national policy as a result of the interdependence of trade in a world economy in which U.S. business and industry appear to be at a decided disadvantage, especially when one measures the capability of American personnel in languages other than English. Due to revolutionary changes in telecommunications, a shrinking world is sure to bring even closer to the American public the linguistic diversity which exists throughout the globe. Third, one can envision varying degrees of de facto bilingualism among large numbers of residents as a condition likely to exist in some regions, given the concentrations of language minorities in them. Such conditions now exist in many cities on the United States-Mexico border, as well as in Miami, New York, San Antonio, San Diego, Los Angeles, Chicago, and other major urban areas. A national language policy does not exist in the United States now, but may eventually emerge from city, state, or regional experiences, especially if current immigration trends and Hispanic fertility rates continue for several decades.

The current debate, which combines the issues of bilingual education for LEP children, maintenance of native language proficiency by former LEP students once English proficiency has been achieved, and second language acquisition by *all* Americans so that the goal of *individual* bilingualism (as opposed to *group* bilingualism à la Quebec) in a variety of languages can be achieved on a large scale in the United States, will go on.[103] However, there may be a bifurcation of issues before they can be joined again. Transitional bilingual education will continue to be the common vehicle employed for LEP children for English language acquisition and instruction in basic subjects, where large enough concentrations of students exist to make it possible for districts to offer such programs. Simultaneously, a parallel policy of language acquisition by *all* students (or maintenance in the case of bilinguals and former LEP students) on a voluntary basis, as an enlightened educational policy promoting individual bilingualism in U.S. schools, may be pursued by some districts and state education agencies, with partial support being provided by the federal government as a stimulus for experimentation and development. As one of the leading spokespersons for bilingual education put it recently: "Bilingual education [i.e., transitional] is *not* for everybody, but everyone should be bilingual!"[104] However, the likelihood of such a policy being universally adopted by states and school districts across the country is nil.

Ironically, if it were, these programs would tend to be targeted for children of middle- and upper-middle-class parents, and would offer little or no benefits for lower-class LEP students whose education would still focus on acquiring English, not on achieving bilingual proficiency.

In the last analysis, the real—the only—question is not whether transitional bilingual education should become maintenance bilingual education for some or all children, or whether ESL is better for LEP students than bilingual education. Rather, the issue is: What is the most effective way to educate the growing number of language minority students in schools so that they can reach the social and economic mainstream of our society? The answer to this question clearly transcends language as an issue. The nation's well-being will no doubt be affected for several decades by the educational policies which are chosen to address these needs.

APPENDIX: DEFINITIONS

Bilingual Education: "in very general terms . . . implies some use of two (or more) languages of instruction in connection with teaching other than language per se."[105] In the United States, an English as a second language program is also included.

Bilingual/Bicultural Program: "A program which utilizes the student's native language [example: Navajo] and cultural factors in instructing, maintaining and further developing all the necessary skills in the student's native language and culture while introducing, maintaining and developing all the necessary skills in the second language and culture [example: English]. The end result is a student who can function, totally, in both languages and cultures."[106]

English as a Second Language: "ESL students are placed in regular submersion instruction for most of the day. During part of the day, however, these students receive extra instruction in English. This extra help is based on a special curriculum designed to teach English as a second language. L1 may or may not be used in conjunction with ESL instruction."[107]

Maintenance: ". . . the child's L1 (home language) and L2 (target language) are used regularly with approximately equal emphasis as mediums of instruction for subject matter."[108]

Structured Immersion: "Instruction is in the second language (L2), as in the case of submersion, but there are important differences. The immersion teacher understands L1, and students can address the teacher in L1; the immersion teacher, however, generally replies only in L2. Furthermore, the curriculum is structured so that prior knowledge of L2 is not assumed as subjects are taught. Content is introduced in a way that can be understood by the students. The students in effect learn L2 and content simultaneously. Most immersion programs also teach L1 language arts for thirty to sixty minutes a day. Structured immersion differs from transitional bilingual education in that L1 is rarely used by the teacher (except where it is a subject) and subject-area instruction is given in L2 from the beginning of the program."[109]

Submersion: "Language-minority children are placed in an ordinary classroom where English is spoken. There is no special program to help them overcome the language problem. Submersion is aptly described as 'sink or swim.' The minority home language (L1) is not used at all in the classroom. In *Lau v. Nichols* the Supreme Court found that the submersion approach violated the civil rights of language-minority students and that schools had to make an extra effort to help overcome the language problems of these students."[110]

Transitional Bilingual Education: "... a program in which the child's L1 language is used only as an interim medium of instruction until he/she acquires fluency in L2."[111]

NOTES

[1]Elementary and Secondary Education Act, P.L. 89-10 (89th Congress, 1st Session).

[2]Other efforts were aimed at adult education, vocational education, and higher education, but the focus of this chapter is on elementary and secondary education.

[3]Susan Gilbert Schneider, *Revolution, Reaction or Reform: The 1974 Bilingual Education Act* (New York: L. A. Publishing Co., Inc., 1976).

[4]Bilingual Education Act, P.L. 90-247 (90th Congress, 1st Session), Title VII.

[5]Sec. 702, P.L. 90-247.

[6]Sec. 704(c), P.L. 90-247.

[7]Quoted in Schneider, op. cit., p. 23.

[8]Raymond V. Padilla, *Federal Policy Shifts in Bilingual Education: Consequences for Local Implementation and National Evaluation* (Los Alamitos, CA: National Center for Bilingual Research, 1984), p. 3.

[9]John C. Molina, "National Policy in Bilingual Education: An Historical View of the Federal Role," in Herman La Fontaine, Barry Persky, and Leonard H. Golubchick, eds., *Bilingual Education* (Wayne, NJ: Avery Publishing Group, 1978), pp. 16-17.

[10]Sec. 701, P.L. 90-247.

[11]Molina, op. cit., p. 17.

[12]Quoted in Molina, ibid.

[13]*Lau* v. *Nichols,* 414 U.S. 563(1974).

[14]Education Amendments of 1974, P.L. 93-380 (93rd Congress, 2nd Session), Title VII.

[15]Padilla, op. cit., p. 19.

[16]Sec. 702(a)(5)(B), P.L. 93-380.

[17]Sec. 703(a)(4)(A)(i), P.L. 93-380.

[18]Sec. 703(a)(4)(B), P.L. 93-380.

[19]Malcolm N. Danoff, *Evaluation of the Impact of ESEA Title VII Spanish/ English Bilingual Education Programs* (Palo Alto, CA: American Institutes for Research, 1978).

[20]Noel Epstein, *Language, Ethnicity and the Schools: Policy Alternatives for Bilingual-Bicultural Education* (Washington, D.C.: Institute for Educational Leadership, 1977).

[21]Education Amendments of 1978, P.L. 95-561 (95th Congress, 2nd Session).

[22]See, e.g., Secs. 702(a)(1) and 703(a)(1), P.L. 95-561, now codified as 20 U.S.C. Secs. 3222(a)(1) and 3223(a)(1).

[23]Sec. 703(a)(4)(B), P.L. 95-561, now codified as 20 U.S.C. Sec. 3223 (a)(4)(B).

[24]Sec. 721(b)(2)(A)(iii), P.L. 95-561, now codified as 20 U.S.C. Sec. 3231(b)(2)(A)(iii).

[25]Sec. 751(a)(1), P.L. 95-561, now codified as 20 U.S.C. Sec. 3261(a) (1).

[26]Sec. 703(a)(1)(F), P.L. 95-561, now codified as 20 U.S.C. Sec. 3223 (a)(1)(F).

[27]Sec. 721(b)(3)(F), P.L. 95-561, now codified as 20 U.S.C. Sec. 3231 (b)(3)(F).

[28]Education Consolidation and Improvement Act of 1981, P.L. 97-35 (97th Congress, 1st Session).

[29]Quoted in Diego Castellanos, *The Best of Two Worlds—Bilingual-Bicultural Education in the U.S.* (Trenton, NJ: New Jersey State Department of Education, 1983), p. 234.

[30]H.R. 2682 was a U.S. Department of Education bill, backed by U.S. English, the anti-bilingual lobbying group, for the purpose of gaining more flexibility in the use of Title VII funds to sponsor nonbilingual instructional approaches.

[31]See James J. Lyons, "Academic Excellence and Equity Through the Bilingual Education Act," *NABE News* 8: 2 (Winter 1985): 1.

[32]Sec. 702, H.B. 5231 (1984).

[33]U.S. Congress, House Committee on Education and Labor, *Education Amendments of 1984, Report* (to accompany H.R. 11), p. 4.

[34]Sec. 703(a)(8), P.L. 98-511, now codified as 20 U.S.C. Sec. 3223 (a)(8).

[35]Sec. 721(a)(1)-(7), P.L. 98-511, now codified as 20 U.S.C. Sec. 3231(a)(1)-(7).

[36]Transitional Bilingual Education Act, codified in Laws of Massachusetts, Ch. 71A, Secs. 1-9.

[37]The state laws and statutes are as follows:

Texas: Acts 1973, 63rd Leg., p. 860, Ch. 362, Sec. 1, amended by Acts 1981, 67th Leg., p. 2138, Ch. 498, Sec. 1; now codified as [Texas] Education Code Sec. 21.451-.463.

Illinois: P.A. 78-727, Sec. 1; now codified as [Illinois Stats.] Ch. 122, Sec. 14C-1 to 14C-12.

California: Bilingual Education Act of 1972; now codified as [California] Education Code, Secs. 52100-52114.

Michigan: P.A. 1976, No. 451, Secs. 1151-1158; now codified as 380.1151-380.1158, Mich. Comp. Laws.

New Jersey: Bilingual Education Act, L. 1974, Ch. 197, Secs. 1-12; now codified as New Jersey Stats. Sec. 18A: 35-15-35-26.

Wisconsin: Bilingual Education Act, L. 1975, c. 395; now codified as Wis. Stats. Secs. 115.95-115.976.

[38]National Clearinghouse on Bilingual Education, "Statistical Files on SEAs," *ESL Information Packet* (Rosslyn, VA: National Clearinghouse on Bilingual Education, 1984). Data from a 1986 survey conducted by NCBE indicate that seventeen states have legislation that requires special instruction for LEP students (but not necessarily a bilingual education instructional program) or teacher certification for ESL and/or bilingual education. Twenty-seven other states and territories have no legislation at all with respect to bilingual education. Only West Virginia still prohibits instruction in a language other than English. (Personal communication, Alex Stein, Senior Education Analyst at NCBE, Feb. 1987). Data were submitted by fifty-seven state or territorial education departments, including those of Guam, American Samoa, Puerto Rico, and the U.S. Virgin Islands.

[39]Sec. 22-24-101, Colo. Rev. Stats.

[40]Sec. 22-24-104(6), Colo. Rev. Stats.

41California's Bilingual Education Improvement and Reform Act of 1980 (Stats. 1980, c. 1339) allows "planned variation programs for the purpose of comparing and improving language development programs for pupils of limited English proficiency." California Education Code Sec. 52163(c)(1)(B). Even though these programs can exist in only 150 classrooms across the state, they do allow experimentation in approaches that are not bilingual in the strict sense, i.e., use of English and the native language is not required.

42J. Stanley Pottinger, "Identification of Discrimination and Denial of Services on the Basis of National Origin," Memorandum to School Districts with More Than Five Percent National Origin-Minority Group Children (Washington, D.C.: Department of Health, Education and Welfare, Director, Office for Civil Rights, May 25, 1970), 35 Fed. Reg. 11595.

43Ibid., p. 2.

44Office for Civil Rights, U.S. Department of Health, Education and Welfare, "Office for Civil Rights Guidelines: Task Force Findings Specifying Remedies Available for Eliminating Past Educational Practices Ruled Unlawful Under Lau v. Nichols" (Washington, D.C.: U.S. Department of Health, Education and Welfare, 1975). The text of the Lau Remedies may be found in Keith A. Baker and Adriana A. de Kanter, Bilingual Education: A Reappraisal of Federal Policy (Lexington, MA: D.C. Heath and Company, 1983), Appendix B.

45Ibid., Sec. III. 1. A.

46Ibid., Sec. III. 1. B.

47Ibid.

48Iris C. Rotberg, "Some Legal and Research Considerations in Establishing Federal Policy in Bilingual Education," Harvard Educational Review 52: 2 (May 1982): 152-154.

49Ibid., p. 153.

50Northwest Arctic v. California, Consent Decree, 1978.

51U.S. Department of Education, Office of the Secretary, "Notice of Proposed Rule Making," 34 CFR Part 100, et seq., 45 Fed. Reg. 52052 (August 5, 1980). The text of this notice may be found in Baker and de Kanter, op. cit., Appendix C.

52Ibid., Sec. 100.30.

53Ibid., Sec. 100.39(c)(1).

54Castellanos, op. cit., p. 227.

55National Clearinghouse on Bilingual Education, "Statistical Files," op. cit.

56Independent School District v. Salvatierra, 33 S.W. 2d 790 (Tex. Civ. App. 1930), rehearing denied.

57Brown v. Board of Education, 347 U.S. 483(1954).

[58]See *Mendez* v. *Westminster School District*, 64 F. Supp. 544 (S.D. Cal. 1946), *aff'd.* 161 F.2d 774 (9th Cir., 1947) and *Gonzalez* v. *Sheely*, F. Supp. 1004 (D. Ariz. 1951) as representative cases.

[59]*United States* v. *State of Texas*, 342 F.Supp. 24 (E.D. Tex. 1971).

[60]*Serna* v. *Portales*, 351 F. Supp. 1279 (D. N.M. 1973), *aff'd.* 499 F.2d 1147 (10th Cir. 1974).

[61]*Aspira of New York, Inc.* v. *Board of Education of the City of New York*, 58 F.R.D. 62 (S.D.N.Y. 1973), Consent Decree (S.D.N.Y. August 29, 1974).

[62]*Lau* v. *Nichols*, 414 U.S. 563(1974).

[63]Ibid., 414 U.S. at 566.

[64]For this analysis, see Herbert Teitelbaum and Richard J. Hiller, "Bilingual Education: The Legal Mandate," *Harvard Educational Review* 47: 2 (May 1977): 138-170; and Peter D. Roos, "Bilingual Education: The Hispanic Response to Unequal Educational Opportunity," *Law and Contemporary Problems* 42: 4 (Autumn 1978): 111-140.

[65]See, for example, *Keyes* v. *Denver*, 521 F.2d 465 (10th Cir. 1975). Cities with similar experiences include Boston, Detroit, Milwaukee, and Wilmington, Delaware.

[66]*Idaho Migrant Council* v. *Board of Education*, 647 F.2d 69 (9th Cir. 1981).

[67]20 U.S.C. Sec. 1703(f) states in pertinent part:

> No state shall deny equal educational opportunity to an individual on account of his or her race, color, sex, or national origin, by . . . the failure of an educational agency to take appropriate action to overcome language barriers that impede equal participation by its students in its instructional programs.

[68]*Idaho Migrant Council*, op. cit., 647 F.2d 71.

[69]*U.S.* v. *Texas*, 506 F.Supp. 405 (E.D. Tex. 1981), *rev'd in part, remanded in part*, 680 F.2d 356 (5th Cir. 1982).

[70]Ibid., 506 F.Supp. at 418-428.

[71]*Castaneda* v. *Pickard*, 648 F.2d 989 (5th Cir. 1981).

[72]Ibid., 648 F.2d at 1011.

[73]Ibid.

[74]Ibid., 648 F.2d at 1009.

[75]Ibid., 648 F.2d at 1010.

[76]Ibid.

[77]*Keyes* v. *School District No. 1, Denver, Colorado*, 576 F.Supp. 1503 (D.Colo. 1983).

[78]Ibid., 576 F.Supp. at 1521.

[79]Michael Novak, *The Rise of the Unmeltable Ethnics* (New York: MacMillan Co., 1971).

[80]Ethnic Heritage Studies Act, Sec. 504, P.L. 92-318 (92nd Congress, 2nd Session), now codified as 20 U.S.C. Secs. 900-900a-5.

[81]Alex Haley, *Roots* (Garden City, NY: Doubleday, 1976).

[82]Rodolfo Gonzales, *I Am Joaquin: An Epic Poem* (New York: Bantam Books, Inc., 1972), originally privately printed in Denver, Colorado, 1967.

[83]Castellanos, op. cit., pp. 196-199.

[84]Ibid., pp. 238-239.

[85]*Plyler* v. *Doe*, 457 U.S. 202(1982).

[86]Gerda Bikales stated recently: "The primacy of English is being challenged. There is a general belief, nurtured to some extent by bilingual education, that English is not all that necessary." "Special Report on English," *U.S. News and World Report* (February 18, 1985), p. 55.

[87]To the date of this writing, Indiana, Kentucky, Illinois, Nebraska, and the Virgin Islands had passed laws declaring English to be the official language. The Maryland Senate defeated a similar bill, which had been passed by its House of Representatives, after intense lobbying by Hispanic groups who claimed that such laws were unnecessary and might lead to discrimination against language minorities. A statewide referendum in California declaring the supremacy of English was approved by two-thirds of the voters in November 1986.

[88]Richard Rodriguez, *Hunger of Memory* (New York: Bantam Books, 1983).

[89]See a discussion of various approaches in Henry T. Trueba, "Bilingual Education Models: Types and Designs," in Henry T. Trueba and Carol Barnett-Mizrahi, eds., *Bilingual Multicultural Education and the Professional: From Theory to Practice* (Rowley, MA: Newbury House, 1979).

[90]U.S. Commission on Civil Rights, *A Better Chance to Learn*, Publication 51 (Washington, D.C.: U.S. Government Printing Office, 1975), p. 137.

[91]Epstein, op. cit.

[92]See Jose Cardenas's critique in the Appendix to Epstein, op. cit., for one rebuttal.

[93]See, for example, Tracy C. Gray and M. Beatriz Arias, "Challenge to the AIR Report" (Arlington, VA: Center for Applied Linguistics, 1978).

[94]Among the most significant studies were the following:

a) Gerald E. De Mauro, *The Impact of Bilingual Education on English Acquisition in New Jersey* (Trenton, NJ: New Jersey State Department of Education, 1981), and *Academic Achievement in Bilingual Education Programs, 1980-81* (Trenton, NJ: New Jersey State Department of Education, 1982);

b) Jacob Silver, *Bilingual Education Evaluation Report* (Lansing, MI: Michigan Department of Education, 1982);

c) Lawrence Egan and Ross Goldsmith, "Bilingual Bicultural Education: The Colorado Success Story," *NABE News* IV: 3 (January 1981): 1, 4, 12, 14; d) Rudolph C. Troike, "Synthesis of Research on Bilingual Education," *Educational Leadership* (March 1981), cited in Castellanos, op. cit., pp. 212-214, 286. See also Lorraine Zappert and B. Roberto Cruz, *Bilingual Education: An Appraisal of Empirical Research* (Berkeley, CA: Bay Area Bilingual Education League, 1980) and Maria del Refugio Robledo, "Bilingual Evaluation Research: Does It Work?" *Intercultural Development Research Association Newsletter* (February 1982): 1-3, 6-7.

[95]Baker and de Kanter, op. cit.

[96]See, for example, Stanley S. Seidner, "Political Expediency or Educational Research: An Analysis of Baker and de Kanter's Review of the Literature of Bilingual Education" (Rosslyn, VA: National Clearinghouse for Bilingual Education, 1981).

[97]James Cummins, "Linguistic Interdependence and the Educational Development of Bilingual Children," *Review of Educational Research* 49: 2 (Spring 1979): 222-251; "The Role of Primary Language Development in Promoting Educational Success for Language Minority Students," in California State Department of Education, *Schooling and Language Minority Students: A Theoretical Framework* (Los Angeles: California State Department of Education, National Dissemination and Assessment Center, 1981), pp. 3-49; *Interdependence and Bicultural Ambivalence: Regarding the Pedagogical Rationale for Bilingual Education* (Rosslyn, VA: National Clearinghouse for Bilingual Education, 1982); and *Basic Principles for the Education of Language Minority Students: An Overview*, 1982 ed. (Sacramento, CA: California State Department of Education, 1983); Stephen Krashen, "Bilingual Education and Second Language Acquisition Theory," in California State Department of Education, *Schooling and Language Minority Students*, op. cit., pp. 51-79; Eduardo Hernandez-Chavez, "The Inadequacy of English Immersion Education as an Educational Approach for Language Minority Students in the United States," in California State Department of Education, *Studies on Immersion Education: A Collection for United States Educators* (Sacramento, CA: California State Department of Education, 1984), pp. 144-183; and Tove Skutnabb-Kangas and Robert Phillipson, "Educational Strategies in Multilingual Contexts," *ROLIG-Papir* (Roskilde, Denmark: Roskilde Universitetcenter, 1985).

[98]Edward Fiske, "One Language or Two? The Controversy Over Bilingual Education in America's Schools," *New York Times* (November 10, 1985), Education Fall Survey, p. 1.

[99]Castellanos, op. cit., p. 187.

[100]Ibid., pp. 197-198.

[101]Paul Simon, *The Tongue-Tied American: Confronting the Foreign Language Crisis* (New York: The Continuum Company, 1980).

[102]U.S. Department of Education, *A Nation At Risk: Report of the National Commission on Excellence in Education* (Washington, D.C.: U.S. Government Printing Office, 1983).

[103]For an excellent analysis of individual versus group bilingualism, see Rolf Kjolseth's perceptive article, "Cultural Politics of Bilingualism," *Society* 20: 4 (May/June 1983): 40-48.

[104]Samuel Betances, keynote address at The National Association of Bilingual Education Conference, San Francisco, California (March 16, 1985).

[105]Joshua A. Fishman, "Bilingual Education: What and Why?" in Trueba and Barnett-Mizrahi, op. cit., p. 12.

[106]*Lau* Remedies, Office for Civil Rights, op. cit., pp. 221-230.

[107]Baker and de Kanter, op. cit., p. 35.

[108]Trueba, op. cit., p. 56.

[109]Baker and de Kanter, op. cit., p. 35.

[110]Ibid.

[111]Trueba, op. cit., p. 56.

THE LANGUAGE NEEDS OF SCHOOL-AGE ASIAN IMMIGRANTS AND REFUGEES IN THE UNITED STATES

Sau-ling C. Wong

University of California, Berkeley

Introduction

The purpose of this chapter is twofold: to give an overview of the language needs of school-age Asian immigrants and refugees in the United States, and to explore certain public policy issues related to the language education of this group by examining several pedagogical options commonly suggested as ways to meet the group's language needs.

First, a definition of the key terms is in order. "Asian" as an ethnic label calls for some clarification. As a group, Asian Americans[1] can claim a long history of settlement in the United States dating back to the mid-nineteenth century when the Chinese first came in large numbers to work in gold mines and build railroads in the West. However, the sense of a common Asian ethnic identity cutting across linguistic, cultural, or national origin boundaries, a concept which makes a study such as this one possible and meaningful, did not crystallize until the late 1960s when the civil rights movement and the ethnic revitalization movement brought about profound changes in the way Americans of all backgrounds conceived of themselves and their country. The rationale for designating various Asian groups by a single name is that, however individual Asian Americans prefer to perceive and define themselves, the white majority in America will continue to perceive and define them as variations of a type clearly distinguishable both from the dominant group and from other ethnic minorities. Whatever their learned cultural traits or achieved social traits, then, their ascribed ethnic traits[2]—primarily a matter of physical appearance—joined Asians in a common fate in the past and will always join them in a common struggle as they try to make a place for themselves in the United States. Both the membership categories and the overall designation of

"yellow" Americans are still constantly under revision, with the latest
label being "Asian and Pacific Americans." Since this study draws on
sources which employ slightly varying definitions of the term Asian,
the picture it tries to present of the language needs of school-age Asian
immigrants and refugees may be fuzzy at the edges. For immigrant
groups, the focus is mainly on the Chinese, Filipinos, and Koreans, all
characterized by a large absolute group size and a rapid rate of growth.
The refugee groups discussed are Vietnamese, Laotians, Cambodians,
and other Indochinese such as the Hmong. Generalizations made in
this chapter about the language needs of Asians Americans are not necessarily applicable to some groups traditionally included in discussions
of Asian-American issues, such as the Japanese.[3]

The terms "immigrant" and "refugee" also require careful delimita-
tion since immigrant, which in its root meaning simply refers to the
direction of population movement (in contrast to emigrant) without
consideration of its nature or causes, is sometimes used to cover refugee
also.[4] James Watson[5] identifies four categories of voluntary immigrants (voluntary in the sense that emigration was not a result of legal
compulsion, physical force, etc.): refugees; settlers; sojourners (e.g.,
businessmen and diplomats); and "educational transients" (known as
foreign students in the United States). While the degree of voluntari-
ness is highly debatable in the case of refugees, there being numerous
forms of coercion besides the legal or physical, Watson's classification
points up a basic similarity between immigrants (settlers) and refugees: members of both categories become permanent residents of the
receiving country, despite the "myth of the return"[6] or the "rhetoric of
the return."[7] As such, both groups will have a legitimate claim on the
receiving country's resources and affect the formulation of its public
policy, including that in language and language education.

The terms immigrant and refugee will be kept distinct; when it is
necessary to refer to both groups together the term "newcomer" will be
used, with the qualification that "new" simply refers to entry into the
United States from one's country of birth. No attempt will be made to
settle the question of at what point after entry one ceases to be considered an immigrant.[8] When it is necessary to speak of the entry of both
immigrants and refugees into the United States, in contexts where implications about the nature and causes of such population movement
are irrelevant or undesirable, the term "in-migration" will be used. The
term "immigrant children" is sometimes taken to mean both foreign-
born children who immigrate with their parents and native-born children of immigrants.[9] Its use will be restricted to the first group, although it will sometimes be necessary to cite research which does not

distinguish between first- and second-generation Asian children. The focus of this inquiry will be school-age Asian newcomers, reflecting the emphasis in current public debates on the commitment of resources to the education of ethnolinguistic minorities. Given this focus, the qualifying phrase "school-age" will not be repeated.

Finally, it should be pointed out that the key term "language needs" in the chapter's title is, in a sense, a deliberately vague one. Discussions of the language problems of newcomers are common in the literature of language education and public policy, but the word "problem," whenever it is used in minority contexts, is likely to have the connotation of a deplorable state of affairs for which those adversely affected are themselves somehow held responsible. As Richard Ruiz suggests in an illuminating theoretical paper, "Orientations in Language Planning,"[10] of the three basic orientations in language planning—language-as-problem, language-as-right, and language-as-resource —it is the prevalence of the first among both policymakers and the general public, and the inherent opposition between the first and the second, which have been responsible for much of the current tension over issues of language policy toward ethnolinguistic minorities, particularly bilingual education. In this chapter, if the word problem is used at all, it should be understood to signify merely an area calling for special attention or special measures. The term language needs does not specify the language(s) involved. Again, this inexactness is intended, since one of the central issues to be considered will be how, or even whether, the ethnic languages of Asian immigrants and refugees fit into the picture of English acquisition. Thus the concept of language needs should be taken to cover any particularities in the Asian newcomers' language situation which inhibit their full participation in American life, be it educational, economic, or political.

Background: American Immigration and Refugee Policy toward Asians

Book-length studies devoted to the education in general, and language education in particular, of Asian Americans as a group seem to be of fairly recent vintage in the United States.[11] This recent but growing interest in their language needs is a reflection of changes in immigration and refugee policy concerning them, changes which have had a direct and dramatic impact on American schools.

American immigration policy toward Asians has traditionally been discriminatory, at times openly so. When their labor was needed for the development of the country, Asian immigrants were admitted in large numbers, although, except in Hawaii, their permanent settlement

was actively discouraged. Hard economic times invariably raised the
specter of the "yellow peril," triggering anti-Asian movements and restrictive legislation aimed at curtailing their numbers as well as their
economic influence. Bob Suzuki[12] identifies two phases of Asian immigration separated by a three-decade hiatus: early immigration between
the late 1840s and 1934, when the Chinese, Japanese, Koreans, and
Filipinos came in successive waves to develop the West; and recent immigration since the liberalization of immigration legislation in 1965.
Beginning with the Chinese Exclusion Act of 1882, a series of exclu-
sionary measures directed explicity against specific Asian groups were
passed. The culmination was the prohibition of Filipino immigration in
1934. Thus between 1934 and 1965, immigration from Asia was virtually at a standstill.

A long tradition of favoring European, especially northern and western European, immigration was not modified until 1965 when a more
equitable immigration law was passed to amend the 1952 McCarran-
Walter Act. This new law replaced a racially-based national origins
system with one based on family and occupational preference categories. Since that law came into full effect in 1967, the number of Asian
immigrants has been growing dramatically. Between 1970 and 1980,
the Chinese population in the United States grew by 87 percent; the
Filipino by 128 percent; the Korean by as much as 417 percent.[13] Overall, the Asian population increased 142 percent.[14] Ironically, the emphasis on family reunification written into the 1965 immigration reform was intended by supporters as a means of preventing a large-scale
influx of Asian immigrants, the reasoning being that, given the small
number of Asian Americans then residing in the United States—less
than one percent of the population—it would be relatively harmless to
allow their relatives to enter.[15] Little did the legislators foresee the
snowballing effect of family reunification. Whereas in the 1950s only 6
percent of all immigrants were from Asia, they now account for 44.5
percent of immigration.[16] The 1980 population of Asians in the United
States was 3.7 million, some 1.5 percent of the total population; 59 percent of Asians were foreign-born.

Not all of the growth in the Asian-American population has been
due to immigration. As a legacy of the Vietnam War, the United States
admitted over 686,000 Indochinese refugees between 1975, when the
Saigon government collapsed, and 1980.[18] The Indochinese refugees,
like the European (notably Hungarian) refugees in the 1950s and the
Cuban refugees in the 1960s, entered under special legislation waiving
regular restrictions concerning numbers and occupational skills.[19] The
first wave of Indochinese refugees consisted mainly of highly educated,

middle- or upper-class, urbanized, and westernized Vietnamese from the South; the second wave of "boat people," whose exodus from Vietnam was precipitated by the 1979 China-Vietnam border conflict, consisted mostly of Vietnamese and ethnic-Chinese Vietnamese from a much more diverse socioeconomic and educational background.[20] Chuong Hoang Chung, in a recent analysis,[21] identifies a third wave, noticeable since 1982, of refugees primarily from Laotian, Cambodian, and highland minority (Hmong and Mien or Yao) backgrounds, many of whom never attended school in their homelands.

Public pressure toward reform of immigration legislation has been strong during the last few years, with most of the proposed provisions aimed at reducing illegal in-migration across the southern border of the United States.[22] Unless drastic reform legislation directed specifically against Asian immigration (such as the once-proposed elimination of the "fifth preference"[23]) is enacted, it is unlikely that the growth of the Asian-American population will slow significantly in at least the next few decades. Of course, it is impossible to predict the rate of this growth accurately, because unanticipated changes in such factors as fertility or mortality rates may occur. The picture is further complicated by the unpredictability of the refugee influx, given the volatility of the situation in Southeast Asia as well as the traditional influence of political expediency on American refugee policy.[24] Nevertheless, by one estimate, it is projected that by the year 2000, Asian Americans will make up as much as 4.2 percent of the national population.[25]

The Impact of Asian In-migration on Language Education in the Schools

Data from the 1980 census indicate that two-thirds of the 3.7 million Asians in the United States speak an Asian language at home; of those aged five and over with an Asian home language, about one-fifth may be limited English proficient (LEP).[26] The presence of LEP students of Asian ancestry in American schools is likely to continue to be strong if present in-migration trends continue. Rebecca Oxford and others[27] project that the number of NELB (non-English language background) Asians will increase from 1.8 million in 1976 to 2.2 million in 2000. They further project that the total number of school-age Asian LEP children will remain constant at about 1.3 million, but the LEP rate (ratio of LEPs to NLEBs) is expected to continue to be high: 0.50 for Chinese, 0.75 for Vietnamese, somewhat lower for Koreans and Filipinos.

The presence of Asian LEP children in the schools is being felt not only in traditional ports of entry for immigrants like San Francisco or New York, but also in areas with no previous history of significant Asian settlement.[28] Despite the small absolute size of the Asian-American group in the national population, the impact of Asian immigrant and refugee students on the public schools cannot be ignored. Several important characteristics of the Asian-American population neutralize the effect of small absolute group size and make it imperative that policymakers recognize them as a group with special language needs.

First of all, the high concentration of Asian Americans in certain geographical areas creates heavy demands on the language education resources of the schools there. In 1980, 64 percent of the Asian-American population lived in the states of California, Hawaii and New York, and fully 40 percent was concentrated in four SMSAs (standard metropolitan statistical areas) alone: Los Angeles/Long Beach, San Francisco/Oakland, New York City, and Honolulu.[29] Asian Americans are expected to remain concentrated in the same three states in the year 2000, with 42 percent expected to live in California, 15 percent in Hawaii, and 8 percent in New York, with Texas adding 5 percent as another favored area of settlement.[30] Since the majority (59 percent) of Asian Americans are now foreign-born and most likely NELB, the number of LEP Asian students in these geographical areas, especially in the urban centers with ethnic enclaves, will be a source of concern for educators and policymakers.

The concentration of Asian immigrants in certain areas is a consequence of their previous settlement history in the United States, the greater economic opportunities offered in these areas, and the advantages of their geography (less severe climate, coastal location, etc.). It is interesting to note that, in the case of latecomers like the Indochinese refugees, even government policy has been insufficient to counteract the attraction of the established centers of settlement. In 1975, when the first Vietnamese refugees began to enter the country, the federal government set up a sponsorship system aimed at dispersing them to all states,[31] not only to facilitate their assimilation,[32] but also to avoid creating tension and a focus of discontent among the local population in a time of economic recession.[33] Soon, however, the phenomenon of secondary migration caused Indochinese refugees to resettle in a handful of states, especially in California, which in 1981 accounted for fully one-third of the nation's Indochinese population.[34]

A second characteristic of the Asian-American population affecting public education, especially language education, is its rapid rate of growth through in-migration, which translates to a rapid rate of growth in the number of LEP students in the schools. Schools are often ill-equipped to meet the language needs of Asian immigrant and refugee students; even if they are ready to commit resources to retrain teachers or hire trained ones for this purpose, there is an inevitable time lag before the problem can be adequately addressed. Chong-Sik Lee[35] gives a vivid account of how public school teachers in Philadelphia were bewildered and frustrated by the sudden influx of Asian immigrant children into their classes. General lack of awareness of Asian immigration led many local people to wonder "who was responsible for bringing them the [Korean immigrants] into the area and how long they might stay."[36] When the school district realized that the Asian immigrant children were there to stay, it had to develop language education resources practically overnight, pressing into service speech therapists and teachers of Spanish as a foreign language to teach the newcomers English as a second language (ESL). Lee's account is hardly that of an isolated incident.

Complicating the picture of staff and program development is a third factor related to the first two: the relative unpredictability of demographic changes in the Asian-American population, hence in the composition and needs of the Asian LEP students. Since refugees account for a significant segment of the Asian LEP population, and since the movement of refugees is, by definition, an act of emergency determined by larger forces such as international politics and American foreign policy, school districts are often caught by surprise by sudden and unpredictable influxes of Asian LEPs. The number of Indochinese children aged five to eighteen in the United States almost doubled between the 1977-78 school year and 1979;[37] almost all Laotians admitted between 1970 and 1980 arrived within three years, between 1977 and 1980.[38] Certainly, language issues aside, all schools have to deal with demographic changes in the communities they serve; in this, schools affected by Asian LEPs are no different from their counterparts unaffected by immigrant and refugee settlement. However, the former are much more at the the mercy of demographic changes because in-migration, unlike factors such as the birth rate of the local population or land development, is subject to sudden and unexpected fluctuations, making long-term planning difficult.

Finally, the heterogeneity of the post-1965 Asian-American population is a source of great strain on the language education resources of the schools. Pre-1965 immigrants from Asia tended to be rather homogenous in background within each ethnic group, since most were laborers recruited to fill specific labor needs such as railroad or sugar cane plantation worker. Post-1965 immigration, being based on both occupational and family reunification preference categories, has resulted in

a much more diverse Asian-American population. The successive
waves of Indochinese refugees add further to the heterogeneity of the
group. Asian newcomers evince great diversity in socioeconomic background, level of education, degree of urbanization, degree of exposure
to Western influence and the English language, and so on, in addition
to more fundamental differences in culture and native language. All of
these have a bearing on the newcomer children's experience in American schools. School with Asian LEPs have a problem on their hands
which is not only great in magnitude and unstable over time, but also
multidimensional in nature.

Of particular interest to the formulation of public policy to meet the
language needs of Asian newcomers is their linguistic diversity. The
number of Asian languages and dialects represented is large.

> Asian languages spoken in the United States include Philippine
> languages (Austronesian), the Mon-Khmer languages, the Miao
> and Yao languages, the various Chinese dialects and languages,
> Korean, Japanese, and Vietnamese. Among just one small group
> of recent immigrants, the so-called "montagnards" of southern
> Vietnam, there are tens of different native languages, ranging
> from the Bahnaric (Mon-Khmer) to Churu (a member of
> Austronesian).[39]

While some of these languages do share grammatical properties which
cause their speakers to experience similar problems with English,[40]
knowledge of this fact can only be applied to the teaching of English
indirectly and is not immediately useful to those faced with the task of
easing Asian newcomers into a new linguistic and cultural environment
during the crucial first years after their entry into the United States.

Another aspect of the heterogeneity of Asian newcomers which
poses a special challenge to the schools is the presence of Indochinese
refugees, especially those of the third wave.[41] Two of the most difficult
problems posed by this group—problems which most American schools
are probably unprepared to deal with—are the refugee children's mixed
literacy backgrounds and their experience of irreversible and often vio-
lent dislocation from their homelands.

The mixed literacy backgrounds of refugees can be classified as: pre-
literate, for those who speak a language for which there is no written
form or whose written form is rare (e.g., Hmong, Mien); non-literate or
illiterate, for those who possess no reading and writing skills in any
language; semi-literate, for those who have had some formal education
or possess minimal literacy skills; and non-Latin (or non-Roman) alphabetic literate, for those who are fully literate in their own language
(e.g., Khmer, Lao, Chinese, etc.), but who need to learn the formation

of the Latin alphabet.[42] Children with no or minimal literacy experience must therefore be taught not only academic skills (like all school children) and English skills (like all LEP children), but also basic literacy skills and adjustment to formal educational settings such as classroom routines.

Schools should be conscious of the fact that refugee children are often direct victims of war and survivors of unspeakable ordeals before arriving in the United States. Some are unaccompanied minors who escaped alone, sometimes with the parents' consent, sometimes without the parents' knowledge.[43] Knowledge about the impact of resettlement on refugee children is limited by the lack of hard data,[44] but there is reason to believe that attention to only the language needs of Indochinese refugee children, without taking into account their psychosocial well-being, may be self-defeating.

The emphasis and priority in service and study of refugee children heretofore focused on their language needs and progress. This might well be the priority for immigrant children, but there is every reason to distinguish refugee children from other immigrants and to recognize that their generally unmet priorities are health care (medical and psychological) and that the unit for service to children should be predominantly the family. Similarly, the focus of research must be shifted to consider the long- and short-term consequences of their prolonged traumatization and the social discontinuities that characterize their settlement.[45]

While a more holistic perspective on the language needs of Indochinese refugee children may provide the only basis for a long-term solution—and this may indeed be true for all Asian LEP children—the fact remains that the schools are having a difficult enough time trying to provide adequate language education conceived of in a narrow, technical sense.

To recapitulate, as a result of in-migration the Asian-American population in the United States is characterized by its high concentration in certain geographical areas, its rapid rate of growth, its relative demographic unpredictability, and its great heterogeneity. This configuration of characteristics creates a challenge for schools affected by the influx of Asian immigrant and refugee LEP children. Any attempt to formulate public policy to meet the language needs of these children must take into account the unique demographic patterns of the group.

The Need to Recognize the Language Needs of Asian Immigrants and Refugees as a Distinct Group

Apart from the numerical insignificance of Asian Americans in the national picture, a number of factors have prevented the full recognition by educational policymakers of Asian immigrants and refugees as a group with distinct language needs. As part of the Asian-American population, school-age Asian newcomers suffer from the same neglect experienced by the entire group. National data on Asian Americans in general are scarce.[46] Before 1970, except for the 1940 census, the census question on mother tongue was not asked of the general population; the concern was with European immigrant populations and their children.[47] Information on the language situation of Asians in the United States suffers from paucity and haphazardness.

In addition, the in-migration experience has not been sufficiently recognized as a significant influence on the Asian immigrants' and refugees' language learning. Even in the field of TESOL (teaching English to speakers of other languages) itself, a holistic view of language learning as a process involving not just cognitive but also social and affective factors is a fairly recent development,[48] and ESL teachers have been largely trained on a generalized "foreign learner" model which makes scant distinction between learners in different social contexts.[49] Using John Schumann's "acculturation model" of language learning[50] as a theoretical framework, I have argued elsewhere[51] that the experience of permanent dislocation, the stresses resulting from resettlement, and the Asian Americans' status as a visible minority in this country are all likely to affect the linguistic adjustment of Asian immigrant students. Asian immigrant and refugee students are often loosely referred to as foreign students. Besides unfairly suggesting the alienness and unassimilability of residents who have been legally admitted as permanent members of the society, this term obscures important differences between the Asian newcomers and foreign students proper, i.e., educational transients, in both the context of their language learning and the characteristics of their English usage and proficiency. Yet the distinction is one that even the College Entrance Examination Board fails to recognize in its compilation of data on SAT scores.[52]

Finally, the common perception of Asian Americans as a "model minority," perpetuated by the media and sometimes embraced by Asian Americans themselves, serves to mask the language needs of Asian immigrants and refugees. On the basis of the often questionable use of statistics,[53] exponents of the model minority thesis hold up Asian Americans as an example of an ethnic minority which has, by dint of hard work alone, become even more successful than whites, especially in education.[54] As part of the model minority idea, Asian Americans are often stereotyped as being quiet by nature, even nonverbal, and gifted in quantitative fields of study.[55] This popular perception may cause some teachers of Asian immigrant and refugee children to take less seriously the newcomers' lack of verbal expressiveness, or to encourage them to concentrate prematurely on technical subjects at the expense of English. While it is true that Asian-American students as a whole are doing well educationally, it must be stressed that Asian immigrant and refugee students constitute a significant exception to the general picture.[56] At the high school level, Asians who have lived in the United States for five or fewer years scored substantially lower than white students in both verbal skills and science, whereas those who have lived here at least six years did as well or better than whites.[57] At the college level, the presence of Asian newcomers contributes to the lower SAT verbal scores of Asian Americans compared to whites; LEP Asians show an imbalance in verbal and math scores.[58] After analyzing the above data and others, Sau-lim Tsang and Linda Wing conclude that "immediate attention must be given to the education of recent immigrants and others whose best language is not English. . . . [B]oth secondary and postsecondary students appear to have difficulties in verbal skills and in areas dependent on a high level of reading comprehension. These difficulties appear to narrow their options for study and career preparation."[59]

Data collected by the Office of Civil Rights for 1978 show that, of the LEPs—presumably mostly newcomers—who constituted 14.5 percent of the Asian-American enrollment in kindergarten through twelfth grade, only 54 percent were receiving ESL or bilingual education services.[60] Extending adequate language education to all newcomers, a prerequisite for providing them an equal and meaningful general education, is therefore a matter of great concern. Before the situation can be addressed, the language needs of Asian newcomers as a distinct group must be fully recognized.

Examining Some Options for Addressing the Language Needs of Asian Immigrants and Refugees

From a public policy standpoint, what is the best way to meet the distinct language needs of Asian newcomers? This question will be explored with reference to several options commonly suggested: submersion, pull-out ESL, bilingual education, and immersion as a particular type of bilingual education.

In the mounting public debate over language issues in the United States, especially over bilingual education, the above programmatic terms have themselves become emotionally loaded. For example, "English as a Second Language," which is simply a term describing the learners' language history (since a person can have only one first language or mother tongue, those whose first language is not English must learn it as a second language), is sometimes taken by laymen to mean an unpatriotic relegation of English to secondary status.[61] The terms may also cause confusion because of their lack of standardization in usage. What the public often refers to as immersion is actually what second language researchers call submersion; what second language researchers call immersion is a form of bilingual education, and is indeed known as such in Canada.[62] It should be stressed that in this chapter, the decision to use the terms listed at the beginning of this section results from an attempt to strike a balance between their popular and specialized usages, a gesture of deference to reality. These terms should not be taken to refer to separate and mutually exclusive alternatives in competition with each other; ESL, for example, is an integral part of bilingual education. Use of a term does not imply automatic endorsement of the pedagogical approach involved.

Several issues must be considered before it can be determined whether a pedagogical approach is applicable on a large scale in meeting the language needs of Asian immigrants and refugees. The first is an issue of rights: Is there a legal basis for claiming access to this type of language education service? Do the newcomers have a legitimate claim to it? Are the schools obligated to allocate public funds to provide it? Second, the theoretical basis for the effectiveness of a method must be examined. What does available research indicate? What does this research mean? What do theories of second language acquisition tell us about the potentials of the method? Third, the feasibility of an option must be determined in the context of the four characteristics of the Asian population outlined previously: geographical concentration, rapid rate of growth, demographic unpredictability, and heterogeneity. Cost and benefit should not be conceived of in narrow, monetary terms; rather, a consideration of the trade-off must take into account the human dimension—with the understanding, however, that some uncertainty necessarily exists here because not all meaningful things can be measured. Ruiz's classification of orientations in language planning—language-as-problem, language-as-right, and language-as-resource—referred to earlier, will be useful to help focus the discussion of each option.

The following is not meant to be a comprehensive review of the pedagogical soundness of each method or its general applicability to LEPs.
Rather, the emphasis of the discussion will be on the public policy, not
the pedagogical, implications of the various options.

Submersion

The substitution of immersion for submersion in the layman's vocabulary is interesting. The scholarly use of the term immersion has somehow never caught on. Perhaps submersion, with its connotations of
"going under," would have made both the speaker and listener more
uncomfortably aware of the "sink-or-swim" threat of the laissez-faire
approach and its implications for LEP students as human beings—an
awareness that advocates of submersion as a cheap, fast, and patriotic
means of solving the language problem might wish to avoid evoking.
    Submersion is more appropriately described as a non-method than a
method; it involves placing LEP students into a class of predominantly
native English-speaking students and leaving the former to their own
devices to "pick up" the new language from the English-only instruction. Advocacy of submersion as a matter of policy stems from a language-as-problem perspective. Immigrant and refugee students are
seen as creating a problem, an extra burden on taxpayers which should
be removed as swiftly as possible, preferably at no expense above what
it would take to educate the other, "normal," native English-speaking
students. Submersion is most often promoted in opposition to bilingual
education; at times any form of language service is rejected even if it
does not involve use of the newcomer's native language. The arguments used by submersion advocates are usually various combinations
of what Heinz Kloss[63] identifies as the "tacit compact" theory, the
"take-and-give" theory, the "anti-ghettoization" theory, and the "national unity" theory. The anti-ghettoization argument, which claims
that the in-migrant stands to benefit from being educated exclusively
in English, is often augmented by the suggestion that forced mingling
with native English speakers facilitates language learning.[64]
    Few if any researchers or theorists in second language acquisition
have publicly advocated submersion as an effective policy to meet the
language needs of in-migrant students. Even Schumann's "acculturation model," which de-emphasizes the role of instruction,[65] does not
warrant such a stand: Informal contact with native speakers does not
automatically lead to acquisition[66] of English, since the learner must
experience "social and psychological proximity" with native speakers
before language "input" can be converted into "intake."[67] For Asian

immigrants and refugees, members of a visible minority with a history
of discrimination in this country, submersion by itself may in fact increase, not decrease, "social and psychological distance" from native
English speakers. In addition, submersion may foster the development
of a superficial fluency in English which masks the in-migrant student's
deeper problems with the language, especially in cognitive/academic
skills.[68]

From a language-as-resource perspective, the submersion approach
is a waste of human resources since it will almost certainly result in
"subtractive" rather than "additive" bilingualism[69] for Asian newcomers, given the state of interethnic relations in the United States.
Perhaps most importantly, from a language-as-right perspective, submersion deprives in-migrant students of equal opportunity in education as established by the Supreme Court's decision in Lau v. Nichols in
1974.[70] While the Lau ruling does not create any language rights in
terms of requiring specific measures of redress, and is based on the 1964
Civil Rights Act prohibiting discrimination due to national origins,[71]
it does establish that "there is no equality of treatment merely by providing students with the same facilities, textbooks, teachers, and curriculum: for students who do not understand English are effectively
foreclosed from any meaningful instruction."[72] It goes on further to
say, "Basic English skills are at the very core of what these public
schools teach. Imposition of a requirement that, before a child can effectively participate in the educational program, he must already have
acquired those basic skills is to make a mockery of public education."[73]

A fact often overlooked by submersion advocates is that immigrants
and refugees have been legally admitted into this country as permanent residents, eligible for naturalization after a period of residence. As
such, they are not foreign elements parasitic on the native population,
but are an integral part of the public the schools are meant to serve.
English proficiency is not a criterion in immigration law for admission
into the United States; lack of English proficiency, then, should not be
used after the admission of immigrants as a basis for penalizing them
and preventing them from enjoying their rights as taxpayers. As Clive
Beck argues, since the receiving country has made the decision to ad-
mit certain immigrants, presumably after considering what it will gain
and lose as a result, "the receiving population must to a large degree
accept the consequences of their action."

Insofar as the action was taken on compassionate grounds, presumably these grounds continue to be relevant. And insofar as
some benefit to the country was expected—a larger population, a

larger work force, a certain type of work force, a better world image, or whatever—there must be a preparedness to accept certain inconvenient aspects of the arrangement.[74]

The recent replacement of the *Lau* Remedies[75] by the May 25th Memorandum,[76] which "requires the schools to provide special help to LEP students, but does not limit the choice of instructional methods which may be used,"[77] represents a significant setback for the education of ethnolinguistic minorities. However, it should be pointed out that the *Lau* Remedies prescribing bilingual education for federally funded programs are not part of the *Lau* v. *Nichols* ruling, which does not specify the means of providing language education services to LEP students. Thus there continues to be no legal basis for implementing submersion as a policy.

If, in the foregoing account, little mention is made of Asian immigrants and refugees as a separate group, it is because discussion of submersion, which is in effect absence of service, necessarily focuses more on the matter of rights than on feasibility. The demographic configuration of Asian newcomers is not a relevant issue for the former, but is so for the latter. However, Asian newcomers, being mostly from developing countries widely perceived by mainstream Americans as traditional beneficiaries of American largesse (the Philippines, Korea, Taiwan, etc.), may be subjected more frequently than other language minorities to Kloss' give-and-take argument based on misconceptions concerning the debt of gratitude owed to the receiving country.[78] It is important for Asian newcomers themselves, especially refugees, to be informed about their right to receive language education services as part of their right to an equal education.

Pull-out ESL

The teaching of ESL (or, to use a more neutral term, teaching English to speakers of other languages, TESOL), unlike bilingual education, does not involve the use of any language other than English. Pull-out ESL programs "pull out" newcomer LEP students from their regular classes for a certain number of hours each week, and group them together for ESL instruction. Providing newcomers with help in content subjects and fostering multiculturalism are not integral to the discipline of TESOL; the focus is on mastering the English language.

Especially when utilized in the early days of bilingual education implementation, ESL is often perceived by proponents of bilingual education as an approach insensitive to the LEP student's needs. It should be stressed that there is nothing inherently damaging to newcomer students in the teaching of English as a language. Schumann suggests that even if one considers acculturation (social and psychological proximity to the target language group) to be the causal variable in second language acquisition, formal instruction may facilitate acquisition by making available more language input, by helping the learner isolate grammatical and lexical elements, and by providing the learner with a "conscious monitor" which can be used in informal use of the second language.[79] The negative connotations attached to ESL probably derive in no small part from the pulling out process, which is a consequence of the need to accommodate the scheduling and staffing demands of the school bureaucracy.

Pulling out results in several disadvantages whose effects on Asian immigrant and refugee students are perhaps particularly acute. The practice stigmatizes LEP students. Pull-out ESL classes are often viewed by native English speakers as "dummy classes," so that the very students they are supposed to help instead develop a psychological resistance to them. To the already precarious psychological well-being of the newcomer students, especially the refugees, is added the burden of finding their proficiency in another language a deficit or handicap. This stigmatization stems partly from the language-as-problem attitude adopted by many school administrators and teachers, and partly from the prevailing ethnocentric sentiments of the larger society which denigrate Asian cultures and languages. In addition to creating psychological damage, the practice of pulling out may reduce interaction between the newcomers and the native English speakers. Since Asian LEPs are likely to be concentrated in certain geographical areas, especially urban centers (a situation which encourages newcomers to interact with those from similar cultural or linguistic backgrounds), pulling out further diminishes opportunities for using English in natural settings.

Two other disadvantages of pull-out ESL are relevant to Asian immigrant and refugee students. When used as the sole means to address the language needs of the group, pull-out ESL may cause newcomers to fall behind in their content subjects, with which they are expected to keep up at the same time they are learning English. Also, ESL courses, considered strictly remedial, are not normally given full academic credit; high school ESL units do not count toward fulfilling university entrance requirements.[80] Both these consequences frustrate the academic aspirations of many Asian immigrant and refugee students. Many Asians immigrate to the United States specifically to give their children a chance for a better education, especially a higher education, which is limited in many Asian countries. Asian-American students tend to have high academic aspirations; in 1982-83, 46 percent of all eighteen-year-old Asian Americans took the SAT, compared to 24 percent of the total eighteen-year-old population.[81] For Asian LEPs in secondary school, it is important to keep up with native English speakers in content subjects and to accumulate enough regular English units to meet university entrance requirements. Yet many of them operate under time constraints; in-migration at the "wrong" age, i.e., too late in their secondary school career, may not give them enough time to catch up on both English and content subjects with the help of pull-out ESL alone.

However, in spite of the above shortcomings, pull-out ESL may be the only feasible option when the LEP students are from heterogeneous linguistic backgrounds, which is the case with Asian immigrants and refugees. Christina Bratt Paulston[82] notes that the field of TESOL has made "large theoretical and methodological advances during the last fifteen years," and that many of its previous abuses are not inherent in the approach. She suggests reconciling the opposition between ESL and bilingual education, since both are components in TESOL: "The worst possible outcome anyone could envisage in TESOL is a return to submersion."[83]

From a language-as-problem perspective, pull-out ESL may be relatively easy to implement, involving minimal retraining of teachers and minimal reorganization of the curriculum and classes. Nevertheless, from a language-as-resource perspective, ESL can do little to counteract subtractive bilingualism, which is a function of larger societal forces. Thus the diverse linguistic resources Asian newcomers bring with them cannot be preserved.

Bilingual Education

From a language-as-resource perspective, maintenance bilingual education is probably the only truly desirable way to provide language education services to Asian immigrants and refugees. Yet it is also the most problematic in theoretical justification and practical implementation.

Since *Lau* v. *Nichols* did not specify the means of helping LEP students overcome the language barrier to an equal and meaningful education, let alone pronounce on the type of bilingual education appropriate for a particular LEP population, it is unclear whether Asian newcomers have a rightful claim to maintenance bilingual education, even if all concerned were to find the option desirable. The right to receive maintenance bilingual education, in Kloss' taxoi >my of language rights, is a "promotion-oriented" (as opposed to "t(lerance-oriented") right to which a group can lay claim only after demonstrating a three-generation commitment to keeping the language alive.[84] By this criterion, newcomers (first generation) have no claim to maintenance bilingual education.

Even if Asians in the United States are taken as an entire group, their record of native language maintenance is weak. A comparison with Hispanics as a group may be instructive here. Dorothy Waggoner suggests that the number of claimants of Spanish as their mother tongue increased between 1970 and 1975.[85] The 1976 Survey of Income and Education (SIE) showed that three out of four Hispanics were native-born, four out of five lived in Spanish-speaking households, and one in three usually spoke Spanish.[86] Although a significantly smaller percentage of the native-born spoke Spanish less frequently than the fore ign-born, and although recently Calvin Veltman, using 1977 SIE data, has argued that Spanish maintenance is due less to intergenerational transmission than to in-migration,[87] taken as a whole the group has been reasonably successful in maintaining Spanish.

In contrast, SIE data showed Asian Americans having a larger percentage of foreign-born than Hispanics (57 percent), but a smaller percentage (two out of three) living in households where the Asian languages were spoken.[88] These data weaken the group's claim to maintenance bilingual education. Joshua Fishman notes:

> In the context of the powerful, participatory reward system that America has traditionally made available to so many of its inhabitants, few immigrant (or other minority) ethnicity reward systems have been able to remain aloof from or impervious to it. Those non-English speaking populations who were outside the national system (for example, most American Indians, Mexican Americans, Puerto Ricans, and small, self-isolating groups such as the Hutterites or Amish) retained their non-English mother tongues. Their language remained part of their ethnicity owing to the absence of severe strains imposed by mobility opportunities.[89]

Asian immigrants and refugees, while frequently faced with initial downward occupational mobility, are clearly within the reward system described by Fishman. For them and their children, language shift from the Asian mother tongue to English within one or two generations is a common occurrence. Asian Americans initially came into contact with native English speakers through migration; Hispanics, through annexation. According to Richard Schermerhorn,[90] the origin and type of contact between subordinate and dominant groups are important factors affecting interethnic relations and the subordinate groups's integration into the larger society (hence the ease of its language maintenance). As an in-migrant group, Asian Americans cannot use the powerful argument that the indigenous Spanish speakers can use in favor of maintenance bilingual education: "We were here first."[91]

In the spirit of *Lau* v. *Nichols* and the anti-discrimination civil rights laws on which it was based, bilingual education in the United States has traditionally been conceived of as transitional, even compensatory, in nature (although the 1974 Bilingual Education Act, which amended the 1968 act, removed low income as a criterion for admitting language minority students into Title VII programs). As such, it can be legitimately claimed by Asian immigrants and refugees. At the same time, the feasibility of transitional bilingual education for Asian newcomers is reduced by the demographic characteristics of rapid rate of growth, unpredictable demographic changes, and heterogeneity, especially linguistic heterogeneity. (Hispanic subgroups, though diverse in many ways, are by contrast at least linguistically more homogeneous.[92]) The practical difficulty in implementing bilingual education of whatever kind, in materials development, teacher training, program design, and related areas, is quite daunting.[93] The Asian newcomers' diversity adds to the implementation problem in that the resources allocated for the Asian LEP population, already limited because of the group's small size, must be further divided among a number of different language groups. This creates the fact of competition even if the intent for it is absent. In competing for a piece of the "national pie" in transitional bilingual education, Asian Americans as a group come up against the greater number of Hispanics. (Spanish-origin persons make up some 14.6 million, or 6 percent of the total American population, four times the number of Asian Americans.[94]) While greater numbers may mean higher visibility in the popular mind and easier attraction of hostility in a conservative political climate, both of which have affected the Spanish speakers' struggle for bilingual education, there is no denying that political clout is based chiefly on numbers. It is also true that the principle of "numerosity"[95] is a crucial, yet problematic, criterion for determining the provision of language education services from a language-as-right perspective.

This discussion of the feasibility of transitional bilingual education for Asian immigrants and refugees is not to be taken as a negation of the concept. It is simply a recognition of the demographic characteristics of the group. It should be emphasized that transitional bilingual

education serves a vital function which ESL cannot serve; that is, helping the newcomer keep up with academic subjects, an important concern for Asian immigrants and refugees and a prerequisite to a meaningful, equal education.

Immersion as a Type of Bilingual Education

The maintenance-transitional controversy in bilingual education is
complicated by research findings which demonstrate that the maintenance of the newcomers' mother tongue through its use as a medium of
instruction may be the only effective way of achieving transition to the
dominant language of the receiving country.[96] In other words, the opposition between transition and maintenance, on which most discussions of bilingual education in the United States are implicitly or explicitly based, turns out to be much less clear-cut than one might
expect. In view of the proven success of immersion in a large number of
programs in Canada and elsewhere[97] (the typical model involves use of
a non-dominant language as a medium of instruction for all subjects,
with the dominant language being gradually introduced as language
arts in the curriculum from second grade up), this approach has been
suggested as a means of meeting the language needs of language minority students.[98] This invalidation of the maintenance-transition dichotomy raises interesting questions about the right of in-migrant groups
to receive education in their native languages, questions which are unanticipated in and unaddressed by Kloss' schema of promotion- versus
tolerance-oriented rights.[99]

It should be noted that the classic cases of immersion have been designed for the enrichment of children from the dominant ethnolinguistic group, as an indirect means of improving interethnic relations and raising the status of the minority language in which
immersion is conducted. The orientation adopted is that of language-
as-resource, but the emphasis is on *development* (of an additional language among monolingual English speakers) rather than on *conversion*
(of a minority language among those who already speak it). Certain
common denominators of successful immersion programs have been
identified by Merrill Swain and James Cummins, Richard Tucker,
Wallace Lambert, and Christina Paulston.[100] Success is associated
with anglophone subjects, members of the majority whose language
and culture are prestigious, socially and economically valued, and
therefore secure. They tend to be of higher socioeconomic status, and
their parents are voluntarily and actively involved in the programs.

Classes are relatively homogeneous in composition and in initial language proficiency, although small numbers of native speakers of the immersion language are sometimes included. In addition, since both the first and second languages are Indo-European, it is possible that the degree of transfer of cognitive/academic skills across languages is enhanced, although the survey literature is not explicit on this subject.

All the aforementioned authors are careful to point out that it is spurious to advocate submersion of LEP students into an all-English environment on the basis of the proven success of immersion programs, for the characteristics of a submersion experience contradict many of the common denominators of successful immersion. The application of the lessons of immersion for LEP students lies, rather, in transforming their subtractive bilingualism into an additive one by establishing a firm cognitive/academic foundation in their native language before introducing English. Wallace Lambert, distinguishing such an application from "typical compensatory education or catch-up-in-English models," describes it as

> a dual-track educational paradigm that emphasizes the use of the non-English home language as the major instructional language in the early grades and eventually introduces a separate English language instructional component when it is certain that the child's home language has taken root and is a secure base for starting the build-up of English, a stage that may not be reached until a child enters the second or third grade.[101]

The attractiveness of this alternative is that it promises to "[bring] two traditionally disparate social groupings—anglophone mainstreamers and ethnolinguistic minorities—together around a new form of bilingualism and biculturism."[102] However, there is as yet little *direct* research evidence on the systematic and large-scale inclusion of LEP students into an immersion program conducted in their native language, which involves a shift in emphasis from the development to the conservation of language resources.

A key question about the pedagogical effectiveness of immersion for Asian Americans concerns the transferability of cognitive/academic skills between languages. Many of the Asian languages used in the United States are nonalphabetic, yet little data are available on how far cognitive/academic skills acquired in nonalphabetic languages are transferable to an alphabetic one like English. Ovid J. L. Tzeng, in a review of studies on the cognitive processing of speakers of languages using different orthographies, cautions:

[R]eading skills acquired in one orthography may not be the same
as those acquired in another orthography, if these two orthographies have different script-speech mapping rules. . . . Thus instructional programs for bilingual children whose first language
has a nonalphabetic orthography should be carefully designed to
facilitate positive transfer and minimize negative interference
due to the orthographic factor.[103]

This crucial issue of transferability is unlikely to be settled by research
involving actual immersion programs in nonalphabetic Asian languages, for there is always the potential human cost to consider:
Should transferability turn out to be limited, students in an experimental group may suffer retardation in their acquisition of English as well
as academic content. It is to forestall any such problems that the Cantonese immersion program at West Portal School in San Francisco, one
of a small number of immersion programs for non-Indo-European languages available in the United States, has elected to introduce English
literacy skills at the kindergarten level rather than the customary second or third grade. This constitutes a departure from the Canadian
model and is known as "two-way immersion"; the program's preliminary results have been described as promising, but the theoretical
question on Chinese/English transfer remains unexplored.[104]

The West Portal School case also brings up another question about
the applicability of immersion for Asian immigrant and refugee children. Like its Canadian counterparts, the Cantonese program is designed for enrichment of primarily anglophone students of various ethnic backgrounds.[105] Thus it will not be able to provide insights on the
switch from language resource development to conservation. Informed
speculation on the subject may be made, however, by contrasting the
situation of Asian newcomer students with that of successful immersion candidates in established programs. Several factors may militate
against the effectiveness of immersion in the native language for Asian
immigrants and refugees. The group has a large proportion of persons
of lower socioeconomic status, and the stresses of newcomer life may
make active participation in decisionmaking by parents difficult, unless a conscious effort is made to involve them. Moreover, an immersion program presupposes a relatively stable student population. The
soundness of the approach derives in no small measure from the grad-
ual, sequential, and systematic introduction of the first and second languages. Asian immigrant and refugee communities may constantly lose
members due to social mobility as well as gain members from continued in-migration, thereby reducing the continuity of the program. On

the other hand, the high geographical concentration of Asian newcomers may work in their favor as candidates for immersion, at least for the more populous ethnolinguistic groups in urban centers.

At this point, direct evidence is limited on the viability of immersion for Asian immigrant and refugee students. Yet on balance, despite some uncertainty concerning its feasibility for specific groups, immersion remains the most adequate public policy alternative for the education of ethnolinguistic minorities. Since teachers using the immersion language need not have native-like proficiency in the dominant language, they are easier to recruit than bilingual teachers, who ideally should be equally proficient in both languages. In terms of costs, immersion should be no more expensive than pull-out ESL, which again calls for only monolingual proficiency (in English). Most attractive of all, because of the language-as-resource orientation which informs immersion, the approach benefits the majority as well as the minorities and minimizes opposition between their interests. If the chief limitation of the language-as-problem perspective is insensitivity to human costs, and if that of the language-as-right perspective is insensitivity to political realities, immersion promises a way to reconcile the conflict between the two approaches. In a global context, many of the Asian languages currently dismissed as minor in the American educational system are in fact highly important, and ignorance of them has been harming America's interests in diplomacy, foreign trade, and general world image.[106] It is therefore in the interest of all Americans, regardless of ethnicity, to see language resources wisely preserved as well as developed. How easy politically it would be to implement immersion is another question. In the 1980s' climate of retrenchment and chauvinism, in which bilingual education is seen by many proponents as having reached "the most critical period" of its history,[107] the American public's resistance to immersion would most likely be intense if the nature of the approach became widely understood. Advocates of immersion as part of the language education policy for newcomers are certain to have a highly difficult task of persuasion and lobbying on their hands.

Conclusion

From the above analysis of the strengths and weaknesses of several common approaches proposed to address the language needs of Asian immigrants and refugees, it can be seen that, except for submersion (which has few merits except as a last resort), all of the options provide necessary language education services in some ways, although none qualifies as the sole solution to be recommended for Asian newcomers under all circumstances. Asian newcomers are not a monolithic group; while the same can be said of any ethnolinguistic minority or indeed of any collectivity, the former do exhibit a unique configuration of demographic characteristics which must be taken into account in the formulation of public policy affecting them. While the grouping together of diverse Asian newcomers does create some problems, the practice is necessary, at least as a tactic, for ensuring adequate recognition of their distinct needs as compared to those of non-Asian ethnolinguistic minorities on the one hand, and those of native-born Asians on the other. Both Asian ethnicity and the in-migration experience are powerful influences on language learning. Flexibility, then, is the key to meeting the language needs of Asian immigrants and refugees.

Flexibility in conceptualization is essential in that, as long as program options are thought of as rigid, self-contained entities, much energy will be expended as proponents of each approach battle one another for exclusive claim to attention and resources. Both attention and resources are limited enough to begin with for Asian newcomers, and competition among those concerned or charged with serving the language needs of the group can only hurt the cause. Flexibility in conceptualization is a prerequisite for flexibility in implementation, which is needed given the rapid growth of the group and the complexity and instability of its composition. This flexibility is to be based on informed attention to details of the group's reality, demographic, political, or otherwise, as well as on a combination of planning and openness to change. "A traditional (and misguided) assumption is that if the policy is well articulated, the subsequent program will reflect that policy."[108] Things in the public realm often do not happen that way. And with regard to the language needs of Asian newcomers, we may add that we are still far from even a well-articulated policy.

It cannot be overemphasized, too, that what is needed is a committed flexibility based on genuine concern for the needs of the newcomers and ungrudging acknowledgment of their right, as legitimate and permanent members of this society, to receive necessary language education services. This does not seem to be part of the basis of the rhetoric of flexibility used by the Reagan administration,[109] which "raised questions of the appropriateness of using Federal funds to enable schools to operate programs of bilingual education in which the native language had to be used, even on a graduated scale," and "[argued] that it was inappropriate for the Federal government to dictate curriculum to the local schools."[110] President Reagan once stated that it is "absolutely wrong and un-American to have a bilingual program that is now openly, admittedly dedicated to preserving their native language, and never getting them adequate in English so that they can go out into the job market and participate."[111] This remark betrays a narrow, historically uninformed view of the language heritage as well as current linguistic realities of the United States,[112] not to mention ignorance about recent research, theory, and practice in the area of language education. Yet it is quite characteristic of the Reagan administration's suspicion of pluralism and of minority rights, which may be seen in other, more acutely debated public policy areas such as affirmative action. Thus it is imperative that, at the same time that flexibility is exercised, those concerned or charged with the language education of Asian newcomers guard against erosion of previous gains in language-related rights[113] under the guise of expanding options.[114]

In the long run, the most effective way to ensure fulfillment of the language needs of Asian immigrants and refugees is to strengthen the concept of multiculturalism and the language-as-resource perspective, both in the consciousness of educational policymakers as well as in that of the general public. Only when Asian ethnicity and newcomer status are no longer considered handicaps, only when newcomers' language rights are fully recognized, only when their potential contributions to the linguistic resources of the nation come to be valued, will language education services for the group be able to go beyond the haphazardness which currently characterizes them and take their place in a far-sighted national education policy serving the interests of all ethnic groups.

NOTES

[1]The term is used in this chapter as a general label for persons of Asian ancestry in the United States, whether native-born or foreign-born.

[2]These three components of ethnic identity are discussed in Lung-Chang Young, "Identity, Conflict, and Survival Mechanisms for Asian Americans," in Edgar B. Gumbert, ed., *Different People: Studies in Ethnicity and Education* (Atlanta: Center for Cross-Cultural Education, College of Education, Georgia State University, 1983), pp. 22-23.

[3]Japanese Americans are excluded because the group is predominantly native-born—72 percent of the total Japanese-American population of over 716,000; see Sau-lim Tsang and Linda C. Wing, *Beyond Angel Island: The Education of Asian Americans*, ERIC/CUE Urban University Series Number 90 (New York: ERIC Clearinghouse on Urban Education, Institute for Urban and Minority Education, Teachers College, Columbia University, 1985), pp. 3-4. Asian Indian Americans, though the fourth most populous group at 360,000, are excluded because they were not classified as a separate group

before the 1980 census and, being heavily concentrated in the Northeast, have
not been studied as extensively as the Asian groups with strong historical roots
in the western United States, where Asian-American studies first gained impetus. See Bob H. Suzuki, "The Education of Asian- and Pacific-Americans: An
Introductory Overview," in Don T. Nakanishi and Marsha Hirano-Nakanishi,
eds., *The Education of Asian- and Pacific-Americans: Historical Perspectives
and Prescriptions for the Future* (Phoenix: Oryx Press, 1983), pp. 4-6, for a brief
demographic overview of Asian Americans. I am indebted to Professor Sucheta
Mazumdar of the Jackson School of International Studies at the University of
Washington, Seattle, for explaining to me the relative lack of information on
the language education of Asian Indians. For a general discussion of the education of Asian Indians in the United States (though one which offers only brief
comments on school-age children), see Ashakant Nimbark, "Some Observations on Asian Indians in an American Educational Setting," in Parmatma
Saran and Edwin Eames, eds., *The New Ethnics: Asian Indians in the United
States* (New York: Praeger, 1980), pp. 247-271.

[4] For example, Gail P. Kelly, "Contemporary American Policies and Practices in the Education of Immigrant Children," in Joti Bhatnagar, ed., *Educating Immigrants* (New York: St. Martin's Press, 1981), pp. 214-232, studies
Hungarian, Cuban, and Vietnamese refugees, but uses the term immigrant.

[5] James L. Watson, ed., *Between Two Cultures: Migrants and Minorities in
Britain* (Oxford: Basil Blackwell, 1977), pp. 5-6.

[6] Ibid., p. 5.

[7] Patricia Jeffery, *Migrants and Refugees* (Cambridge, England: Cambridge
University Press, 1976), p. 144.

[8] Clive Beck, in "Is Immigrant Education Only for Immigrants?," in Aaron
Wolfgang, ed., *Education of Immigrant Students: Issues and Answers* (Toronto:
The Ontario Institute for Studies in Education, 1975), p. 6, likewise finds it
problematic to give an exact cutoff point.

[9] This is the usage adopted in A. J. Cropley, *The Education of Immigrant
Children: A Social-Psychological Introduction* (London: Croom Helm, 1983),
pp. 29-31.

[10] Richard Ruiz, "Orientations in Language Planning," *NABE Journal* 8: 2
(Winter 1984): 15-34.

[11] For example, Chong-Sik Lee, ed., *Asian Immigrant Children in Schools:
Reflections of Teachers and Administrators* (Elkins Park, PA: The Philip
Jaisohn Memorial Center, 1979); John H. Koo and Robert N. St. Clair, eds.,
Bilingual Education for Asian Americans: Problems and Strategies (Hiroshima:
Bunka Hyoron Publishing Company, 1980); Mae Chu-Chang, ed., *Asian- and
Pacific-American Perspectives in Bilingual Education: Comparative Research*
(New York: Teachers College Press, 1983); and Nakanishi and Hirano-Naka-
nishi, op. cit.

[12] Suzuki, "Overview," op. cit., pp. 2-4.

[13]Bureau of the Census, *1980 Census of Population Supplementary Report, Race of the Population by States: 1980*, Supplementary Report Number PC80-Sl-3 (Washington, D.C.: Bureau of the Census, U.S. Department of Commerce, July 1981), and *1980 Census of Population, Volume I, Characteristics of the Population, Chapter C, General Social and Economic Characteristics, Part I, United States Summary*, Report Number PC80-1-Cl (Washington, D.C.: Bureau of the Census, U.S. Department of Commerce, December 1983), cited in Tsang and Wing, op. cit., p. 4.

[14]Suzuki, "Overview," op. cit., p. 5, gives slightly different figures based on the same census data, but the general picture is the same.

[15]This analysis is made by David Reimers in "South and East Asian Immigration into the United States: From Exclusion to Inclusion," *Immigrants and Minorities* 3: 1 (March 1984): 30-48. See especially pp. 38-39.

[16]Immigration and Naturalization Service, *1980 Statistical Yearbook of the Immigration and Naturalization Service* (Washington, D.C.: Immigration and Naturalization Service, U.S. Department of Justice, 1980), cited in Tsang and Wing, op. cit., p. 2.

[17]Bureau of the Census, *1980 Census of Population Supplementary Report, Race of the Population by States: 1980*, Supplementary Report Number PC80-Sl-3 (Washington, D.C.: Bureau of the Census, U.S. Department of Commerce, July 1981), and *1980 Census of Population, Volume I, Characteristics of the Population, Chapter D, Detailed Population Characteristics, Part I, United States Summary, Section A: United States*, Report Number PC80-1-D1-A (Washington, D.C.: Bureau of the Census, U.S. Department of Commerce, December 1984), cited in Tsang and Wing, op. cit., p. 2.

[18]Immigration and Naturalization Service, op. cit., cited in Tsang and Wing, op. cit., p. 3.

[19]Kelly, op. cit., p. 214, and Reimers, op. cit., p. 40.

[20]Joan Rubin, *Meeting the Educational Needs of Indochinese Refugee Children* (Los Alamitos, CA: National Center for Bilingual Research, 1981), pp. 3-15, provides a useful, brief overview on Indochinese in-migration up to 1980.

[21]Chuong Hoang Chung, "Bilingual Education and the Vietnamese Student" (Unpublished Manuscript, 1984).

[22]Since this writing, the Immigration Reform and Control Act of 1986 has been passed by Congress.

[23]The fifth preference, one of the family reunification preference categories created by the 1965 immigration reform, allows brothers and sisters of adult United States citizens to apply for immigrant visas. Favored by Asians, whose kinship systems posit a much closer relationship between siblings than those in Western societies, it has been partially responsible for the unforeseen "snowball effect" in Asian immigration discussed in Reimers, op. cit., p. 42. The proposal to eliminate the fifth preference met with strong opposition from the Asian-American community; see, for example, Peter Chau's report, "Community Gears Up Again to Fight Immigration Bill," in *East/West* (March 16, 1983).

[24]Kelly, op. cit., especially pp. 227-230.

[25]Report by the Center for Continuing Study of the California Economy, cited in "Palo Alto Study Predicts Minority Population Growth," *East/West* (August 11, 1983).

[26]Tsang and Wing, op. cit., pp. 2, 5.

[27]Rebecca Oxford, Louis Pol, David Lopez, Paul Stupp, Murray Gendell, and Samuel Peng, "Projections in Non-English Language Background and Limited English Proficient Persons in the United States to the Year 2000: Educational Planning in the Demographic Context," *NABE Journal* 5: 3 (Spring 1981): 1-29.

[28]This is particularly true in the case of refugee students, since an initial policy of geographical dispersal of refugees caused the settlement of many Indochinese in rather unlikely areas of the American continent (in terms of climate, historical ethnic makeup, etc.). Thus Wisconsin, for example, an inland state which one does not traditionally associate with Asian in-migration, is now host to enough Indochinese students to make a state-sponsored information manual on them (for school personnel) necessary. See Constance K. Knop, *Limited English Proficiency Students in Wisconsin: Cultural Background and Educational Needs, Part II: Indochinese Students (Hmong and Vietnamese)* (Madison, WI: State of Wisconsin Department of Public Instruction, 1982). Lee, op. cit., p. 2, notes that the presence of Korean immigrant students in the greater Philadelphia area in the late 1970s came as a surprise to school administrators and teachers, who at first attempted to treat it as a temporary phenomenon. In 1970, Pennsylvania's total Korean population was only 656; by 1980, it had grown to 12,503. See "Analysis: Asians in California and United States [sic]: 1980 U.S. Census," *Asian Week* (April 8, 1982): unpaged.

[29]Tsang and Wing, op. cit., pp. 2 and 7, based on Bureau of the Census, *1980 Census of Population and Housing Census Tracts Reports, Standard Metropolitan Statistical Areas,* Report Number PHC80-2-347 (Washington, D.C.: Bureau of the Census, U.S. Department of Commerce, August 1983).

[30]Oxford, et al., op. cit., pp. 16-17.

[31]Darrel Montero, *Vietnamese Americans: Patterns of Resettlement and Socioeconomic Adaption in the U.S.* (Boulder, CO: Westview Press, 1979), pp. 26-30.

[32]Chung, op. cit.

[33]Montero, op. cit., p. 28.

[34]Rubin, op. cit., pp. 5-7.

[35]See, for example, the presentations by various school district personnel from the North Penn School District in the "Record of the Seminar on Teaching Asian Immigrant Children," October 7, 1978, in Lee, op. cit., pp. 1-42.

[36]Lee, op. cit., p. 2.

[37]Oxford, et al., op. cit., p. 24.

[38]Tsang and Wing, op. cit., p. 4; based on Immigration and Naturalization Service, op. cit. A dramatic example of how such fluctuations affect the schools is San Francisco's Newcomer High School, which hired two Laotian teachers in 1984 in response to an influx of Laotian students, only to find the Laotian enrollment dropping drastically the following year; personal communication with Lydia Stack, Newcomer High School, San Francisco Unified School District.

[39]Charles Li, "The Basic Grammatical Structures of Selected Asian Languages and English," in Chu-Chang, op. cit., p. 4.

[40]For example, monosyllabicity, lack of articles, use of classifiers before nouns, aspectual rather than tense system in verbs, relative morphological simplicity, and subject prominence. See Li, op. cit.

[41]For a more detailed discussion of the subject, see Chung, op. cit., Rubin, op. cit., and Nguyen Dang Liem, "Bilingual-Bicultural Education for Indochinese," paper presented at the Annual Conference of the National Association of Asian and Pacific American Education (Los Angeles: April 1979).

[42]The classification is from Don Banard and Wayne Haverson's analysis of the language needs of Indochinese adults, "Teaching ESL to Illiterate Adults," Adult Education Series No. 9, Indochinese Refugee Education Guides (Washington, D.C.: Center for Applied Linguistics, 1981). However, the scheme is useful for describing the language needs of school-age Indochinese as well.

[43]Chung, op. cit.

[44]Earl E. Hyuck and Rona Fields, "Impact of Resettlement on Refugee Children," International Migration Review 15: 1 (Spring-Summer 1981): 246-254.

[45]Ibid.

[46]Tsang and Wing, op. cit., p. 9.

[47]Dorothy Waggoner, "Statistics on Language Use," in Charles A. Ferguson and Shirley Brice Heath, eds., Language in the U.S.A. (Cambridge, MA: Cambridge University Press, 1981), p. 487.

[48]For an introduction to recent developments in a "whole person" approach to language teaching, see Earl W. Stevick, Memory, Meaning and Method: Some Psychological Perspectives on Language Learning (Rowley, MA: Newbury House, 1976).

[49]Many popular introductory teacher-training works in the TESOL field, such as Christina Bratt Paulston and Mary Newton Bruder, Teaching English as a Second Language: Techniques and Procedures (Cambridge, MA: Winthrop, 1976), or Wilga M. Rivers and Mary S. Temperley, A Practical Guide to the Teaching of English as a Second or Foreign Language (New York: Oxford University Press, 1978), implicitly adopt a model of second language teaching which does not distinguish between learners from differenct sociocultural milieus. Teacher trainees have to turn to more specialized works, such as J. B. Pride, ed., Sociolinguistic Aspects of Language Learning and Teaching (Oxford: Oxford University Press, 1979), in order to move beyond the undifferentiated "foreign learner" model.

[50]John H. Schumann, "The Acculturation Model for Second Language Acquisition," in Rosario C. Gingras, ed., *Second Language Acquisition and Foreign Language Teaching* (Arlington, VA: Center for Applied Linguistics, 1978), pp. 27-50.

[51]Sau-ling C. Wong, "The Language Learning Situation of Asian Immigrant Students in the U.S.: A Socio- and Psychological Perspective," paper presented at the Eighth Annual Convention of the National Association of Asian and Pacific American Education (Los Angeles: April 1986).

[52]Tsang and Wing, op. cit., p. 10.

[53]For some representative critiques of this practice, see Bob H. Suzuki, "Education and the Socialization of Asian Americans: A Revisionist Analysis of the 'Model Minority' Thesis," *Amerasia Journal* 4: 2 (November 2, 1977): 23-51; Ki-Taek Chun, "The Myth of Asian American Success and Its Educational Ramifications," *IRCD Bulletin* 15 (Winter/Spring 1980): 1-2; Ronald Takaki, "Comparisons between Blacks and Asian Americans Unfair," *Seattle Post-Intelligencer* (March 21, 1985), p. A15.

[54]Some recent examples of this portrayal of Asian Americans in the national media are "Asian Americans: 'A Model Minority,' " *Newsweek* (December 6, 1982); "Confucian Work Ethic," *Time* (March 16, 1983); "Asian Americans: The Drive to Excel," *Newsweek on Campus* (April 1984).

[55]For an analysis and critique of this stereotype, see Elaine H. Kim, "Yellow English," *Asian American Review* (Berkeley, CA: Asian American Studies Program, University of California, Berkeley, 1976), pp. 44-63.

[56]Tsang and Wing, op. cit., pp. 12, 29-30.

[57]Samuel S. Peng, Owings A. Jeffrey, and William B. Fetters, *School Experiences and Performance of Asian American High School Students* (Washington, D.C.: U.S. Department of Education, Office of Educational Research and Improvement, April 1984).

[58]Leonard Ramist and Solomon Arbeiter, *Profiles, College-Bound Seniors, 1982* (New York: College Entrance Examination Board, 1984). See also Sucheng Chan, "Contemporary Asian Immigration and Its Impact on Undergraduate Education at the University of California, Berkeley" (Unpublished Manuscript, 1982).

[59]Tsang and Wing, op. cit., p. 37.

[60]Suzuki, "Overview," op. cit., p. 5.

[61]See Lee, op. cit., pp. 47-48, for an account of how a school administrator in Philadelphia was forced to change the name of her ESL program to ESOL (English for Speakers of Other Languages) as a result of strong criticism from parents and the board of education, who were offended by the "un-American" flavor of the term ESL. Stanley S. Seidner and Maria Medina Seidner, "In the Wake of Conservative Reaction: An Analysis," in Raymond V. Padilla, ed., *Theory, Technology, and Public Policy in Bilingual Education* (Rosslyn, VA: National Clearinghouse for Bilingual Education, 1983), cites the following response by a school board president to an ESL training program brochure:

"... I don't find your program the least bit exciting or have any enthusiasm over the idea of having English as a second language. This is America we live in and the language is English. ..." (John R. Pellegrini, Concerned Citizens of Cicero and Berwyn, to Dr. Stanley Seidner, March 15, 1981).

[62]This is the usage adopted in G. Richard Tucker, "Implications for U.S. Bilingual Education: Evidence from Canadian Research," *Focus* (Papers from the National Clearinghouse for Bilingual Education, Rosslyn, VA) 2 (February 1980): 1-4.

[63]Heinz Kloss, "Language Rights of Immigrant Groups," *International Migration Review* 5 (Spring 1971): 250-268.

[64]Kloss' refutation of the four arguments against the language rights of immigrants may be summarized as follows:

(i) The "tacit compact" theory: Judging from the historical behavior of both receiving countries and immigrant groups, no such compact can be said to exist. In fact, sometimes the immigrant languages have been cultivated more vigorously in the receiving country than in the land of origin.

(ii) The "take-and-give" theory: Although immigrants typically improve their economic situation in the receiving country, they also give back much in the form of contributing labor, creating new dimensions in the economy, and participating in consumption. Thus the demand that they repay what they take by yielding language rights is untenable.

(iii) The "anti-ghettoization" theory: The ghettoization of immigrants is often caused by the receiving country's restrictive language policy (which easily creates "functional illiteracy in two tongues"), rather than by native language retention per se. "It depends largely on the spiritual climate fostered by school and society whether the descendants of immigrants will be hampered by ghettoization or by 'foreign accents.' "

(iv) The "national unity" theory: Counterexamples of linguistically homogeneous but politically unified nations do exist. Moreover, centrifugal tendencies among ethnic minorities are often caused by outright discrimination, including that in language. Finally, modern immigrants seldom outnumber speakers of other languages and are typically dispersed, leading to assimilation within a relatively short period; thus their threat to national unity is limited. Id. at pp. 255-258.

[65]Schumann, op. cit., pp. 44-47, 49-50.

[66]Here the term "acquisition" is used in the narrow sense, adopted in Krashen's "monitor model" of second language acquisition, to refer to a largely unconscious, informal process distinguished from "learning," which involves formal instruction and conscious efforts. See Stephen Krashen, "The Monitor Model for Second Language Acquisition," in Gingras, op. cit., pp. 1-26.

[67]The distinction between "input" and "intake" is made by Stephen Krashen in "The Input Hypothesis," in James E. Alatis, ed., *Current Issues in Bilingual Education: Georgetown University Roundtable on Languages and Linguistics* (Washington, D.C.: Georgetown University Press, 1980), pp. 168-180.

[68]James Cummins, "Four Misconceptions about Language Proficiency in Bilingual Education," *NABE Journal* 5: 3 (Spring 1981): 31-45.

[69]Wallace E. Lambert, "The Effects of Bilingualism on the Individual:
Cognitive and Sociocultural Consequences," in Peter A. Hornby, ed., *Bilingualism: Psychological, Social and Educational Implications* (New York:
Academic Press, 1977), pp. 15-27.

[70]*Lau* v. *Nichols*, 414 U.S. 563 (1974).

[71]Reynaldo F. Macias, "Language Choice and Human Rights in the U.S.,"
in James E. Alatis and G. Richard Tucker, eds., *Language in Public Life:
Georgetown University Roundtable on Languages and Linguistics* (Washington,
D.C.: Georgetown University Press, 1979), pp. 86-101, provides a detailed discussion of the type and extent of language rights for ethnolinguistic minorities
in the United States; see especially the analysis of the legal basis of *Lau* v.
Nichols on p. 92.

[72]*Lau* v. *Nichols*, 414 U.S. at 566.

[73]Ibid.

[74]Beck, op. cit., p. 8.

[75]The *Lau* Remedies derive from the 1975 report, "Task Force Findings
Specifying Remedies for Eliminating Past Educational Practices Ruled Unlawful Under *Lau* v. *Nichols*" (Washington, D.C.: Office of Civil Rights, U.S.
Department of Health, Education and Welfare, 1975).

[76]The May 25th Memorandum was published by the U.S. Department of
Health, Education and Welfare in 35 Fed. Reg. 11595 (May 25, 1970).

[77]U.S. Department of Education, *The Condition of Bilingual Education in
the Nation, 1984: A Report from the Secretary of Education to the President and
the Congress* (prepared by the Office of Minority Languages Affairs, U.S. Department of Education, 1984; disseminated by the National Clearinghouse for
Bilingual Education, Rosslyn, VA), p. 95.

[78]For a critique of the "debt of gratitude" concept, see Kloss, op. cit., pp.
255-256; and Beck, op. cit., pp. 6-8.

[79]Schumann, op. cit., p. 50.

[80]This point is made in the charges made by the Asian American Task Force
on University Admissions against the University of California, Berkeley, for
discriminatory admission practices against Asian-American students; see its
Task Force Report (San Francisco: Asian Incorporated, 1985), p. 16. The task
force also points out that since the College Board does not have achievement
tests on Asian languages, Asian immigrant applicants to universities with foreign language requirements who are proficient in their native languages are in
effect penalized by having to study a third language while mastering English.

[81]Tsang and Wing, op. cit., p. 13.

[82]Christina Bratt Paulston, "Bilingualism and Education," in Ferguson
and Heath, op. cit., pp. 469-485.

[83]Ibid., p. 482.

[84]Kloss, op. cit., pp. 259-260. Briefly, promotion-oriented rights concern the authorities' active and official use of the minority language at public expense; examples include translating laws, erecting street signs, purchasing public library books, and teaching children in public schools in the minority language. Tolerance-oriented rights give minorities leeway to use their language in private spheres, in such ways as operating private language schools or circulating newspapers and magazines in the minority language.

[85]Waggoner, op. cit., pp. 491-492.

[86]National Center for Education Statistics, "Place of Birth and Language Characteristics of Persons of Hispanic Origin in the United States, Spring 1976," *National Center for Education Statistics Bulletin 78B-6* (Washington, D.C.: National Center for Education Statistics, 1978), p. 1.

[87]Calvin Veltman, *Language Shift in the United States* (New York: Mouton, 1983). I am indebted to Professor Donald W. Larmouth of the University of Wisconsin-Green Bay for pointing out the significance of this study.

[88]National Center for Education Statistics, "Place of Birth and Language Characteristics of Persons of Chinese, Korean, Filipino, and Vietnamese Origin in the United States, Spring 1976," *National Center for Education Statistics Bulletin 79B-12* (Washington, D.C.: National Center for Education Statistics, 1979), p. 2.

[89]Joshua A. Fishman, "Language Maintenance," in Stephan Thernstrom, ed., *Harvard Encyclopedia of American Ethnic Groups* (Cambridge, MA: Belknap Press, 1980), p. 630.

[90]Richard Alonzo Schermerhorn, *Comparative Ethnic Relations: A Framework for Theory and Research* (New York: Random House, 1970), p. 68, cited in Paulston, op. cit., p. 245.

[91]A. Bruce Gaarder, *Bilingual Schooling and the Survival of Spanish in the United States* (Rowley, MA: Newbury House, 1977), p. 131.

[92]The concept of linguistic homogeneity is, of course, relative; within the Spanish-speaking segment of the United States great diversity exists. For a brief historical-linguistic overview of the Spanish-speaking subgroups in the United States, see Nancy F. Conklin and Margaret A. Lourie, *A Host of Tongues: Language Communities in the United States* (New York: The Free Press, 1983), pp. 10-18.

[93]The difficulties described by Nam-Kil Kim in "Some Problems in Bilingual Education: The Korean Case," in Koo and St. Clair, op. cit., pp. 163-176, are quite typical of Asian-American groups.

[94]U.S. Bureau of the Census, *Persons of Spanish Origin in the United States,* March 1979, Advance Report (Washington, D.C.: Bureau of the Census, U.S. Department of Commerce, 1979).

[95]Ruiz, op. cit., p. 24.

[96]Tove Skutnabb-Kangas and Pertti Toukomaa, *Teaching Migrant Children's Mother Tongue and Learning the Language of the Host Country in the Context of the Sociocultural Situation of the Migrant Family* (Helsinki: Finnish National Commission for UNESCO, 1976); James Cummins, "Linguistic Interdependency and the Educational Development of Bilingual Children," *Review of Educational Research* 49: 2 (Spring 1979): 222-251; and James Cummins, "The Cross-lingual Dimensions of Language Proficiency: Implications for Bilingual Education and the Optimal Age Issue," *TESOL Quarterly* 14: 2 (June 1980): 175-187.

[97]Findings are summarized in Wallace E. Lambert and G. Richard Tucker, *Bilingual Education of Children: The St. Lambert Experiment* (Rowley, MA: Newbury House, 1972); Merrill Swain and James Cummins, "Bilingualism, Cognitive Functioning and Education," *Language Teaching and Linguistics: Abstracts* 12: 1 (January 1979): 4-18; Wallace E. Lambert, "Deciding on Languages of Instruction: Psychological and Social Considerations," in Torsten Husen and Susan Opper, eds., *Multicultural and Multilingual Education in Immigrant Countries: Proceedings of an International Symposium Held at the Wenner-Gren Center, Stockholm, August 2 and 3, 1982* (Oxford: Pergamon Press, 1983), pp. 96-101; and Wallace E. Lambert, "An Overview of Issues in Immersion Education," in California State Department of Education, *Studies in Immersion Education: A Collection for U.S. Educators* (Sacramento: California State Department of Education, 1984), pp. 9-30.

[98]Cummins, "Four Misconceptions," op. cit., pp. 42-43.

[99]Kloss, op. cit., pp. 259-260.

[100]See Swain and Cummins, op. cit.; Tucker, op. cit.; Lambert, "Deciding on Languages"; and Christina Bratt Paulston, "Ethnic Relations and Bilingual Education: Accounting for Contradictory Data," in Alatis and Twaddell, op. cit., pp. 235-262.

[101]Lambert, "Overview," op. cit., pp. 26-27.

[102]Ibid., p. 27.

[103]Ovid J. L. Tzeng, "Cognitive Processing of Various Orthographies," in Chu-Chang, op. cit., p. 92.

[104]David Dolson and Liana Szeto, "Two-Way Immersion Education: An Enrichment Program for All Children," paper presented at the Eleventh Annual Conference of the California Association for Asian/Pacific Bilingual Education (Palo Alto, CA: November 1985).

[105]The initial enrollment consisted mostly of anglophone Chinese-American children, with a small number of Caucasians and blacks (Personal communication with Winnie Tang, Bilingual Office, San Francisco Unified School District, April 1, 1986). In the program's second year of operation, only seven of the twenty-four incoming kindergarteners were Chinese; see Dolson and Szeto, op. cit. Overall, Cantonese speakers constituted a minority of the enrollees.

[106]Under President Carter, the President's Commission on Foreign Languages and International Studies issued a report in 1979 strongly criticizing

the inadequacy of foreign language education in the United States, pointing to harmful effects on the nation's international standing, diplomacy, and trade relations. See James A. Perkins, ed., *Strength through Wisdom: A Critique of U.S. Capability* (Washington, D.C.: President's Commission on Foreign Languages and International Studies, 1979). Under President Reagan, the National Advisory Board on International Education Programs also issued a report deploring an "indifference [toward foreign languages] . . . that should be a source of national embarrassment" as well as "woefully inadequate" citizen knowledge of foreign affairs and cultures. However, this 1984 report, unlike the earlier one, de-emphasizes federal responsibility for improving foreign language education. See Becky T. York, "Panel Urges More Foreign-Language Instruction," *Education Week* 3: 24 (March 7, 1984): 8.

[107]Muhammad A. Shuraydi, "Bilingual Bicultural Education: A Humanistic Multiethnic Challenge," in Padilla, op. cit., p. 395.

[108]R. C. Rist, "The Social Context of Multicultural and Multilinguistic Education in Immigrant Countries: Some Program and Policy Considerations," in Husen and Opper, op. cit., p. 48.

[109]For a detailed analysis of the current conservative political sentiment against bilingual education, particularly the Reagan administration's rhetoric and policy on the subject, see Seidner and Seidner, op. cit.

[110]U.S. Department of Education, op. cit., p. 95.

[111]Cited in *NABE News Release* (March 2, 1980).

[112]For accounts of the United States' tradition of linguistic diversity, see Shirley Brice Heath, "English in Our Language Heritage," in Ferguson and Heath, op. cit., pp. 6-20; Conklin and Lourie, op. cit.; and Heinz Kloss, *The American Bilingual Tradition* (Rowley, MA: Newbury House, 1977).

[113]L. Ling-Chi Wang, "*Lau v. Nichols*: History of a Struggle for Equal and Quality Education," in Emma Gee, ed., *Counterpoint: Perspectives on Asian America* (Los Angeles: Asian American Studies Center, University of California, Los Angeles, 1976), pp. 240-263, details the kind of struggle against the educational establishment which must be waged in order to make the slightest gain in public policy changes on behalf of ethnolinguistic minorities.

[114]California, the state most affected by Asian in-migration, provides some interesting examples of flexibility which take newcomer students' interests into account. At the state level, the recent legislation to certify language development specialists (Language Development Specialist Act of 1982, California Education Code, Secs. 4443.75-4443.81) provides, on the one hand, much needed institutional recognition that "teaching English to LEP students requires specialized knowledge and training," and, on the other, equally needed flexibility in implementing language education services in situations where compliance with the state's bilingual education requirements is not feasible (as, for example, in schools with LEP students speaking many different languages). See Lydia Stack and James Stack, "Language Development Specialist Legislation Passes," *CATESOL News* 14: 3 (October 1982): 1-2. At the local level, Newcomer High School in San Francisco provides a one-year transitional program for LEP newcomers designed to teach them enough English to function in regular schools, orient them to American culture, and prepare them

academically for higher education. See Alina Tugend, "From War-torn Nations to 'Newcomer' School," *Education Week* 4: 22 (February 20, 1985): 1-37.
It is a program which takes advantage of the small size and high in-migrant
concentration of the city, and Asian immigrants and refugees have benefited
much from it.

THE POLITICS OF THE BLACK CHILD'S LANGUAGE: A STUDY OF ATTITUDES IN SCHOOL AND SOCIETY

Shirley Stennis Williams

University of Wisconsin-Oshkosh

Introduction

An examination of Black English in American society should not be concerned primarily with counting verbs and adjectives in the oral or written discourse of black indigenous people, attempting to trace the survival of African features in the American version of English, or analyzing such surface variations in black speech as "playing the dozens," "rapping," and "getting over." To discuss Black English without including its cultural, philosophical, and political milieux would result in the kind of knowledge one would have of black physical traits without studying genetics or of gospel music without studying rhythm.[1] As Frantz Fanon points out:

> To speak means to be in a position to use a certain syntax, to grasp the morphology of this or that language, but it means above all to assume a culture. A man who has a language consequently possesses the world expressed and implied by the language. Mastery of language affords remarkable power.[2]

Black American English has an interactive history. It is uniquely derived from both Africa and America, and is the sum of what happened to the language of black people of diverse African linguistic stock when they were thrown into subservient states, forcibly prevented from speaking their own languages, and later legally denied opportunities to learn, at more than a rudimentary level, the language of their enslavers. Moreover, in recent years there have been serious debates on whether it would not be best for the culture and the country to develop new educational policies for the adaptive codes that black American speakers have devised.

The linguistic experiences of blacks in America have not been parallel to those of any bilingual immigrants. No statehood enabling act protected black languages. No teachers were trained to be specialists in the use of Black English or any African language. Few blacks can speak Swahili or any other African *lingua franca*. The reasons why Black English speakers have not been assimilated linguistically, as the language immigrants of the nineteenth century have been primarily, are related to *interference, isolation,* and *choice.* The forces that have shaped present-day attitudes toward the language of the black child can be found in history, education, the media, and black culture.

The term Black English, used interchangeably with the terms Black American English, Black Language, and Black Speech, was coined during the revisionist sixties. Black English is the label for the dialect that is spoken by most native-born Americans of African descent.[3] Dialect is properly defined as one of the varieties of English spoken in America by a regional or ethnic group. (References to specific black languages usually designate them by name such as Wolof, Yoruba, etc.) Blacks have registered resentment that among all the varieties of English spoken in the United States, theirs alone was commonly referred to as a dialect. The term developed such negative connotations that even some linguists spoke out against its continued use.[4]

The Linguistic Background

Many major linguists have called into question the beliefs and assumptions that have been advanced by the schools about dialects in general, and the black dialect in particular.[5] They have found no linguistic basis for assuming that the grammatical system of one dialect is superior to the other. However, they have recognized the linguistic ethnocentrism that allows each group to think that its manner of speech should be preferred in everyday discourse, if not in commerce.

The term Standard English is linguistically vague and as difficult to define as Black English. There seem to be two views of what is standard. One view is that Standard English is defined descriptively with reference to parameters of social level and style. It is, therefore, the variety of English spoken in formal situations or in certain settings such as the classroom. This view allows a number of sub-varieties of Standard English to be recognized. These include regional varieties, such as southern and eastern, and ethnic varieties, such as Anglo and black.[6] Another view of Standard English is that it is perceptive, an absolute, the repository of the prestigious vernacular toward which all speakers should strive.[7] (The former is the definition that will be used in this chapter, although there is evidence that authors in some citations were referring to the latter.)

Clyde Kluckhohn[8] has stated that culture is a giant mirror for man, and that the customs, traits, mores, and adaptive language found in one culture are usually found in some variation in others. An example of adaptive language is the fact that the native Alaskan has more than thirty different words to describe snow, while other Americans have about five. American Indian peoples had no language to express the selling of property and had difficulty comprehending what this meant to the English, but in the twentieth century every tribe has language to describe elaborately the confiscation of what they now define as their own.

In Europe, the discourse about the best forms of language began in the eighteenth century when the King's English was held up as a model for the common folk. It began in this country when the northeastern region established its dialect as the linguistic aristocracy. This claim was based upon the fact that the Massachusetts Laws of 1642 and 1647 were the first educational laws passed in this country. These laws stated that in order for citizens to be allowed to read their Bibles, in every community of thirty households there must be a reading and writing school, and in every community of fifty, a Latin Grammar (secondary) school. Thus, being from Massachusetts became synonymous with being educated.

The literature suggests two prevailing notions about the origin of Black English. The most common is that Black English is an offshoot of the southern dialect that found its way north during the three post-World War II migrations along the Atlantic and Pacific Oceans and along or somewhat near the Mississippi River to Chicago and other midwestern cities.[9] The second, postulated by Melville Hershkovits,[10] is that Black English is a creolized English pidgin that came from West Africa to the Caribbean and America.

The three main contemporary theoretical positions about the nature of Black English are: (1) the linguistic creole position; (2) the dialect geographer's position; and (3) the deficit theorist position.[11] A creole is a pidgin which has become the native language of a speech community. Pidgins and creoles became widely used as contact languages in the bustling West African-American-European slave trade. J. L. Dillard found abundant records of pidgin varieties of English, French, and Portuguese in all of these areas which, through a process of relexification, could be changed from one version to the other.[12]

The purest present-day forms of this early Black English can be found among the black Gullah-speaking residents of the Sea Islands of South Carolina and Georgia, and among French Creole residents of certain sections of southeastern Louisiana. The linguistic creole position is that Black English is, or has been, a distict language with its own rules. Like other languages, it has a number of varieties. Comparative studies are often made between Black English and African and Caribbean languages. Major adherents of this school of thought are William Stewart and J. L. Dillard. Joan Fickett,[13] who has coined the term " 'Merican,"[14] has also gained recognition.

The dialect geographer's position is that Black English is not a universal dialect but a regional variation that is defined by the same geographic areas as white speech. Adherents to this position argue that the rules identified by creolists to prove that Black English is a language are also found in other dialects of English. They also believe that while black speech reflects black culture, it is impossible to prove that all blacks share a common language.[15] Among major adherents of this position, one of the best known is William Labov.

The most widely known and accepted position is that of the deficit theorists. Some educators and social scientists believe that Black English speakers have both linguistic and cognitive deficiencies that will seriously affect their potential for success in American society. These professionals may or may not accept the other theoretical positions, but are not as concerned with those as they are with correcting the "bad" speech forms that they hear. Those who essentially hold this position are Carl Bereiter, Siegfried Engelmann, and Basil Bernstein.

The oldest theoretical position about Black English is the Anglican theory which holds that Black English is a direct derivative of British English. Those who hold this position state that when slaves were brought to America, they were deliberately mixed with slaves from other language backgrounds as a means of control. Because their primary language contacts were with overseers who controlled their food and safety, slaves struggled to learn their language. Over the years, slave proficiency in English increased until all traces of their original languages were eliminated. Gullah is explained as a frozen form of seventeenth century-British English spoken by blacks who were isolated on the Sea Islands.[16] John Bennett felt that Gullah was very similar to Shakespearean English:

This dialect spoken by low-country plantation negroes is strangely akin to the English dialects; quite as akin to England's provincial dialect as was the best English spoken in the Southern states, settled in William Shakespeare's days or immediately thereafter, to the English of Shakespearean plays.[17]

Hershkovits, considered the father of the creolists, reported being appalled at what he termed Anglican myths that were based on conjecture rather than research.[18] After his 1941 book entitled *The Myth of the Negro Past*, other research on Black English began to appear. The first of these was Lorenzo Dow Turner's *Africanisms in the Gullah Dialect*.[19] The subsequent work of creolists hypothesized that Black English is a separate language, with a separate history and a different pattern of development, that progressed through four stages: (1) native West African language; (2) contact with English-pidgin; (3) pidgin-creole; and (4) decreolization.[20]

The creolists further theorized that when proficient West African speakers had to trade with proficient Portuguese speakers, they developed a pidgin: a form that combined and simplified the two, and that became the most widely used West African trading language in the fifteenth and sixteenth centuries. As England replaced Portugal as the dominant trading partner, English words infiltrated the pidgin to produce a Portuguese-English-multiple West African languages pidgin that became the *lingua franca* of the slave trade. This is the most widespread of the pidgin origin theories. With the end of the slave trade came the end of the African-English pidgin.[21] Since there was no chance for renewed African influence, slaves born after 1830 used their parents' pidgin, not as a second language, but as their first. The pidgin had thus become creolized.

The pidgin stage is characterized by: a simplified syntax; a rigid word order; and reduced redundancy. It lacks: passive construction; reversed-order questions; a way to express connotative information; and individual expressions and style. When blacks reached the point in their acculturation at which they wished to make statements in these ways, the pidgin was expanded to meet their needs for expressing abstract, subjective, philosophical, and literary ideas. When this transformation was completed, the language was a creolized pidgin or simply a creole. Grammatically, a creole may have no endings to indicate plurality, case, gender, tense, or mood. Often the copular, or helping verb *to be*, is omitted. In the phonological context, the creole speaker tends to avoid consonant-vowel-consonant cluster patterns (CVCC) and to favor consonant-vowel-consonant patterns (CVC), e.g., *hol'* (CVC) instead of *hold* (CVCC).[22]

Since English is the dominant language, by a process of acculturation creole speakers gradually assimilated the patterns of Standard English, but held on to the grammatical structures that were most engraved. Thus decreolization—the final stage in the development of contemporary Black English—occurred on a continuum for individuals and families. The process continued only with constant exposure to Standard English and a desire by the speaker to adopt the dominant standard. The concern that some urban black speakers show signs of being stalled or actually regressing to an earlier stage is an effect of renewed isolation and is another form of relexification.[23]

The dialect geographers believe that black speech did, indeed, begin in Africa, and that it developed somewhat like the pidgin creole model. They also believe that once the West Africans were in this country, their speech was shaped by the mode of speech of other West Africans already in their region, and that this in turn led to a number of black adaptive codes. The similarities of regional Black English dialects, they believe, are not unlike the structural and surface similarities of African languages.[24]

The theory most widely accepted, especially by teachers and social scientists, is the deficit theorist model which holds that Black English speakers are disadvantaged, culturally deprived, and deficient, not only linguistically but cognitively as well. All problems of the child, whether educational or sociological, may be viewed through this filter. Children who speak non-standard Black English may not be expected to learn how to read, and when they do not, the self-fulfilling prophecy has been realized. This view has led to large-scale programs of intervention designed to correct this postulated verbal deficit. Arthur Jensen based his genetic inferiority report on the linguistic behavior of ghetto children in testing situations,[25] and Carl Bereiter and Siegfried Engelmann did much the same thing in their research.[26]

Yet despite the debunking of these myths by noted linguists, they continue.[27] Dillard observes that the assertion that Black English is southern or rural is patently false. He also rejects the notion that there is a literary conspiracy to represent all non-standard black speakers by a kind of standardized "pseudo Gullah." He cites as proof the use of the Gullah pidgin for certain black fictional characters by such notable black writers as Charles W. Chestnutt, Zora Neal Hurston, and Ralph Ellison.[28] One major difference in the use of the pidgins by black writers and white writers is that black writers primarily use it for blacks considered uneducated by the black community, while some white writers use it to denote any black speaker.

Among the West African languages which survived for a time in the New World, Wolof had a special *lingua franca* status, but pidgin English rapidly replaced it and became the language of the slave masses. By 1715, African pidgin English was used throughout the domain of the slave trade. The American development of pidgin English can be traced most accurately through a study of the language of plantation slaves. Linguistically, slaves on a plantation were divided into those who could speak the language of the owner and were most comfortable in this culture, and those who could not and were thus removed as far as possible to the fields. While house slaves often could speak a highly standardized English for the day, learning to read was rigidly proscribed. Those who did learn to read had to be careful to keep this knowledge hidden. Caution was the guiding tenet for all slaves, and they often developed elaborate alternative verbal and non-verbal means of communication. The calls and responses of the eighteenth century were often codes used by slaves to communicate across these barriers. Many of the pidgin speakers could understand Standard English and all of the Creoles could understand pidgin.[29]

Sojourner Truth (formerly named Isabella) is perhaps the most famous user of the "Dutch Patois" as reported by Harriet Beecher Stowe in the *Atlantic Monthly*:

> I journeys round to camp meetins, an' wherever folks is, an' I sets up my banner, an' then I sings, an' then folks always comes up round me, an' then I preaches to 'em. I tells 'em about Jesus, an' I tells 'em about the sins of this people. A great many always come to hear me; an' they're right good to me, too, an' say they want to hear me agin.[30]

Nat Turner and Sojourner Truth and other slaves who could read were the leaders of the most historically significant rebellions against slavery. Accordingly, the white South joined in opposition to any spread of literacy. So fearful were the planters of education among blacks that even free blacks who could read and write were considered dangerous and often forced to leave the area. However, by the end of the eighteenth century, slaves used varieties of English that ranged from pidgin to a standard that was more elaborated than that of the average white. Some slave owners considered it a status symbol to have slaves who were well-dressed, articulate, and well-mannered.

Even after slavery, blacks continued to mask their feelings and cultural system from whites. This meant that sometimes they avoided revealing their true feelings or interpreting an event for a white researcher.[31] In *Drylongso*, a speaker says,

> The white man must pretend to know more than he does, but we must always show less than we know . . . what excites the white man does not move most of us. Now partly that is because most of us don't want white people to know when something does move us . . . most people who have worked in service have to learn how to talk at great length about nothing. I never have been very good at that, so I don't speak normally unless I am asked something. Some people I have worked for think I am slow-witted because I talk very little on the job.[32]

Although there was little research on Black English prior to 1950, many writers, black and white, used a stylized dialect for fictional characters. Some of the best known of these were Joel Chandler Harris, Mark Twain, and Charles Chestnutt. When serious research on black speech did begin, there was no consensus on what to call it. Terms included Negro dialect, Negro English, non-standard Negro English, Negro non-standard English, black folk speech, black dialect, home speech (as opposed to school speech), or black folk speech. Black English, coined by Dillard,[33] is currently preferred and least offensive. Cultivated Black English or Black Standard English is used to describe the equivalent of White Standard English. Ebonics was suggested by Robert Williams to suggest ebony phonics.[34] 'Merican and Pan-African Language in the Western Hemisphere are not yet widely used. Finally, Black English Vernacular was coined by William Labov[35] to label the colorful slang and rapping speech of urban male youth.[36]

Black English in the Schools

Through a process of enculturation, there is a linear transmission of Black English from one generation to the next. Through the process of acculturation, Black English remains dynamic and able to change to meet the new language needs of each succeeding generation.

The features of Black English that are most noted by educators are:

- Variant use of verbs, especially the verb *to be*; zero copula: (E.g., *My father be working. I be done. He happy.*)
- Multiple negatives: (E.g., *Didn't nobody see it. Nothing wouldn't stop it.*)
- Simplification of final consonant clusters: (E.g., *Hol* for *hold. Gon,* as in, *I'm gon eat this apple. Goin,* as in, *I'm goin to the store.*) (It should be noted here that blacks have questioned the wide acceptance of *gonna* and the non-acceptance of *gon* and *goin* in informal speech.)
- Sound substitution or elaboration or omission: (E.g., *Pin* for *pen. Ghos-tes* for *ghosts. He look* for *he looks. Mouf* for *mouth. Follin* for *following.*)
- R-lessness and L-lessness: (E.g., *You* for *your. They* for *their. Hep* for *help.*)
- Variant use of pronouns: (E.g., *Hisself. Her'n.*)
- Dialect-specific vocabulary and idioms, especially teenage varieties like slang, rapping, signifying, and the dozens: (E.g., *Clean* for *well-dressed. Fox* for a *beautiful woman. Pop* for *kill.*) However, the teenage varieties should be considered adjuncts to the dialect since they are not used across all age groups.[37]

Among the varieties of Black English are standard, nonstandard, restricted, elaborated, and regional; the possible combinations are many:

- northern-standard elaborated
- northern-standard restricted
- northern-nonstandard elaborated
- northern-nonstandard restricted
- southern-standard elaborated
- southern-standard restricted
- southern-nonstandard elaborated
- southern-nonstandard restricted
- midwestern-standard elablorated (AKA general American)
- midwestern-standard restricted
- midwestern-nonstandard elaborated
- midwestern-nonstandard restricted

Using the above construction, it is easy to see that the speech of the black native Bostonian is probably more similar to that of the white native Bostonian than to that of the black native southerner or midwesterner. The grammatical structure in the nonstandard forms of all of these remains constant though they may differ phonologically. As Thomas Sowell reports on his childhood migration from North Carolina to New York:

> There were many unhappy afternoons agonizing over my homework and sometimes crying. Although we were all black kids in Harlem, I was from the South and talked "funny" and everybody knew that Southern kids were "dumb" and reminded me at every opportunity.[38]

The author recalls similar treatment of black children from Mississippi, who enrolled in the 1960s in the Chicago Public Schools. Not only were they ridiculed by the other children, despite the fact that many of their parents had the same linguistic roots, but they were often put into special education classes from which, after a few semesters of linguistic acculturation, they tested out. This writer herself was cautioned that she might not pass the required and dreaded Chicago Teacher's Exam for a permanent license because of possible examiner hostility toward her black southern dialect.

Geneva Smitherman has identified four traditions that have shaped Black English. Her list includes: West African language background; servitude and oppression; music and "cool talk"; and the traditional black church.[39] Within these traditions, variations in Black English are achieved through a number of devices. Manipulation dates back to slavery when coded languages served as a protective maneuver.[40] Early manipulation was achieved by Pig Latin.[41] Today's manipulation is achieved by "cool talk." A typical example is:

> 'Twas the night before Christmas and
> all through the pad, cocaine and
> heroin was all the cats had . . .[42]

Metonymy, the use of a part for the whole, is a commonly used figure of speech, as in *threads* for *clothes* or *bread* for *money*. Metaphors which may use language describing anatomy and bodily functions are also widely used. In the black church, terms of address like brother and sister are used to address another member of the "church family."[43]

Black speakers also use punning to derive meaning. Names with a double entendre are often used for woman, for example, *I want my Fanny Brown*. In *Song of Solomon*,[44] Milkman gets his nickname from his desire to suckle long after he reaches school age.[45] Labels like *woman, baby,* or *mother* are used in sexual ways or in obscenities.

Black speech users also may be categorized as receptive, expressive, or situational. The expressive Black English speaker will converse in cultural speech with others both within and outside of the culture. The receptive Black English speaker might not use cultural speech, but is able to converse easily with others who do. The situational Black English speaker will use his most cultural speech with other members of the culture, and switch to a more standardized code with non-members. Studies show that some blacks use only a few of the unique Black English forms, others use many, and still others none.[46]

Basil Bernstein[47] noted that nonverbal clues are important in the speech of the low-income child. Martin Deutsch[48] further noted that blacks are much more concrete than abstract in their language and language-related activities. Unfortunately, black speech often suffers the same stereotyping to which other parts of the culture are subjected. This contributes to a widely held conception that only stereotypic black is truly black. Thus, the linguistic purist would maintain that only the pidgin/creolized versions most commonly labeled nonstandard are truly black. If this premise were accepted, Black English would be confined to a certain point in time. It could not grow in response to these times. This would be akin to saying that hamburgers (or pizza or cola) are not truly American because they were not known in 1776.

In the nineteenth century, American English teachers faced a polyglot of language students. European immigration became a groundswell in the 1890s that continued until the 1920s saw the closing of Ellis Island. Foreigners came in such large numbers that there was concern that American cities might not continue to be American. There was special concern about the linguistic assimilation of so many foreigners.

In 1920 in the Chicago Public Schools, there were 57 different racial or ethnic groups represented, yet there was no first language study for 56 of these groups. Having the clout of numbers, the Germans, who comprised 400,000 of the school population while the American-born totalled only 332,100, persuaded the Chicago Board of Education to add a German elective to any school district upon petition of 150 parents.[49] All other children were presented a rigid program of English rules to be mastered. Research can find no mention of any special language program for any of the native language groups. The language of blacks, who also spoke English, was never considered a problem. Even after the European spigot closed in the 1920s and the great black migration from the rural South began, there is no mention in the literature of the special language needs of blacks.

The following table shows the breakdown of ethnic change in the school population of Chicago:

SCHOOL ENROLLMENTS IN THE CITY OF CHICAGO, 1930-1963

(Age 5 through 18)

	1930	1940	1950	1960	1963
Total Chicago School Enrollment[a]	630,000	567,000	512,000 [b]	685,000	740,000 [c]
White and Other	596,000	517,000	436,000	497,000	490,000 [c]
Black	34,000	50,000	77,000	189,000	250,000
Chicago Public Schools[d]	470,000	420,000	350,000	476,000	536,000
White and Other	440,000 [c]	374,000 [c]	276,000 [c]	290,000 [c]	286,000
Black	30,000 [c]	46,000 [c]	74,000 [c]	186,000 [c]	250,000
Chicago Catholic Schools[e]	157,000	143,000	184,000	232,000	234,000

Source: Robert Havighurst, *The Public Schools of Chicago: A Survey for the Board of Education of the City of Chicago* (Chicago: Board of Education for the City of Chicago, 1964), p. 54.

[a]Data from the United States Census Bureau, in the age group 5 through 18.
[b]Kindergarten pupils were under-enumerated in 1950.
[c]Estimated by Havighurst.
[d]Data from the Chicago Public Schools.
[e]Data from the Catholic School Board of Chicago.

Similar growth occurred in most large urban school systems, so that by the end of the 1970s, Black English had become the predominant dialect in these schools. This linguistic reversal was of great magnitude, but not until 1967 can one find the first *Chicago Schools Journal* article specifically related to the black learner. This resulted from a census report that indicated there were enough *new* black children enrolling in the Chicago Public Schools each month to fill a new school.[50]

In the 1920s the English teachers of the United States held the common belief that there was only one "correct" form of English. Their goal was to see that all learners from all ethnic backgrounds eliminated incorrect forms and had adequate drill to master the correct ones. In 1946 when Robert Pooley wrote his widely used volume that explained what history shows about attitudes toward Standard English, he was influenced by the studies of Charles C. Fries, who also protested the rigidity of attitudes toward divergent users.[51] Pooley described the varieties of expression related to cultural levels in society and introduced his widely quoted five levels of usage: the illiterate level; colloquial level; Standard English-informal level; Standard English-formal level; and literary level. He also espoused a linguistic policy of toleration for divergent speech in informal situations.[52] This action by Pooley helped to establish a national education policy of acceptance of cultural speech. Especially important was his recognition that teachers are themselves linguistically ethnocentric.

Pooley also led a statewide study of the English language arts in Wisconsin that was commissioned by the Department of Public Instruction. In it he emphasized the importance of providing the language user with choices in pronunciation, morphology, syntax, and lexicon.[53] The Executive Committee of the Conference on College Composition and Communication of the National Council of Teachers of English established a position far left of what some already viewed as Pooley's sellout when it issued a controversial resolution which stated that the student has a right to his/her own language. The English profession became involved in furious debate over what was now termed levels of bidialectism.[54] Black English had now moved from being the "invisible man" of English to being on the cutting edge of its new philosophy.

Reading, Writing, and Racism

In 1967 Representative Adam Clayton Powell of New York led a congressional hearing on books for schools and the treatment of minorities.[55] In opening the hearing, Powell said that its purpose was to generate pressure for

> a new and more wholesome image in textbooks of minority groups in America—not only for their pride, but for the pride of all Americans in the eclectic society we know as the United States.[56]

Harold Howe II, then head of the U.S. Office of Education, condemned the all-white world of children's books and the Look-Jane-Look view of a white suburban world. The hearing committee also heard condemnation of textbook publishers who had, in essence, created a national curriculum that excluded, trivialized, and/or humiliated black Americans. Especially condemned were northern, southern, and cathedral editions of texts used across the nation that pandered to local prejudices. As a result, a wide range of multi-ethnic readers and other school materials were published. The most notable of the pacesetters was the *Bank Street Reader* by the MacMillan Company which showed ethnically diverse people in a variety of settings and locales. Others included the Great Cities Reading Program by Follett and the Zenith Series by Doubleday.[57]

Pressure for books to be different was not limited to the absence or stereotyping of pictures. There was even more criticism of the written representation of Black English. Throughout the nineteenth century both white and black writers struggled with how to represent pidgin or creolized Black English in print. This was even more difficult for those who were attempting to represent regional and class variations, as well as Gullah and Creole influences. The reader of dialect was also required to understand code switching, and was often put off by the foreign look of a passage. Since dialects change over time, those from an earlier era look even more strange. Given the racism of the era, many blacks perceived any written representation of Black English as vulnerable to being stereotyped or ridiculed.

Throughout his life, W.E.B. DuBois[58] denounced both white and black writers who used black dialect. He felt that standard spelling should be used rather than phonological representations of Black English. Joel Chandler Harris, who was known as the best dialect writer of the nineteenth century and wrote in a black dialect that included both mainland Creole and Gullah, was a special object of DuBois' scorn. Yet, Harris was a careful transcriber and wrote of his representation of Gullah:

> Gullah . . . is an admirable vehicle for storytelling. It recognizes no gender, and scorns the use of the plural number except accidentally. "E" stands for "he", "she", or "it" and "dem" may attend to one thing or may include a thousand.[59]

An example of Uncle Jack's Gullah speech is:

> Bumbye, B'er Geter, 'e come drowsy; 'e do nod, un 'e head sway down, tel ma 'sh-grass tickles 'e nose, un 'e do cough sem lak 'e teer up da crik by da root.[60]

Well into the twentieth century, followers of the DuBois philosophy loudly criticized any black dialect writing even by such established black writers as Langston Hughes in his "Jess B. Simple" column in the *Chicago Defender*.[61]

On the other hand, Harriet Beecher Stowe's *Uncle Tom's Cabin* was well accepted by blacks, not only because of its positive attitudes and powerful social statement, but because of the relatively little detail in the black dialect used. Both her poor white and poor black characters spoke with almost the same accent. This in itself might have contributed to a black perception that white friends saw black speech not as strangely spelled and incomprehensible, even to readers who were black, but almost the same as theirs. While it would be easy to criticize DuBois for linguistic intransigence, it should be remembered that he felt that he must be unrelenting in ensuring that Booker T. Washington's accommodations did not allow the entire race to become a servant class. He wanted educated whites to see that blacks, too, were literate and refined and had a "talented tenth" not unlike their own. Yet, acceptance of a new standard did not come easily. One of the earliest breakthroughs came when some publishers added an integrated line for large urban school systems, but continued to sell "star" or "little white" editions in the South. Some merely "grayed" a few pictures or added a single picture of a sports figure like Jackie Robinson. Some published books like *Two is a Team* in Standard English. By 1980, every major publisher had a truly integrated line and had published guidelines for presentation of minorities and women in their publications.[62]

Censorship or threats to ban certain books from their schools became real in states such as Texas that had state-adopted texts. A censorship order could mean the success or failure of a business year.[63] Some groups tried to blunt criticism of these actions by averring that they were not protesting the black child, but the "non-standard" language used by black characters in the books. The Council on Interracial Books for Children played a leading role in sharply criticizing both the traditional and the newer books that held the black child's language and culture up to ridicule by other children. Libraries and teachers were shocked when the Council's negative evaluations included such enduring favorites as *Little Black Sambo* and *Dr. Doolittle.*

Once the pictures in the picture books had been integrated, there began a movement of greater sensitivity toward differences in language. As mentioned earlier, prior to 1965 there was almost no direct reference to any special language problems of the black child. In the early 1960s there were veiled allusions to the "divergent speaker."[64] However, by the late 1960s and early 1970s Black English was widely discussed.

One of the earliest and most controversial approaches to teaching black children to read was espoused by Carl Bereiter and Siegfried Engelmann at the University of Illinois.[65] They developed and marketed a highly structured, behavioristic approach that combined speech and reading. The teacher in a Bereiter-Engelmann class is a veritable drill sergeant. He/she introduces a verbal pattern with appropriate hand signals and claps and the children are to parrot him/her *on the beat.* There were reports that children were severely chastised if they did not respond as programmed. Some teachers felt that this approach was diametrically opposed to the child-centered, sensitive approaches that were favored by followers of Martin Deutsch. Yet the method, minus the punishment, has endured and is still being used in some districts. Another controversial approach was the beginning dialect reader (discussed later) that, in effect, resegregated the newly integrated schools.

Linguists and Teachers

Literacy is usually built on the base of the child's existing language. Kenneth Goodman developed an approach based on the child's own speech that focused on decoding, that is, getting meaning from the printed word, rather than correcting the child's oral language patterns. He felt that the child who was made to accept another dialect for learning had to first accept the view that his own language was inferior. In a very real sense, since this was the language of his parents, his family, and his community, he had to reject his own culture and identity in order to become something else. This is unhealthy, and many educators believe that in reading, the focus must be on learning to read, and no attempt to change the child's language should be permitted to enter into this process.[66] Goodman points out that dialects are primarily oral divergencies:

English orthography has one great virtue in its uniformity across dialects. No matter how words are pronounced, printers across the country usually spell them the same. . . . [W]e spell *pumpkin* the same whether we say *pəŋkin* or *pəmpkən* and *something* the same whether we say *səmpthin* or *səmpm.*[67]

Goodman believes that above all, reading teachers should allow children to read in their own dialect and should avoid sending children to speech correction classes when the speech needs no correction, but just is not like the teacher's.[68] Furthermore, very young children cannot identify points of interference clearly enough to change their dialects, even if they want to. Therefore, such choices should not be presented to a child before fifth grade.[69]

One of the most controversial approaches to date for teaching reading to black children was developed by Joan Baratz. Her Black English reader created a dialect orthography, vocabulary, and syntax for the beginning reader. Only black children in a school district were to use this special material. After they had gained proficiency in reading the Black English readers, they then would be introduced to traditional materials.

Even if such a program were educationally defensible, it failed to take into account the tremendous mobility of urban families. Unless black readers were adopted nationwide, which they were not, the child who started this reading program in one school and then moved to another that did not use the Black English Reader would be doubly handicapped. (When the author taught in the Chicago Public Schools, such moves often occurred in October or April when rental leases expired.) Also, if the black child already spoke Standard English, then he/she would be forced to use a speech form that the school would soon deem no longer acceptable.

Yet, when black parents and groups predictably raised a storm of protest, Baratz[70] strongly defended this drastic change in school policy and practice and compared it to the similarly controversial Initial Teaching Alphabet Readers that were created by Sir James Pitman for English school children and exported to a number of American schools.[71] Black parents were especially wary of the Black Language Reader, since they wanted their children to get the same education as whites, and they were not sure that this was not a ploy to resegregate the classes.

William Stewart also favored a dialect-based text, but he was never as convinced as Baratz that it was "doable."[72] He became convinced that the dialectal reader was the best approach when a black female visitor, known as a problem reader, happened to see the following dialect translation of Clement Moore's poem, *The Night Before Christmas*, in his typewriter, and for the first time was able to read fluently:

> It's the night before Christmas, and here in our house,
> It ain't nothing moving, not even no mouse,
> There go we-all stockings, hanging high up off the floor,
> So Santa can full them up, if he walk in through our door.[73]

One could argue that only a few of the divergencies are Black American English phrases (*we-all, walk,* and *full*), since *ain't* and double negatives are commonly used in non-black speech as well. The decoding tasks presented by these words are not as significant as interpreting *so* for *sore* or *tol* for *told*.

According to William Labov,[74] any problem that the black child has in reading should be examined closely and the teacher should become as dialectal as the child. He also believes that school problems with black speakers can often be traced to the child's ignorance of Standard English rules, the teacher's ignorance of nonstandard English rules, or both.

The priorities for the reading program are to read, comprehend, write, and spell Standard English, and to speak with a prestige pattern of pronunciation that does not include stigmatized forms.[75] But, is the latter phase reading? And, is not part of Labov's problem, and that of the deficit theorists in general, the commingling of reading, which is decoding graphic symbols to interpret a written message, with speech, which is translating one's own thoughts into nongraphic symbols?

Legislation and Public Policy

The most important court rulings affecting language policy for Black English speakers can be found in *Plessy* v. *Ferguson,*[76] *Brown* v. *Board of Education,*[77] *Lau* v. *Nichols,*[78] and *Martin Luther King, Jr.* v. *Ann Arbor School District.*[79]

Plessy established the "cake of custom" that institutionalized the isolation of blacks in schools and communities. This caused their linguistic assimilation to occur at a much slower pace than that of immigrants, and allowed their language to continue to develop unique forms. When Kenneth Clark used the deficit theory to prove that proximity was important in intellectual development in the *Brown* case, this was the first time that courts allowed sociological data to be introduced in a federal case.

Lau reformulated the principles even more by stating that cultural imperatives must also be recognized by the schools and, when necessary, dual languages must be used. Non-English-speaking students of Chinese ancestry in the San Francisco Public Schools charged that they were being denied equal educational opportunities because 1707 of the 3457 Chinese-origin pupils who spoke little or no English were not receiving special instruction. Some options pointed out during the district court hearings were to teach them English or give them instructions in Chinese. The Court ruled that these children did, indeed, receive fewer benefits than did the English-speaking majority, and thus there was a discriminatory effect even though there might have been no such intent. The decree also stated that the school is obliged to deal with language minority needs in a manner that does not force these pupils into a permanent separate track that will prevent their full participation in educational programs.[80]

In the *Ann Arbor* case, an action was brought in behalf of black school children because the schools had not recognized their "black vernacular," and had not even taken it into account when some speakers had reading problems. The important principle in this case was not that the school should teach Black American English, or that a dual language program should be developed, but that the school had a duty to teach the children to read Standard English so that they would have an equal chance for success in the arts, sciences, commerce, and the professions. If making the transition from the language of their speech community was a barrier, it was the school's responsibility to use its professionals to ensure that all groups could make normal academic progress.[81]

These four cases established the foundation for public policy affecting Black English for this century. All are related to the Equal Protection Clause of the Fourteenth Amendment and, with the exception of *Plessy* and *Brown*, the 1964 Civil Rights Act.

Before 1960, black educators had to be restrained in their interactions with the black community to avoid increasing the hostility of whites, many of whom feared that educated blacks could upset the status quo. Despite these conditions, some black intelligentsia, W.E.B. DuBois, E. Franklin Frazier, Allison Davis, Sinclair Drake, Carter G. Woodson and Kenneth Clark, among others, were able to publish studies on the education and sociology of blacks that were read widely.[82] Most of the educational research related to blacks followed the intellectual deficit theory that attempted to prove and prove again that blacks were innately inferior to whites. While Frantz Fanon[83] and Nathan Hare[84] have accused black educators of being "whiter than whites," Thomas Sowell[85] and Joyce Ladner[86] believe that black educators have done much to disprove the inferiority theories and to establish a black theory of education and sociology. It is evident that this evolving theory and sociology have had an impact on the courts.

Events surrounding the Montgomery bus boycott led to two presidential platforms that for the first time included planks on civil rights and poverty. With these two contiguous victories, a bimodal and sustained attack was made on what blacks perceived to be their major problems. The result was that the Supreme Court continued to make rulings that struck down racist policies and practices, and the federal government enacted massive economic programs in its War on Poverty. A new alliance between the federal government and blacks was created that made it possible for black educators to become more aggressive. They used this relationship to fight racism while requesting protection from the federal government.

Studies by contemporary black educators during this time involved attacks on white writers and attempts to repair the perceived damage that was done to blacks by racism. (Black educators often found previous research by whites to be inhospitable or irrelevant.) These studies by blacks focused on the social system instead of groups, and assumed the social system to be corrupt. Moreover, they gave priority to changing the system rather than individuals.[87] Youth development projects, community action programs, neighborhood service programs, revision of welfare regulations, the complete dismantling of residential bastions of segregation in schools, housing, public accommodations and jobs, and the hiring and retaining of black school administrators were seen as top priorities.[88]

Among the Great Society programs of the Lyndon Johnson administration, the one that had the greatest impact on the black child's language development was Head Start. This community action program was designed to enhance the probability of verbal school achievement of low-income children through a subsidized program of enrichment, nutrition, and parental involvement. Today it is almost the only program of that era that has survived intact. Head Start programs in the North became pre-kindergartens and in the South they often became a state's first kindergarten. The Head Start Program was later supplemented with a heavily researched Follow Through Program that was designed to provide data on the improved performance in reading and other verbal skills of Head Start graduates. Most importantly, both of these programs insisted that black parents play an active role in the newly desegregated schools in the North and South.[89]

The advent of Marshall Mc Luhan's television age in the late 1950s and early 1960s coincided with the climactic changes that were occurring in American culture. Prior to this time, each classroom in the school was largely individualistic with little concern for the sociocultural dimensions of the larger world. Television brought the world into the classroom and into the homes of the children. The educational question of the 1950s had been, "Dare the schools build a new social order?" The public policy question of the 1960s and 1970s was, "How can the schools prevent television from usurping the school's educational prerogative to mold the national character?"

Carefully and consciously designed to have the greatest influence on the black child's acquisition of language and language skills was the Sesame Street program that was developed by the Children's Television Workshop. The program had a multi-ethnic cast, an urban, inner-city setting, black and white and bilingual authority figures, and memorable fantasy characters. The program was heavily language-based and was designed to nationalize the kinds of language development activities that had been started in the Head Start Program. So controversial were the social aspects of the program that it was banned in a number of southern cities, but it was also translated into more than a dozen languages and is considered the most highly successful children's program in the world. The Head Start model was used by its staff to develop The Electric Company to teach beginning reading and speech. Its language was even more heavily ethnic than that of Sesame Street.[90]

Throughout the post-*Brown* era, one openly stated position was that black speech patterns would somehow contaminate white language patterns, although linguistic borrowing began long before schools were desegregated and, as discussed earlier, can be traced back to black African interaction with other American speech communities. The borrowing has never been one-way. All languages are constantly changing and change is influenced by the social milieu. The black language has also been one of the richest sources for phrases and idioms that are considered purely American.[91] The oft-stated concern of white teachers that black children *must* learn the white dialect if they are ever to succeed in white society is rendered null when television daily shows blacks in various fictional and real roles whose speech, like that of their slave forefathers, ranges from nearly pidgin to highly elaborated standard.

Interference and Choice

In any public policy discussion, the matter of who has the right to choose and who has the power to implement the choices one makes must be determined. The school has long felt that it had both the right and the duty to establish language policies and practices. But this right is a delegated one. White parents have in large measure accepted and thus legitimized the right of white teachers to decide. In the dual school system of the South, black parents had apparently delegated these rights to black teachers. Not even in the 1950s and 1960s, when blacks had established their right to integrate the classroom, was there any outcry about the white language studies of the schools. But eventually the following attitudes of white teachers began to become evident to blacks:

1. Because of their own linguistic interference, they could not understand the black child's dialect.
2. They did not choose to learn the black child's dialect in either receptive or expressive modes, and knew few linguistic theories about the origin and development of black speech or black culture.
3. They would withhold rewards from those children who did not make every effort to eliminate their own cultural speech and make the teacher's regional or ethnic dialect theirs.

The absurdity of these attitudes is seen when one understands that many black children live in a bimodal language world. School and commerce are one language world; the second is their speech community—usually isolated—which contains only other speakers of similar ethnicity, education, income, and origin. Most blacks belong to what DuBois and, more recently, John Gwaltney call "a nation within a nation." As one black respondent told Gwaltney: "We are a nation because we think of ourselves as a nation."[92]

After manumission was completed, blacks began to develop a social infrastructure and have continued to do this for more than a century. Today there are black schools and universities, black churches and press, black social clubs and fraternal orders, black professional associations and black hospitals. The strongest, oldest, most influential and most purely black institution is the black church. Every major denomination is represented, but the Baptists are by far the largest. Baptist churches are among the least hierarchial in the world. Each has its own personality and is free to establish a form of service that pleases the congregation. Most importantly for this study, unadulterated Black English is widely accepted.

Vine Deloria, Jr.,[93] has attacked the proverbial gathering of whites on reservations to seek knowledge for knowledge's sake, and many blacks share similar sentiments. Studies on regional and social dialectation have found that blacks are increasingly asking the following sort of questions:

(1) Should the speech of minority groups be studied?

(2) What was the justification for so much time, energy, and resources?

(3) Were not there more pressing issues of racial prejudices and discrimination that should take precedence?

(4) Why should a child choose to give up the *lingua franca* of his extended family and his speech community for that of a hostile neighboring world?

(5) Could the young child who leaves this world for a brief six hours for five days per week do this even if he/she wished? Would not the interference be too great? (Kenneth Johnson believes that not before fifth grade can a child choose to make his speech conform to a greater degree to another code.[94])

One has only to look at national leaders such as Henry Kissinger and Zbigniew Brzezinski to see that despite several college degrees and complete immersion in the Standard English-speaking worlds of Harvard and the federal government, they have not given up the sounds that they learned at their mothers' knees. Perhaps because of dialect loyalty they have not *chosen* to do so. This same dialect loyalty is found among black children and their parents. Often they choose not to acquire the dialect or vocabulary of the school for fear that they will be ridiculed for being "oreos."[95]

The position of most black educators has always been that the language of the school should be Standard English. DuBois, one of the founders of the Niagara movement and of the NAACP, in his long tenure as editor of *Crisis*, roundly denounced any efforts by whites to portray blacks in fiction with white interpretations of black speech. He insisted that blacks strive to speak Standard English. As late as 1971 the *Crisis* position was little changed. DuBois articulated what was surely the viewpoint of most black parents, even those who spoke nonstandard themselves, that their children should have the same opportunities for full political and economic participation as dominant culture children, and that dominant culture teachers and minority teachers should prepare the children for this change.

The position of most black educators and parents seems to be that the schools should not try to eliminate Black English, but should improve the students' linguistic versatility so that they can function in both worlds. Most have rejected the social pathology model. Some black parents, like some bilingual parents, feel that the proper role of the school is to teach Standard English. Some feel that they can teach the child cultural speech, and others view any support of Black English as a way of maintaining cultural division. Middle-class parents who speak black standard English at home often feel that only standard speech should be used in writing and in speech. However, respect for the black culture is expected, no matter what linguistic policy is favored. These differences among black parents are not unlike those found among Hispanic and American Indian parents. Colonized people usually spend a great deal of time discussing the best way to succeed in the dominant culture which controls both economic rewards and survival.[96]

Johnson has suggested three things that must be done by teachers of the Black English speaker: understand the black culture; understand the black dialect; and adapt teaching strategies.[97] Important questions that the teachers of Black English speakers should ask are: Does the child's language fulfill its purpose? Is the child able to communicate ideas to others? Is the child's speech consistent with that of the educated members of the community? Does the child find satisfaction and joy in the use of language?[98]

The most important tasks for the teachers of Black English speakers are to rid the students' psyches and those of the nation of notions of cultural dominance, work to eliminate ethnic isolation, fully accept the philosophy of no-one-model America, and help each child to achieve his or her fullest potential. This should lead to a welcome linguistic self-fulfilling prophecy.

NOTES

[1] Jack L. Daniel, ed., *Black Communication: Dimensions of Research and Instruction* (New York: Speech Communication Association, 1974), p. x.

[2] Frantz Fanon, trans. Constance Farrington, *The Wretched of the Earth* (New York: Grove Press, 1968, original copyright 1963), pp. 17-18.

[3] Joyce A. Joyce has written an interesting account in which he contrasts the symbolism in the use of the word "black" in Ralph Ellison's *Invisible Man* with its use in Richard Wright's *Black Boy*. See Joyce A. Joyce, "Semantic Development of the Word Black: A History from Indo-European to the Present," *Journal of Black Studies* 2:1 (March 1981): 307-312.

[4] See, for instance, Raven McDavid, "A Theory of Dialect," in James E. Alatis, ed., *Report of the Twentieth Annual Roundtable Meeting on Linguistics and Language Studies: Linguistics and the Teaching of Standard English to Speakers of Other Languages or Dialects* (Washington, D.C.: Georgetown University Press, 1970), pp. 45-62.

[5] See Neil Postman and Charles Weingartner, *Linguistics: A Revolution in Teaching* (New York: Dell Publishing, 1966).

[6]Elizabeth C. Traugott, "Principles in the History of American English—A Reply," *Florida Foreign Language Reporter* 56 (Spring/Fall 1972): 5-6.

[7]Robert C. Pooley, *The Teaching of English Usage*, 2nd ed. (Urbana, IL: National Council of Teachers of English), p. 5.

[8]Clyde Kluckhohn, *Mirror for Man: The Relation of Anthropology to Modern Life* (Greenwich, CT: Fawcett Publications, 1965), p. 19.

[9]J. L. Dillard, "Black English in New York," in Rodolfo Jacobson, *The English Record: Studies in Teaching English to Speakers of Other Languages and Standard English to Speakers of a Non-Standard Dialect*, Vol. 21 (April 1971) (New York: The New York State English Council, 1971), pp. 114-120.

[10]Melville Hershkovits, *The Myth of the Negro Past* (New York: Knopf Publishing Co., 1941).

[11]Joan C. Baratz, *Beginning Reading for Speakers of Divergent Dialects*, Vol. 14 (International Reading Association Conference Paper on Reading Goals for the Disadvantaged, 1970), pp. 77-83.

[12]Dillard, "Black English in New York," op. cit.

[13]Joan Fickett, "Ain't, Not, and Don't in Black English," in J. L. Dillard, ed., *Perspectives on Black English* (The Hague: Mouton, 1975), pp. 31-34

[14]Insightfully, Fickett's term utilizes Black English by substituting an apostrophe for the beginning letter "A".

[15]Joan C. Baratz and Roger W. Shuy, eds., *Teaching Black Children to Read* (Washington, D.C.: Center for Applied Linguistics, 1969), p. 18.

[16]Sylvia W. Holton, *Down Home and Uptown: The Representation of Black Speech in American Fiction* (Rutherford, Madison, and Teaneck, NJ: Fairleigh Dickinson University Press; London: Associated University Presses, 1984), p. 19.

[17]Quoted in Holton, ibid., p. 20.

[18]Hershkovits, op. cit., p. 2.

[19]Lorenzo Dow Turner, *Africanisms in the Gullah Dialect* (Chicago: University of Chicago Press, 1949).

[20]Holton, op. cit., p. 25.

[21]Mary Berry and John Blassingame, *Long Memory: The Black Experience in America* (New York: Oxford University Press, 1982), p. 24.

[22]Holton, op. cit., p. 28.

[23]Ibid.

[24]J. L. Dillard reports that J. Dyneley Price has done similar work on American Indian language pidgins which he assumes they learned from blacks during the short period when both were slaves. Dillard, "Black English in New York," op. cit.

[25] Arthur Jensen, "How Much Can We Boost I.Q. and Scholastic Achievement?" *Harvard Education Review* XXXIX: 1 (Winter 1969): 1-123.

[26] Carl Bereiter and Siegfried Engelmann, *Language Learning Activities for the Disadvantaged Child* (New York: Anti-Defamation League of B'nai B'rith, 1966); and *Teaching Disadvantaged Children in the Preschool* (Englewood Cliffs, NJ: Prentice Hall, 1966).

[27] William Labov, "The Logic of Non-Standard English," in Alatis, op. cit., p. 2.

[28] J. L. Dillard, "Black English in New York," op. cit., p. 118.

[29] Melville Hershkovits and Lorenzo Turner have written two of the most useful foundation studies. See also Raven McDavid's theory that Black English is a divergence from British English, and William Stewart's view that Black English derived from West African languages and is now beginning to converge with the British-derived American English.

[30] Harriet Beecher Stowe, "Sojourner Truth, The Libyan Sibyl," *Atlantic Monthly* 11 (April 1863): 473-481 at 478.

[31] J. L. Dillard, *Black English: Its History and Usage in the United States* (New York: Vintage Books, 1973, ©1972), p. 28.

[32] John L. Gwaltney, ed., *Drylongso: A Self-Portrait of Black America* (New York: Vintage Books, 1980), pp. 7, 28, 99.

[33] J. L. Dillard, "Black English in New York," op. cit.

[34] Robert L. Williams, ed., *Ebonics: The True Language of Black Folks* (St. Louis, MO: Institute of Black Studies, 1975).

[35] William Labov, *Language in the Inner City: Studies in the Black English Vernacular* (Philadelphia: University of Pennsylvania Press, 1972).

[36] Holton, op. cit., p. 18.

[37] William Labov, *A Study of the Non-Standard English of Negro and Puerto Rican Speakers in New York City* (New York: Columbia University Press, 1968), Vol. I, pp. 280-286.

[38] Thomas Sowell, *Black Education: Myths and Tragedies* (New York: David McKay and Company, 1972), p. 5.

[39] Geneva Smitherman, *Talkin & Testifyin: The Language of Black America* (Boston: Houghton Mifflin, 1977), p. 43.

[40] Ibid., p. 49.

[41] Pig Latin became very popular in black communities in the 1920s and 1930s because of its versatility and ease of use. The first letter of a word is moved to the end and -ay is added. Thus, from "foe" we get "ofay," the common designation for a white man. "I am a boy" becomes "Iay amay ay oybay."

[42] This adaptation of Clement Moore's poem, *The Night Before Christmas*, can be found in Smitherman, *Talkin & Testifyin*, op. cit., p. 49.

[43]Ibid., p. 50.

[44]Toni Morrison, *Song of Solomon* (New York: Knopf, 1977).

[45]Smitherman, *Talkin & Testifyin*, op. cit.

[46]Jane W. Torrey, "Black Children's Knowledge of Standard English," *American Educational Research Journal* 20:4 (Winter 1983): 627-643.

[47]Harry Rosen, "Language and Class: A Critical Look at the Theories of Basil Bernstein," *Urban Review* 7 (April 1974): 97-114.

[48]Martin P. Deutsch, *The Disadvantaged Child: Selected Papers of Martin Deutsch and Associates* (New York: Basic Books, 1967), pp. xii.

[49]Shirley Stennis Williams, "Student Teaching in the Chicago Public Schools, 1856-1964" (Ph.D. Dissertation, George Peabody College of Vanderbilt University, 1972), p. 396.

[50]Ibid., p. 404.

[51]Robert Pooley, *The Teaching of English Usage* (Urbana, IL: National Council of Teachers of English, 1974), p. xii.

[52]Ibid., p. 19.

[53]See Robert Pooley and Robert D. Williams, *The Teaching of English in Wisconsin, A Survey of Methods and Materials of Instruction and of Teaching Personnel in the Elementary and Secondary Schools, 1944-45* (Madison, WI: University of Wisconsin Press, 1948).

[54]Pooley, *The Teaching of English Usage*, op. cit., p. xiii.

[55]Lerone Bennett, "Reading, 'Riting and Racism," *Ebony* (March 1967): 130-138, at 136.

[56]Ibid.

[57]Ibid., p. 137.

[58]W.E.B. DuBois, *The Souls of Black Folk: Essays and Sketches* (Chicago: A. C. McClurg, 1903), p. 124.

[59]Quoted in Holton, op. cit., p. 82.

[60]Joel Chandler Harris, *Uncle Remus, His Songs and His Sayings: The Folklore of the Old Plantation* (New York: D. Appleton, 1881), p. 146.

[61]Langston Hughes, "Jess Be Simple," *Chicago Defender* (1949). The black readers were based on research done on the language of black school children in Detroit.

[62]See, for example, Nancy Roberts, *Guidelines for Creating Positive Sexual and Racial Images in Educational Materials*, prepared under the direction of the MacMillan Publishing Company, Inc., School Division Committee for Creating Positive Sexual and Racial Images in Educational Materials (New York: MacMillan Publishing Company, Inc.; London: Collier MacMillan Publishers, 1975).

[63]Shirley Stennis Williams, *Ethnicity and Censorship*, Unpublished Manuscript (Oshkosh, WI: University of Wisconsin-Oshkosh, 1980), p. 2.

[64]Kenneth S. Goodman, "Dialect Barriers to Reading Comprehension," *Elementary English* XIII: 8 (December 1965): 853.

[65]Bereiter and Engelmann, op. cit.

[66]Kenneth Goodman, "Dialect Barriers to Reading Comprehension," in Baratz and Shuy, op. cit., p. 27.

[67]Ibid., pp. 18-19.

[68]Kenneth Goodman, "Who Gave Us the Right?" in Jacobson, *The English Record*, op. cit., p. 91.

[69]Kenneth R. Johnson, *Teaching the Culturally Disadvantaged: A Rational Approach* (Palo Alto, CA: Science Research Associates, 1970).

[70]Joan Baratz, "Teaching Reading in an Urban Negro School System," in Baratz and Shuy, op. cit., p. 113.

[71]This now defunct experiment also proved to be ill-advised. The Pitman Initial Teaching Alphabet (ITA) program used an expanded alphabet of forty-four symbols rather than twenty-six symbols in order to ensure better grapheme-phoneme correspondence in words. ITA was supposed to be particularly advantageous for the black American English speaker who reportedly had great difficulty with the phonics approach used in some schools.

[72]William A. Stewart, "Urban Negro Speech: Sociolinguistic Factors Affecting English Teaching," in Roger Shuy, ed., *Social Dialects and Language Learning: Proceedings of the Bloomington, Indiana Conference* (Champaign, IL: National Council of Teachers of English, 1965), pp. 10-19.

[73]Found in William A. Stewart, "On the Use of Negro Dialect in the Teaching of Reading," in Baratz and Shuy, op. cit., p. 171.

[74]See also Kenneth Johnson's discussion of black kinesics, including walking and soul handshakes. Elementary teachers should especially note the use of lowered eyes to show respect. "Black Kinesics—Some Non-Verbal Communication Patterns in the Black Culture," in J. L. Dillard, *Perspectives on Black English* (The Hague: Mouton, 1974).

[75]William Labov, "Some Sources of Reading Problems for Negro Speakers of Nonstandard English," in Baratz and Shuy, op. cit., p. 31.

[76]*Plessy* v. *Ferguson*, 163 U.S. 537 (1896).

[77]*Brown* v. *Board of Education*, 347 U.S. 483 (1954), 349 U.S. 294 (1955).

[78]*Lau* v. *Nichols*, 414 U.S. 563 (1974).

[79]*Martin Luther King, Jr.* v. *Ann Arbor School District*, 473 F. Supp. 1371 (E.D. Mich. 1979).

[80]Richard Ruiz, "Ethnic Group Interests and the Social Good: Law and Language in Education," in Winston Van Horne, ed., Thomas V. Tonnesen, man. ed., *Ethnicity, Law and the Social Good* (Milwaukee, WI: University of

Wisconsin System American Ethnic Studies Coordinating Committee, 1983), p. 52; *Lau* v. *Nichols*, op. cit.

[81]*Ann Arbor School District*, op. cit.

[82]Art and Annette M. Evans, "Black Educators Before and After 1960," *Phylon: A Review of Race and Culture* 43: 3 (September 1982): 254-261, at 256.

[83]Fanon, op. cit., p. 144.

[84]See Nathan Hare, "The Challenge of the Black Scholar," *The Black Scholar* 30: 1 (December 1973): 59-63, cited in Evans, op. cit.

[85]See Thomas Sowell, "Education and Ghetto Schools: Patterns of Black Excellence," *Public Interest* 43 (Spring 1976): 26-58, cited in Evans, op. cit., p. 254.

[86]Joyce Ladner, ed., *The Death of White Sociology* (New York: Random House, 1973).

[87]John Bracey, August Meier, and Elliott Rudwick, "The Black Sociologists: The First Half Century," in Ladner, ibid., pp. 3-22 at p. 18.

[88]Marjorie B. Smiley, "Objectives of Educational Programs for the Educationally Retarded and the Disadvantaged," in Paul A. Witty, ed., *The Educationally Retarded and Disadvantaged* (Chicago: National Society for the Study of Education, distributed by the University of Chicago Press, 1967), pp. 130-132.

[89]Ibid., pp. 133-138.

[90]Edward L. Palmer, *Formative Research in the Production of Television for Children in Media and Symbol: The Forms of Expression, Communication, and Education* (Chicago, IL.: National Society for the Study of Education, 1974), pp. 302-309.

[91]See J. L. Dillard, *American Talk: Where Our Words Came From* (New York: Random House, 1976), pp. 117-134.

[92]Gwaltney, op. cit., p. 4.

[93]Vine Deloria, Jr., *We Talk, You Listen: New Tribes, New Turf* (New York: Doubleday, 1975).

[94]Johnson, op. cit., p. 190.

[95]Zola Neale Hurston had several degrees, one in anthropology, but chose to write about the working poor in the South. After DuBois and his followers criticized her for writing in a nonstandard southern dialect, she labeled them the "Niggerati" and ridiculed their pretensions of grandeur. See her "Story in Harlem Slang," *American Mercury* LV (July 1942): 84-89.

[96]Robbins Burling, *English in Black and White* (New York: Holt, Rinehart and Winston, 1974), p. 111.

[97]Johnson, op. cit., pp. 288-290.

[98]Deborah Sears Harrison and Tom Trabasso, eds., *Black English: A Seminar* (Hillsdale, NJ: Lawrence Erlbaum Associates, distributed by the Halsted Press Division of John Wiley and Sons, 1976), p. 285.

PUBLIC POLICIES AND ETHNIC INFLUENCES UPON FOREIGN LANGUAGE STUDY IN THE PUBLIC SCHOOLS

Frank M. Grittner

Wisconsin Department of Public Instruction

It is estimated that 70 percent of all Americans trace their ancestry back to an immigrant who arrived in this country speaking a language other than English. Over the centuries, tens of millions of people have arrived speaking only German, Spanish, French, Polish, and many other European and Asian languages. Given this multi-ethnic background, one might have assumed that an educational tradition would have developed in which the study of foreign languages would have been an important element, one which would be strongly supported by public policies regarding education. It might also have been assumed that the more academically talented from among the various non-English speaking groups would have generally capitalized upon the rich language resources of their parents and grandparents, and would have gone on to become students, teachers, and scholars in the language of their heritage.

As a matter of historical fact, this scenario was in evidence in many parts of the United States with regard to German ethnics. School laws in the 1800s in Ohio (1839), Wisconsin (1848), Colorado (1867), Oregon (1872), Maryland (1874), and Minnesota (1877) dealt specifically with language in the curriculum either as a medium of instruction or as a subject to be taught. Although the efforts were concentrated in the Midwest, the ethnic push of German groups extended as far west as Oregon where, in 1872, state legislation permitted public schools to exist in which instruction was given completely in German.[1] Bilingual schools in Cincinnati (1840), Milwaukee (1846), and Baltimore (1874) reflected the desire by the German population to have their children instructed in the German language. In fact, so powerful was the influence of the German language that a Wisconsin law was passed in 1846 which recognized as public only those Milwaukee schools that taught at least one course of English as subject matter. The state of Missouri also felt it necessary to pass a law requiring that some English be taught in the schools. This law resulted from an 1887 report by the state supervisor of education in which he testified that the German population was so large and influential in some school districts that instruction was mainly or entirely in German.[2]

This early public policy of permitting school subjects to be taught mostly in a foreign language was largely a defensive move on the part of local school boards of the day. Many of the Germans who had arrived in the mid-1800s felt that their parochial schools were superior to anything available in the public schools. This attitude, coupled with a strong desire to maintain the language and the cultural traditions of the homeland, made it nearly impossible for the monolingual English public schools to compete with the parochial schools for students in those areas which were populated predominantly by recent German immigrants. In those localities, many public school boards competed head-on by offering bilingual programs which at least met the state requirement that some course work be taught in English. This policy provided parents with a very attractive option: Their children could now become literate and fluent in the language of the cultural heritage while learning to speak, read, write, and understand the English language. And they could do this in the local public schools at little cost to the parents.

German Americans had evolved a model which flourished from the mid-1800s until well into the twentieth century in those areas where German ethnics predominated. This model of cultural and linguistic maintenance reemerged with less success in the 1960s and 1970s. The basic problem with the nineteenth-century model in German (as well as with subsequent attempts to implement "maintenance" bilingual programs) was that, although such programs had the support of a strong minority, the group was, in fact, a minority, and other linguistic minorities were not in a position to replicate the model for their own people. Monolingual English-speaking Americans naturally could not relate to the model at all. As a result, even in the nineteenth century a groundswell began against the use of German for instruction in public schools. The result was a new public policy which favored English over German. Even in Wisconsin—that most German of all states—the non-German majority managed to get the Bennett Law passed in 1889 in the Wisconsin legislature. The Bennett Law required that all children between the ages of seven and fourteen attend school, public or private, in the district where they resided. Section five of the law declared, "No school shall be regarded as a school unless there shall be taught therein, as part of the elementary education of children, reading, writing, arithmetic, and United States history in the English language."[3]

Policies For and Against Foreign Languages

Apparently, the supporters of the Bennett Law had overplayed their hand. For if the law were to be enforced, not only public schools but also the private and parochial schools which taught their curricula partly or totally in German would have been outlawed. Heavy political lobbying by German ethnic groups at the time succeeded in changing the political makeup of the legislature and the governor's office from Republican to Democratic in the election year 1890. The Bennett Law was repealed in 1891, thus permitting the German language to retain its status in many public and private schools across the state, a domination which lasted into the early part of the twentieth century. The German ethnic community had won the battle against the emerging public policy regarding the use of English in the schools. They could not know that within thirty years they would lose the language war while the armies of Kaiser Wilhelm were losing the shooting war.

The experience with the Bennett Law helps to illustrate the manner in which public policy on foreign language education has been (and continues to be) implemented in the schools of Wisconsin and the nation. In this regard the following principles apply:

- The final decisionmaking with respect to whether a foreign language will be offered, which foreign language or languages will be available, and how many years of study will be provided, are decisions which are ultimately made by the local school board. State and national commissions, governmental units and/or public agencies can make recommendations, but the power to accept or reject lies with the local school system. Thus, public policy is decentralized and dispersed among sixteen thousand school boards across the nation.

- The prevailing mood within mainstream American society tends to become incorporated into the state statutes governing educational policy. For example, as the move to anglicize all non-English-speaking immigrants became fixed in the public mind through the 1800s, the inclination to implement it within the legal system became irresistible.

Through a quirk of history, the successful efforts of German ethnics over a half century to establish German as the main language in many public schools were cancelled almost overnight. Prior to World War I, German was the leading modern language in the high schools: Over 24 percent of all high school students were enrolled in the study of German in 1916. Then came 1917, and

> ... in the spring of that year, when the United States declared war on Germany, all hell broke loose. The propaganda, which had concentrated upon the German emperor, his army and submarines, with many allegations of atrocities, turned immediately, now that we were at war, against the language, its literature as a whole and, in some cases, even against its teachers who were confronted with the sweeping accusation of being "pro-German." Groups of vigilantes visited the libraries and removed German books; others came to the departmental offices in the universities and confiscated textbooks containing pictures of Emperor William II or equally "subversive" material. . . . State legislatures (twenty-two in number. . .) and a score of cities vied with one another in forbidding the teaching of German in the public elementary and high schools, or even in prohibiting the speaking of German.[4]

But German did not suffer by itself; French and Latin went down with it. Forty years later, when the downward plunge in enrollments finally ended, Spanish had won the largest share of a very small slice of pie. For in the mid-1950s, a little more than 20 percent of all students were now electing foreign languages as compared with 80 percent before World War I. The enrollment figures below tell their own story.

FOREIGN LANGUAGE ENROLLMENT TRENDS AFTER WORLD WAR I
Modern Language

Year	Total Enrollment	Latin	French	German	Spanish	Total
1915	1,328,984	37.3%	8.8%	24.4%	2.7%	35.9%
1922	2,230,000	27.5	15.5	.6	11.3	27.4
1928	3,354,473	22.0	14.0	1.8	9.4	25.2
1934	5,620,625	16.0	10.9	2.4	6.2	19.5
1949	5,399,452	7.8	4.7	.8	8.2	13.7
1954	6,582,300	6.9	5.6	.8	7.3	14.2

Source: William R. Parker, *The National Interest and Foreign Languages*, 3rd ed. (Washington, D.C.: Government Printing Office, U.S. Department of State Publication 7234, 1961), p. 86.

It is important to note that German remained virtually out of the public school curriculum despite the fact that people of German ancestry remained the largest single ethnic group in the nation and that, until as late as 1960, the U.S. Census Reports continued to show German as the most widely spoken language in the nation after English. (In the 1970 census, Spanish finally replaced German as the second most widely spoken language.) The loss of German from the curriculum and the diminished enrollments in other languages were accompanied by another major change in policy regarding foreign language programs in the schools. The ethnic-oriented German programs had tended to use German as a means of communication in the classroom and to emphasize what were called "direct" and "natural" methods of teaching the language itself. Thus speaking and listening comprehension tended to be balanced with reading and writing skills. However, as the long sequence courses starting in elementary school and continuing on into high school vanished, so too did the emphasis upon the spoken language. Research in the 1920s showed that 83 percent of all high schools offered only two years of foreign language instruction.[5] With so little exposure to language instruction, it was considered futile to attempt to teach students how to understand, read, write, and speak a foreign language. This was the conclusion reached by a series of investigations conducted by grants from the Carnegie Corporation. Known as the *Coleman Report*, this publication had a profound effect upon the teaching of foreign languages. According to William Parker, " . . . it is a fact that from 1929 until World War II most modern language instruction in American schools and colleges stressed the 'reading aims' and produced a generation largely unable to speak French, German or Spanish or even to read a newspaper or magazine article in these languages beyond the ability of a fifth grade pupil in English."[6]

The Wisconsin Department of Public Instruction joined the national movement to use the war effort as a means of anglicizing immigrant children and programming the foreign language and culture out of them. In 1918 that agency published a bulletin entitled *The First School Days of the Non-English Child*. The booklet was clearly targeted toward German ethnics, and it implied that their lack of English rendered them incapable of comprehending the principles of democracy and the American way of life. As the bulletin expressed it:

> In 1917 there were in Wisconsin 512,569 foreign born inhabitants. They live in all parts of the state and their children attend school in every county. The findings in our recent draft registration revealed conditions that are most startling. In one county of the state 76 men presented themselves to the draft board for examination. Of these, 60 spoke German only, or a very few words of English. . . . These men are all of voting age. What do they know of American ideals? What knowledge have they of national needs?[7]

And the bulletin went on to say that

> We must make sure also that every child who attends any school learns sufficient English to read newspapers and magazines and to

carry on ordinary conversation in the language of the nation. We must urge that every little six-year old foreign child who is physically fit come to school in order that he or she may not become a badly retarded pupil because of inability to speak English.

Adults should be gathered into night schools or home study classes. Every teacher in Wisconsin must work untiringly to wipe out illiteracy and to encourage the use of English in every home in her community. She can do much toward accomplishing this by beginning in her classroom to teach English to the timid little people who cling to older brothers and sisters who are in turn only a trifle less shy. They, too, must receive help from their teachers in the mastery of the new tongue so that they can learn to think in the language of democracy.[8]

The bulletin suggested all kinds of ways of making people learn the "language of democracy." In kindergarten, for example, it was noted that, "Skillful seating does much to increase facility in the use of English. By putting a bashful foreign child next to an aggressive little American, the stimulation is given to the former to pick up the language habits of the latter."[9]

At times the bulletin even took on a patriotic fervor as the author urged the classroom teacher on toward an all-out effort to stamp out non-English-speaking habits. In the author's words, "The teacher who assumes the responsibility of teaching in a community where languages other than English are spoken owes it to her country to study her particular problems and to do her utmost to make English the language of Wisconsin."[10]

A number of public policy issues combined with the factors previously mentioned to work to the disadvantage of foreign language programs. Chief among these was the efficiency movement in which educators moved toward business management thinking and the "efficiency expert" mentality. Somehow, in the rhetoric and actions of school boards and school administrators, cheap education became equated with good education. Thus, for example, large classes meant lower per pupil costs. As foreign languages were downplayed into the role of miscellaneous elective, they became vulnerable to the efficiency-minded school official.

School administrators all over the country, not excluding Wisconsin, began computing the cost of teaching foreign languages and other subjects on a per hour or per minute basis. One administrator had even analyzed the "market price" of Latin in various cities throughout the Midwest. He found that some schools, such as Maple Lake, Minnesota, were paying as much as $244.00 per one thousand student hours for Latin while—in Greensburg, Indiana—you could buy it for only $46.00! The so-called "zone of safety" was a median figure of $71.00.[11]

In his book *Education and the Cult of Efficiency*, Raymond Callahan discussed the impact that this kind of thinking had on foreign language study. He also pointed out the connection between the efficiency movement, the war hysteria, and the foreign language program. As he put it:

> Clearly the way to economize was to get more work out of teachers, either by increasing the size of their classes or by increasing the number of classes they taught or both.

> In this effort the very small classes of ten to fifteen students, especially in the classics or the foreign languages, were doomed. And when some fortunate circumstance such as the anti-German sentiment during and after World War I occurred even fairly popular courses could be dropped. Significantly, when this happened the financial saving which was effected was included in the reporting of the event. Thus the *Journal of Education* reported in a news item that the Cincinnati Schools had eliminated German and had saved $75,000 a year thereby.[12]

The hysteria generated by World War I is a significant landmark in the American public's attitude toward language. It marks the point at which the new "melting pot" theory came to be widely practiced. Even though only 30 percent of the people of this nation were of English-speaking origin, the new unwritten—but nonetheless real—policy was that henceforth, English spoken the American way was to be the mark of full citizenship. As Teddy Roosevelt expressed it, "We want no more hyphenated Americans; no more German-Americans, Italian-Americans, or Polish-Americans. You *will* be Americanized, and that means to be Anglicized. And that means to speak English to the exclusion of any other language."

Hence, the paradox developed that to speak a second language *well* was to be marked as an immigrant, as a person of inferior status. However, to have a sophisticated theoretical knowledge *about* a second language and its literature (even though one might speak it poorly or not at all) was the mark of an educated person. It is not an exaggeration, then, to say that after the World War I period, the public would support those languages only insofar as the aim was to produce linguistic incompetence with respect to listening and speaking skills.[13]

Legislative Policies on Foreign Language Use in the Schools

Between the two world wars the climate grew increasingly inhospitable to foreign language study. The causes for the anti-language trend are difficult to trace and harder to prove. Among the reasons often cited are anti-intellectualism and xenophobia in American society, utilitarianism in education, isolationism in politics, and the immigrant's tendency to reject the culture of the "old country" and (in the second generation) the non-English language of the parents. The rather narrow objectives and limited methodology employed by many foreign language teachers of the period may also have contributed greatly to the deterioration. Further, the absence of any strong, organized group representing the interests of the foreign language profession at the secondary level, as well as the resulting inability of many scattered and isolated language teachers to contend with a changing high school curriculum, may partly explain the downfall. But, whatever the causes, the decline continued even beyond World War II, reaching such catastrophic proportions by the 1950s that over half the high schools in America offered no modern language during the postwar decade. In these bleak years, foreign languages tended to be referred to as "peripheral" subjects or were simply ignored. As late as 1950, a book on secondary education contained the following statement:

> It is difficult to justify languages for all youth. True, languages can help students understand various cultures. A great deal of instruction in language, however, is concerned with reading and speaking skills, and in face of so many urgent needs, use of the time and effort necessary to master these skills is questionable.... The time saved might be used for study of the current social problems completely overlooked by the classical curriculum.... Actually, about the only valid justification the authors can find for inclusion of foreign languages in the high school curriculum is that of satisfying the intellectual curiosity of a few students who are interested in developing their linguistic interests and abilities.[14]

With regard to public policy, the sequence of events followed in accordance with the power of various groups to act. Thus, the elimination or reduction of foreign language programs began with local school board and administrative actions. This was followed by various actions in the state legislatures, twenty-five of which passed laws restricting the teaching of foreign languages. In some instances the statutes actually forbade the teaching of a foreign language below the high school level. Although these more extreme laws were eventually overturned in the courts, virtually all states soon passed laws restricting the use of foreign languages in the curriculum. For example, Wisconsin—which had once required only that *some* of the instruction be in English—changed its curriculum requirements to read as follows:

118.01 Curriculum requirements. (1) FUNDAMENTAL COURSE. Reading, writing, spelling, English grammar and composition, geography, arithmetic, elements of agriculture and conservation of natural resources, history and civil government of the United States and Wisconsin, citizenship and such other subjects as the school board determines shall be taught in every elementary school. All instruction shall be in the English language, except: The school board may cause any foreign language to be taught to pupils who desire it.[15]

Thus state statutes came to reflect the local practices and policies which made foreign language a peripheral subject, not to be used as the means of instruction but to be offered according to the desires of the individual pupils who might wish to study a language other than English.

In summary, World War I had the effect of shifting the emphasis away from ethnic ties with foreign language education and from the use of the everyday spoken language. Academically-oriented foreign language programs, which can be simply defined as language programs in which the primary purpose is *not* to maintain the linguistic or cultural heritage of a particular ethnic group, became the norm in high schools and in higher education. In fact, many academically-oriented programs came into existence in the past precisely *because* there were so many different ethnic groups within a given school district. For political reasons, it was often wise to offer a foreign language which was neutral, so as not to offend the groups who would be left out if an "ethnic" language were chosen. One of the surest ways to obtain neutrality was to find a language which was no longer spoken by anyone, anywhere. In this regard, Latin, for many decades, was in the happy position of being both academically respectable and ethnically neutral. Throughout the history of the state—until very recently in fact—Latin was by far the most popular language in Wisconsin's public high schools. For a good part of Wisconsin's history, Latin outdrew all modern languages combined. It then declined into only a first-place ranking. It retained its first-place position until 1964 when Spanish passed it as the top language in high school. In 1965, Latin dropped to third place behind Spanish and French. Then, in 1967 it fell to fourth place behind Spanish, French and German in that order. The Wisconsin Department of Public Instruction's last collection of data on foreign language enrollments showed that Spanish was in first place, French had moved to second, German to third, and Latin to fourth. Enrollments are mentioned here because they give perhaps the best index of how the public will support a language. In the present climate, it is often a matter of economics. Many school boards have passed regulations that classes below a certain size (i.e., fifteen to twenty-five pupils) will not be offered. The languages which are most popular with the students tend to be the ones with the largest classes and, therefore, the ones that will receive local board support.

When local policies changed during the late 1970s and thus became incompatible with state law, the affected school districts found it relatively simple to change state law to conform to the desires of the local school districts' needs. In Wisconsin, bilingual education was established under subchapter seven of chapter 115 under which the state pays 75 percent of the cost of operating a bilingual program. Under Wisconsin statutes the student's home language may be used in the instructional process until such time as the student is able to function completely in English. Also, as part of a desegregation plan, the Milwaukee Public Schools have developed immersion programs in which English-speaking students are taught the curriculum in French, German, or Spanish. To accommodate these needs of the local school boards, state law was expanded to provide that:

> All instruction shall be in the English language except:
> (1) Those programs established under subch. VII of ch. 115 where instruction shall be in the English language and in the non-English language of the bilingual-bicultural education program.
> (2) The school board may cause any foreign language to be taught to pupils who desire it.
> (3) The school board may cause any course to be taught in a foreign language if the purpose is to facilitate the instruction of English speaking pupils in that language.[16]

What is significant about these changes in legally stated policy is that the ultimate outcome of each of the programs is to produce people who are basically literate speakers of English, but who may or may not acquire fluency and literacy in a foreign language. The not-so-hidden agenda is that, while languages are tolerable as an elective for those who are interested, they are in no way to be required.

Apparently the immigrant heritage with its mandatory rejection of languages other than English has led us to a strange paradox: While to be Americanized means that one must learn American English, the use of that language has not become a matter of ethnic pride. As Joshua Fishman expressed it:

> Just as there is hardly any ethnic foundation to American nationalism, so there is no special language awareness in the use of English. . . . Americans have no particular regard for English, no particular pride in English as an exquisite instrument, no particular concern for its purity, subtlety, or correctness. Even the fact that so few Americans command any other language than English—if, indeed, they can be said to command English itself—

is largely a result of educational failure, cultural provincialism, and the absence of pragmatic utility for bilingualism.[17]

It would be difficult to imagine Americans passing laws and establishing policies on the purity of the American mother tongue as happened in Germany under national socialism or has currently been the case in France under both liberal and conservative leadership. It is almost as if American English were thought of as a neutral force which hovers over the continent and permeates the thinking of those who live there. The paradox lies in the fact that those who deal with educational policies in the United States live in constant terror that somebody will use local, state or federal funds to instruct the youth of the United States in the use of an ethnic foreign language. For example, in the early drafts of the Wisconsin bilingual-bicultural law, there was permissive language to the effect that the school district might include content and activities in the bilingual-bicultural program that reflect the cultural background of the limited English-speaking students, and might include instruction intended to improve the skills of the students in the use of their native language.[18] This proposed provision of the law received strong objections from various groups who testified against it. In the final version (before it officially became a statute), this language was modified to exclude all references to the teaching of the native culture, but permitted instruction "through the use of the native language of the limited-English-speaking pupil, in the subjects necessary to permit the pupil to progress effectively through the educational system."[19] However, the final version of the law makes it clear that a pupil will be eligible for the program "only until such time as the pupil is able to perform ordinary classwork in English."[20]

At the federal level, Title VII of the Elementary and Secondary Education Act of 1965 contained legislation in support of bilingual education.[21] The act was amended in 1968, 1974 and 1978 in response to various kinds of lobbying. This law, which provided for competitive grant proposals rather than outright federal aid, was also transitional in nature. For example, the 1974 version of the law stated that "In no event shall the program be designed for the purpose of teaching a foreign language to English-speaking children."[22] Nevertheless, a report by Noel Epstein that was highly critical of bilingual education included the accusation that:

> It is all so clear that bilingual-bicultural advocates want to provide such instruction to students who are proficient in English. They oppose using the native language only temporarily as a bridge to English instruction. Rather, they long have sought to give equal importance to the mother-tongue and culture, pressing

for what are called "language and cultural maintenance" programs.[23]

Historically, a major part of the foreign language teaching enterprise in the United States was by design as ethnically neutral as possible. This was partly because traditions inherited from European models called for Latin or Greek to be the principal languages offered. These languages were considered to be the ideal vehicle for developing "mental discipline," the main purpose of the grammar school and high school program. In the entire history of the state of Wisconsin, Latin enrollments remained higher than that of any other foreign language, including German at its peak. As noted earlier, this dominance by a classical language continued until the mid-1960s when Spanish at last went ahead as the leading foreign language taught in the state. Modern foreign languages became part of the curriculum of schools in the 1800s only with great reluctance. Usually a modern language was added only on condition that it have the same kind of rigorous traditional grammar, vocabulary memorization, reading, and translation drills that were an integral part of the teaching of Latin.

It is worthy of note here that the policy of identifying foreign language with college preparation did not become so firmly entrenched as it is today until well into the depression years of the mid-1930s. Earlier, foreign language study was thought to be an essential mind-developing experience for all students who went on to high school. In the nineteenth and early twentieth centuries, the high school diploma was a terminal degree for a large majority of students who attended. Only a few, mostly well-to-do, middle-class students went on to higher education.

Part of the reason for the decline in foreign languages were the facts that mental discipline went out of vogue and that many of the students who flooded the high schools during the depression were there primarily because educational laws and policies required them to stay in school longer. The high schools now had to contend with large masses of students, many of whom were not academically motivated. To cope with this situation, schools began to offer differentiated curricula in an attempt to meet the varying needs of students. From this came the policy of tracking students into general, vocational, and college preparatory "streams." Foreign language study tended to fall into the latter category almost by default because of the weakening of the ethnic and mental-discipline rationales for studying them.

Federal Legislation

Except for the personal opinions of prominent national figures such as Thomas Jefferson and Benjamin Franklin, the federal government did little about policymaking in the area of foreign language before the 1950s. Perhaps the first major effort in this direction came almost as a matter of accident. In the hysteria which followed the launching of the Soviet Sputnik in 1957, Congress threw together what was called the National Defense Education Act or NDEA[24]. The success of the Soviet rocket was interpreted as an indication of inferior math and science education in the United States. As a result, the National Defense Education Act as implemented after 1958 included large amounts of money to improve instruction in mathematics and science. Almost as an afterthought, foreign languages were included in the law which provided tens of millions of dollars for equipment, materials, and teacher retraining in the three target areas. In the rhetoric of the NDEA years, foreign language study was no longer seen as a vehicle for maintaining linguistic and cultural ties, for developing the mind, or even for the altruistic purpose of international understanding. Rather, foreign language study was a vehicle for defending the nation. The impact of the federal policies emerging from the NDEA was rather dramatic. Between 1958 and 1968, enrollments in modern languages increased at both the high school and university levels. Foreign languages in the elementary schools and the study of Latin showed initial growth, but these programs began to fade rapidly after 1964. By the late 1960s, many of the smaller high schools had established four-year programs in one of the modern languages. In larger school districts, sequences of four or more years soon became the established norm. The enrollment figures below help to clarify the impact of NDEA policies on foreign languages in the high schools.

MODERN FOREIGN LANGUAGE ENROLLMENTS IN THE NDEA YEARS

Year	High School Population	Modern Foreign Language Students	Percent Enrolled
1958	7,906,679	1,300,882	16.5
1968	12,721,352	3,418,413	27.7

Source: Wesley Childers, *Foreign Language Offerings and Enrollments in Public Secondary Schools, Fall 1958* (New York: Modern Language Association, 1969), pp. 1-16.

Julia G. Kant, "Foreign Language Offerings and Enrollments in Public Secondary Schools, Fall 1968," *Foreign Language Annals* (March 1970): 400-476.

However, the enrollment gains which, at first glance, appear quite impressive, become somewhat less so when classical languages are included.

MODERN AND CLASSICAL LANGUAGE ENROLLMENTS IN THE NDEA YEARS

Year	High School Population	Modern and Classical Language Students	Percent Enrolled
1958	7,906,679	1,920,722	24.3
1968	12,721,352	3,890,924	30.6

Source: Childers, op. cit.; Kant, op. cit.

In fact, an analysis of enrollments in certain key years shows a rapid decline for Latin, the language that had been dominant through most of the history of the high school.

LATIN ENROLLMENTS IN THE NDEA YEARS

Year	Latin Students in Grades 9-12	Percent of High School Population
1958	618,222	7.8
1968	371,977	2.9

Source: Childers, op. cit.; Kant, op. cit.

The message is clear. The new-found prosperity of the modern languages was to a considerable extent realized at the expense of Latin.

Interest in and funding for foreign languages began to wane after 1968 as the nation became more and more obsessed with the problems of the war in Southeast Asia. By the late 1970s foreign language studies were again in a period of decline, even though the war had ended. In response to pressures to deal with this problem, President Carter issued an executive order in April 1978 to establish "The President's Commission on Foreign Language and International Studies," a commission whose responsibility was to "recommend means for directing public attention to the importance of foreign language and international studies for the improvement of communications and understanding with other nations in an increasingly interdependent world."[25] The commission went to work, and by November 1979 it issued its printed report under the title *Strength Through Wisdom: A Critique of U.S. Capabilities.*[26]

The introduction to this report criticized the lack of foreign language teaching in the elementary schools, the short sequence of study offered by most secondary schools, the lack of effective teacher education programs in higher education, and a general lack of effective teaching methods at all levels of instruction. The introduction also criticized past and present policies toward foreign language study in the United States and specified in detail the potential harm that these policies would bring in the future.

> The President's Commission believes that our lack of foreign language competence diminishes our capabilities in diplomacy, in foreign trade, and in citizen comprehension of the world in which we live and compete. Americans' unwillingness to learn foreign languages is often viewed by others, not without cause, as arrogance. The melting-pot tradition that denigrates immigrants' maintenance of their skill to speak their native tongue still lingers, and this unfortunately causes linguistic minorities at home to be ignored as a potential asset.[27]

In addition, the commission cited certain statistical findings to illustrate the sad state of affairs. A sample of these items includes:

- Only 15 percent of American high school students now study a foreign language—down from 24 percent in 1965. The decline continues.

- Only one out of 20 high school students studies French, German, or Russian beyond the second year. (Four years is considered a minimum prerequisite for usable language competence.)

- Only 8 percent of American colleges and universities now require a foreign language for admission, compared with 34 percent in 1966.

- It is estimated that there are 10,000 English-speaking Japanese business representatives on assignment in the United States. There are fewer than 900 American counterparts in Japan—and only a handful of those have a working knowledge of Japanese.

- The foreign affairs agencies of the U.S. government are deeply concerned that declining foreign language enrollments in our schools and colleges will lower the quality of new recruits for their services and will increase language training costs, already at a level of $100 million in 1978.[28]

The bulk of the commission report consisted of recommendations with supporting rationale and projected costs for carrying out the recommendations. Among other things the commission called for the establishment of regional centers intended to "reinvestigate and upgrade foreign language and teaching competencies of foreign language teachers at all levels." The report also called for summer institutes abroad for foreign language teachers and teachers in other disciplines, the reinstatement of foreign language requirements, incentive funding to schools and post-secondary institutions to improve foreign language teaching, and the establishment of international studies in high schools, along with many other specific recommendations.[29]

The commission report was another attempt (similar to the National Defense Education Act) to influence public policies at the state and local levels through pressure from the top down. Although it undoubtedly had some impact, the full effectiveness of the commission was limited due to several unforeseen factors. The most obvious was the failure of President Carter to win reelection. A set of recommendations commissioned by a former president from the opposition party is not the most effective document for promoting a cause. Also, many people in foreign languages were disenchanted by the composition of the commission; most of the members were not specifically oriented toward the teaching of foreign languages. In a dissenting view, one of the commission members pointed out that the expenditures were likely to go for non-foreign language purposes and that, in many of the recommendations, foreign languages were neglected or omitted completely. It almost seemed that the commission report suffered from some of the same monolingual myopia that it was initially set up to correct. On the positive side, though, the report did receive considerable public attention when it was first released and, although it is difficult to measure such outcomes, it appears to have raised public consciousness to a considerable degree.

With regard to education in general, the Reagan administration has adhered to its stated position that education is a state and local matter, one in which the federal government should not get involved. However, former Secretary of Education Terrel Bell publicly campaigned in favor of improved and increased foreign language study in schools and colleges of the nation. He made it clear, though, that the funding for these efforts should come from the state and local governments. In spite of all this Reagan did sign an education bill (Public Law 98-377), the purpose of which was "to improve the quality of mathematics and science teaching and instruction in the United States."[30] This law provided for money to flow through state departments of education and institutions of higher education for improving instruction in mathematics and science. The law also included a provision for directing this funding toward "critical foreign languages."[31] In effect the language of the statute allowed for "no more than 15 percent of the funding" to be used to strengthen instruction in foreign languages, but only if it could be demonstrated that a local school's needs had already been met in the areas of mathematics and science instruction.[32] The law also permitted this "leftover" money to be expended for the use of computers and computerized instruction. This is a clear statement of public policy showing foreign language to be in a secondary position behind mathematics and science education, but apparently ahead of most other subject matter areas. At this writing there is no way to measure what the effect of Public Law 98-377 will have on the teaching of foreign languages. There is not even a clear definition available for the term "critical foreign language."

President Reagan had his own presidential commission report which was much less narrowly focused than was President Carter's. The title of the Reagan commission report is *A Nation at Risk: The Imperative for Educational Reform*. The introduction of this report included strong rhetorical language from which the reader could only conclude that American public education was a disaster area. The report listed a series of "new basics" which included English, mathematics, science, social studies, and computer science. The report stated that instruction in these subjects should be required and the quality improved. In one section of the report there is a reference to "other important curriculum matters" which must be addressed. In this regard there is the following statement applying to foreign languages:

> Achieving proficiency in a foreign language ordinarily requires from 4 to 6 years of study and should, therefore, be started in the elementary grades. We believe it is desirable that students achieve such proficiency because study of a foreign language introduces students to non-English-speaking cultures, heightens awareness and comprehension of one's native tongue, and serves the Nation's needs in commerce, diplomacy, defense, and education.[33]

The report also contains a statement that foreign language should be offered in elementary and junior high school programs. In addition it is recommended that four-year colleges and universities should raise their admission requirements and demand higher performance in these areas. Foreign language is mentioned among the subjects which should be required.

Other Educational Commissions and Task Forces

In addition to *A Nation at Risk*, ten other recent reports on American education were examined in preparing this chapter. Some of these are highly supportive of expanding and improving foreign language programs at all levels, while others focus on foreign languages as being of value to college preparatory students only. Still other reports are concerned with matters such as vocational education, and simply do not mention or appear to be concerned with the study of foreign languages.

Ernest Boyer's report, entitled *High School: A Report on Secondary Education in America*, recommends that all students study a foreign language, preferably beginning at the elementary school level, with the requirement that all students have at least two years study at the high school level. The report takes a stand in favor of Spanish:

> Foreign Language: All students should become familiar with the language of another culture. Such studies should ideally begin in elementary school and at least two years of foreign language study should be required of all high school students. By the year 2000, the United States could be home to the world's fifth largest population of persons of Hispanic origin. It does seem reasonable for all schools in the United States to offer Spanish.[34]

Another report entitled *Making the Grade* emphasizes the importance of students having improved proficiency in English, mathematics, social studies, science, and other such courses taught in the English language. The members of the committee that wrote this report disagreed, however, on whether foreign languages should be required of all American students. A Mr. Yalow disagreed strenuously with the concept of requiring foreign languages. As he expressed it:

> I am in complete agreement with the Task Force recommendation about the essentiality of all Americans acquiring proficiency in English. In addition, it is desirable to develop a cadre with proficiency in foreign languages. Therefore, I accept that every American public school student should have the opportunity to acquire proficiency in a foreign language. But I really doubt the desirability of recommending that all high school students be required to study a foreign language. Is such competency really necessary for a farmer in Iowa, a coal miner in West Virginia, or a factory worker in the textile mills of the South? It might be highly desirable for a shopkeeper or a secretary in a bilingual community. The extent of competency, whether it should be ability to read, write, or speak fluently, should depend on personal and professional interests.[35]

In effect, this commentator goes on record as favoring the approach of offering foreign languages only for those who "need" them. Presumably these are college-bound students and those who might have a vocational application of the language.

New State Laws Regarding Foreign Language Teaching

By 1984 a number of states had attempted to establish policies favorable to foreign language education. For example, the California code states that "Commencing with the 1986-87 school year, no pupil shall receive a diploma of graduation from high school who, . . . has not completed . . . one course in visual or performing arts or foreign language."[36] The same code also requires that foreign language study shall be offered beginning not later than grade seven.[37] Similarly, New York state requires all public schools to make instruction in a second language available to students beginning in grade seven and continuing through grade twelve. This provision becomes effective in September 1988. The New York requirement for the future is even stronger. It states that "all public school students starting with the class of 1992 would be required to have at least one unit of instruction in a second language at some time during grades K-9."[38] Two units would be required by the year 1994. Thus, New York has, by far, taken the strongest stand among the states in favor of foreign languages. As in many other nations of the world, the study of foreign language would become an absolute requirement.[39]

Other states (Wisconsin and Minnesota, for example) have moved toward requiring that foreign language be offered in junior high school or senior high school or both. It is one thing to require an offering; it is quite another to require that a student study a foreign language as a prerequisite for graduation. According to Paul Turner, the attitudes against studying a foreign language (or especially studying subjects by means of a foreign language) are so deeply embedded in American culture that they could only be reversed by a major reeducation effort of a substantial majority of Americans.[40] If Turner is correct, then the New York approach to assuring that all Americans study a foreign language will be the exception in public policy. If that is true, then the ethnic heritage will have worked against itself to prevent still another generation of the descendants of immigrants from realizing the educational values which come to those who study more than one language. Perhaps only time can erase the negative effects of long-term and deeply embedded attitudes deriving from the immigrant heritage.

The other factors affecting foreign language education such as program costs, class size, and the problems of an interdependent world society, also cannot be easily solved. Foreign language education is also affected by the problem of a constantly changing social order. It appears that educators may have to consider major curricular revisions every five or six years and make minor adjustments annually. It will no longer be possible to continue teaching the same old curriculum in the same way year after year in an elective subject, and still have enough students to satisfy those who demand "efficiency." Meanwhile, students are pushing for electives even within the old "required" subjects. Thus, in foreign languages, the formula for public support is quite simple. To have public support, one must have students. To have students, the program must either be required or else appear relevant to the generation in question. To make a program relevant requires massive curricular change at increasingly shorter intervals. This, in turn, requires money. To get money, though, public support is needed. Thus, we seem to have a kind of vicious circle. What is the answer? Unfortunately, there is no easy solution. In this regard the final paragraph from Callahan's *Education and the Cult of Efficiency* can be cited. He said,

> It is true that some kinds of teaching and learning can be carried out in large lecture classes or through television, but other vital aspects of the education of free men cannot. Until every child has part of his work in small classes or seminars with fine teachers who have a reasonable teaching load, we will not really have given the American high school, or democracy for that matter, a fair trial. To do this, America will need to break with its traditional practice, (strengthened so much in the age of efficiency), of asking how our schools can be operated most *economically* and begin asking, instead, what steps need to be taken to provide an *excellent* education for our children. We must face the fact that there is no cheap, easy way to educate a human being, and that a free society cannot endure without educated men.[41]

NOTES

[1]Anthony Gradisnik, "Bilingual Education," in Frank M. Grittner, ed., *NSSE Yearbook, Learning A Second Language* (Chicago: University of Chicago Press, 1980), pp. 104-127.

[2]Ibid.

[3]1889 Laws of Wisconsin, Ch. 519, Sec. 5, cited in Roland B. Day, "The German Language in Wisconsin," a speech before the German Language and School Society (Milwaukee: May 1, 1977), p. 7.

[4]Edwin H. Zeydel, *The Teaching of German in the United States—A Historical Survey* (New York: Modern Language Association Materials Center, 1961), p. 298.

[5]William R. Parker, *The National Interest and Foreign Languages*, 3rd ed. (Washington, D.C.: Government Printing Office, U.S. Department of State Publication 7324, 1961), p. 87.

[6]Ibid.

[7]Maybell G. Bush, *The First School Days of the Non-English Child* (Madison, WI: Wisconsin Department of Public Instruction, 1918), p. 7.

[8]Ibid., p. 8.

[9]Ibid., p. 9.

[10]Ibid., p. 10.

[11]Raymond E. Callahan, *Education and the Cult of Efficiency* (Chicago: University of Chicago Press, 1962), p. 163.

[12]Ibid., p. 233.

[13]Frank M. Grittner, *Teaching Foreign Languages* (New York: Harper and Row, 1969), p. 17.

[14]J. G. Saylor, *Secondary Education: Basic Principles and Practices*, quoted in Parker, op. cit., p. 90.

[15]Wis. Stats. 118.01(1).

[16]Wis. Stats. 118.017.

[17]Joshua Fishman, *Language Loyalty in the United States: The Maintenance and Perpetuation of Non-English Mother Tongues by American Ethnic and Religious Groups* (The Hague: Mouton, 1966), p. 30.

[18]See, for example, Senate Substitute Amendment 1 to 1975 Senate Bill 126, Sec. 4, p. 9, lines 17-22, and Assembly Substitute Amendment 1 to 1975 Senate Bill 126, Sec. 3, p. 5, lines 14-19.

[19]Wis. Stats. 115.955(8)(b).

[20]Wis. Stats. 115.95(4).

[21]The Elementary and Secondary Education Act of 1965 is codified as 20 U.S.C. 3221-3261.

[22]Education Amendments of 1974, P.L. 93-380 (93rd Congress, 2nd Session), Title VII, Sec. 703(a)(4)(B).

[23]Noel Epstein, *Language, Ethnicity and the Schools: Policy Alternatives for Bilingual Education* (Washington, D.C.: George Washington University Institute for Educational Leadership, 1977), p. iv.

[24]The NDEA is codified as 20 U.S.C. 401-602.

[25]Executive Order No. 12054, Sec. 2(b)(1) (April 21, 1978), 43 Fed. Reg. 17457.

[26]James A. Perkins, ed., *Strength Through Wisdom: A Critique of U.S. Capability* (Washington, D.C.: President's Commission on Foreign Language and International Studies, November 1979).

[27]Ibid., p. 6.

[28]Ibid.

[29]Ibid., p. 7.

[30]20 U.S.C. 3901.

[31]See, for example, 20 U.S.C. 3972(c).

[32]20 U.S.C. 3966(c)(2).

[33] National Commission on Excellence in Education, *A Nation At Risk: The Imperative for Educational Reform* (Washington, D.C.: U.S. Department of Education, 1984), p. 25.

[34] Ernest L. Boyer, *High School: A Report on Secondary Education in America* (New York: Harper and Row, 1984), p. 304.

[35] Paul E. Peterson, ed., *Making the Grade: Report of the Twentieth Century Fund Task Force on Federal Elementary and Secondary Education Policy* (New York: The Twentieth Century Fund, 1983), p. 22.

[36] California Education Code, Sec. 51225.3.

[37] Ibid., Sec. 51220(c).

[38] Bureau of Foreign Languages Education, "Summary of Foreign Language Provisions in New York State Board of Regents' Action Plan to Improve Elementary and Secondary Education Results in New York," attached to Paul E. Dammer, "Foreign Language Requirements in New York State," Memorandum to State Foreign Language Supervisors (Albany, NY: New York State Education Department, Assistant Commissioner for General Education, May 9, 1984).

[39] Anthony Papalia, ed., *Futuring: Languages for A Richer Tomorrow* (New York: New York State Association of Foreign Language Teachers, 1984), p. 2.

[40] Paul R. Turner, "Why Johnny Doesn't Want to Learn A Foreign Language," *The Modern Language Journal* LVIII: 4 (April 1974): 191-196.

[41] Callahan, op. cit., p. 264.

PERTINENT EDUCATIONAL REPORTS

Adler, Mortimer J. *The Paideia Proposal: An Educational Manifesto.* New York: MacMillan Publishing, 1982.

Boyer, Ernest L. *High School: A Report on Secondary Education in America.* New York: Harper and Row, 1983.

The College Board, Office of Academic Affairs. *Academic Preparation for College: What Students Need To Know and Be Able To Do.* New York: The College Board, 1983.

Goodlad, John. *A Place Called School: Prospects for the Future.* New York: McGraw-Hill, 1984.

Hunt, James B., Jr., and David Hamburg. *Education and Economic Progress: Toward A National Education Policy.* New York: The Carnegie Corporation, 1983.

National Commission on Excellence in Education, U.S. Department of Education. *A Nation At Risk: The Imperative for Educational Reform.* Washington, D.C.: U.S. Government Printing Office, 1983.

National Science Board Commission. *Educating Americans for the 21st Century.* Washington, D.C.: National Science Board, 1983.

Peterson, Paul E. *Making the Grade: Report of the Twentieth Century Fund Task Force on Federal Elementary and Secondary Education Policy.* New York: The Twentieth Century Fund, 1983.

Sizer, Theodore R. *A Celebration of Teaching: High School in the 1980s.* New York: Houghton Mifflin, 1983.

Task Force on Education for Economic Growth, Education Commission of the States. *Action for Excellence: A Comprehensive Plan to Improve Our Nation's Schools.* Denver, CO: Education Commission of the States, 1983.

EPILOGUE*

Winston A. Van Horne

University of Wisconsin-Milwaukee

Rome, says Saint Augustine, "endeavored to impose on subject nations not only her yoke, but her language, as a bond of peace, so that interpreters, far from being scarce, [would be] numberless."[1] As a bond of peace, Rome sought to use her language as an instrument to convey to the many whom she had conquered and swallowed up in her empire her laws, customs, traditions, norms, mores, and ethos. Through her language she sought not only to lighten the weight of her yoke, but also to bond together the many and diverse strangers whom she had swallowed. To satisfy her voracious and insatiable appetite, she swallowed up ever more and more strange and diverse peoples in her empire, only to suffer the torment that she could swallow them but not digest them. How strikingly is this called out by Saint Augustine when he observes that the very extent of the empire itself produced wars of a most "obnoxious description—social and civil wars—and with these the whole race has been agitated, either by the actual conflict or the fear of renewed outbreak."[2]

Rome endeavored to impose her language upon strangers in her midst to the end that she might create numberless interpreters of and participants in the metaphysical and valuational assumptions that animated the behavior of her people. And who were her people? Those whom she bound together by reason, common sentiments of affection, and a partnership in activities to the end of the good and love of Rome. Language, then, was one means by which Rome sought to expand the size of her people, and in doing so secure her own internal peace. But many were they who succumbed to the imposition of her language and became speakers of it, yet did not become interpreters of it in the sense of being digested into the body of her people. Rome did not, and perhaps could not, expand the size of her people to cover the four corners of the empire through the imposition of her language on the ones whom she had swallowed.

In this there is a lesson of singular importance for the United States—especially in the light of the all too many striking similarities between its history and that of Rome. Having swallowed many strange and diverse peoples with a multitude of alien tongues, the United States could, via the English language, well trod the ground once trodden by Rome. But it should not expect that such will melt those who are unmeltable due to their race and ethnicity, nor ground shared metaphysical and valuational assumptions that foster behaviors which nurture the peace of the society, as well as the peace of the individual's soul. After many generations of imposition, the English language proved to be weak as a bond of peace between the British and the Kenyans as the latter struggled to free themselves from the colonial domination of the former, just as the Americans had done almost two centuries earlier. And surely, the English language has been anything but a bond of peace between England and Ireland, more particularly Northern Ireland. Like examples have abound over historical time. The crucial point that is being called out here is that the imposition of a natural language (for example, Latin, English, Yoruba, etc.) upon human beings whose cultures make them strangers to one another does not meld them into a people, and is no assurance of societal tranquility, much less social peace.

Every people has its own peace, the peace that knits it together as a people; and every people has its own common language, the language of its peace. A common language does not assure the peace of a people, but without it a people—who are made known by the things and objects of their love—have no peace. A common love with bonds more strong than a common language knits together the souls of a people in a striving purpose that animates the activity of life for the sake of ends most sublime and desirable to their souls. Still, a people cannot be forged and will not persist without a common language.

Does a common language imply one official natural language for a given society and nation-state, or does it entail a set of signs, symbols, and meanings sufficient to enable individuals to recognize, interpret, know, and understand the phenomena of subjective reality and objective reality? As one not only reads but reflects upon the chapters of this volume, one cannot but conclude that a common language does not imply logically, conceptually, nor empirically one official natural language, the pervasiveness of the belief that such is true notwithstanding. A common language could be one, two, three or more natural languages in a given society, as long as most, if not all, of its members are able to use each interchangeably in listening, speaking, reading, and writing in relation to inquiry and discourse pertaining to a particular phenomenon or range of phenomena. The success of Wallace Lambert's language immersion activities with youngsters in Canada reinforces the soundness of this observation. A common language is not intrinsically one official or unofficial natural language, but the capacity and ability of large numbers of persons to make common sense of a given phenomenon or range of phenomena and share like sentiments pertaining to it. This is so regardless of whether one, two or more natural languages are used in the emergence of such common sense and sentiments. The conflation of the terms "common language" and "natural language" corrupts and distorts the idea of a common language, and has been the source of all too many irritations, vexations, torments, vulgarities, brutalities, and horrors. In this context, everyone who reads Kai Nielsen's chapter should pause and ponder long and hard the significance of his disquietude concerning "our current overfascination with language." This overfascination with language tends to pervert common sense, transforming it all too often into common sense of the most trite and self-righteous sort. Richard Ruiz and Donald Larmouth are acutely conscious of this, and so with loud and unequivocal voices they call upon their countrymen and fellow citizens to ponder the dangers of the unintended consequences of making English the official natural language of the United States through an amendment to the Constitution.

This is, perhaps, the single most important point in public policy that emerges from this book. Racially, ethnically, and linguistically pluralistic America—where more than one hundred languages are spoken in the greater Los Angeles area alone—is likely to have less rather than more social peace and societal unity if English were to become the *sole* constitutionally official language of the land, both Ruiz and Larmouth warn. The reasons and grounds for their warning need not be restated here. Will their warning blow in the wind and still not be heard, and if heard, not heeded? And what is the potential cost of this? It may be well to return to the observations of Saint Augustine cited at the outset.

Rome endeavored to give those whom she swallowed not only her yoke but also her language. She sought to have her language as a bond of peace between the "we" and the "they"; to bond the we and the they into the "one" through one peace—the peace of all. But was Rome's language a bond of peace or simply an instrument of tranquility, a weapon of order?

The spread of Latin did not bring peace to the empire. Through her language she made her dictates known, and by her arms she had them obeyed. Her language, like arms, was a weapon of order, an instrument to foster the tranquility of the empire. But such tranquility that the empire did enjoy was not true peace, which "between man and God is the well-ordered obedience of faith to eternal law," and "between man and man is *well-ordered* concord."[3] The concord of the empire was anything but well-ordered in the sense that individuals—bound together by right reason and sharing common sentiments of affection in relation to like things and objects of love—acted intentionally, deliberately, and voluntarily to promote and protect that which was deemed to be in the interest and good of Rome. There was no well-ordered concord in the empire, even though it did enjoy a measure of tranquility and order. This is a point of singular importance, for it should be remembered always that tranquility and order are neither the conceptual nor empirical equivalent of well-ordered concord in a political society. Great is the tranquility and order of the graveyard, but such is not well-ordered concord, which is possible only among the living, not the dead. By her arms and her language Rome did succeed in imposing upon the world that she had conquered a measure of tranquility and order, but she failed to give the world the laws of her own peace, for this it could not impose. She could impose her language, and this she did. She could impose her laws, and this she also did. But she could not impose her peace—the laws of her own peace. The language she endeavored to impose was in reality no bond of peace, but an instrument to the end of the preservation of order and tranquility in her far-flung empire. She was to be consumed in part by those who knew of her order and tranquility, but not of her peace. Of what significance is this for the United States?

Human beings tend to be naturally wary of strangers. Nature perhaps uses this as one means of assuring the survival of the species, for wariness tends to become more acute the fewer the similarities one senses and discerns between oneself and a stranger. Now, a political society is an assemblage of strangers who come together and continue to stay together for the sake of mutual beneficence by submitting themselves to public authorities whose decisions are binding upon all. Such strangers become a people when by right reason and common sentiments of affection, they form a partnership in like things and objects of love. A people are thus at once strangers and fellows, as paradoxial as this may seem. At the level of the individual, they are, for the most part, strangers. At the level of the collective, they are fellows. As the relation of stranger becomes progressively stronger and that of fellow becomes progressively weaker at the level of the collective, a people are weakened ever more and more, regardless of the robustness of its individual members. An inverse relation thus obtains between the strength of the relation of fellow, the weakness of the relation of stranger, and the strength of a people, judged in terms of the well-ordered concord that knits them together. The persistence of a people thus necessitates not only the robustness of its individual members, but also the clear dominance of the relation of fellow over that of stranger at the level of the collective. A people who fail persistently to take the kinds of action and engage in the sorts of behavior that strengthen the relation of fellow, and correspondingly weaken that of stranger at the level of the collective, assures its dissolution as a people, even though the political society in which its individual members live may persist. For there is no people where mutual beneficence does not abound, but political society persists as long as a sufficiently large number of individuals are constrained to obey the dictates of public authorities. As the racial, ethnic, and linguistic diversity of the United States becomes ever more and more pronounced, the ones who live there confront one challenge of which there is no greater, to wit, the simultaneous persistence of the people and the political society. By what alchemy are strangers so different by race, ethnicity, and language at the level of the individual to be made fellows at the level of the collective? Here the ideals and values of American democracy come into play full force.

When the president of the United States begins a speech with the words "My fellow Americans", he is not simply extending a salutation. He is doing something more, much more. In conjoining the terms fellow and American(s), he calls out that Americans are fellows at the level of the collective, even though they may be strangers at the level of the individual. As fellows, they participate in a partnership of shared sentiments pertaining to common things and objects of love, such as the ideals of individual liberty, social equality, social justice, equity, the rule of law, fair play, and the pursuit of happiness. It matters not that conceptual incommensurateness obtains between some of these ideals, and it matters not that individuals may love these ideals *qua* ideals but dislike, even hate, particular empirical instantiations of them. What is of critical import is the fact that as fellows, Americans participate together in the love of these ideals, and this love constitutes one of the key, if not the ultimate, defining attribute(s) of them as people. In reality, then, the phrase "my fellow Americans" is synonymous with the phrase "we the American people."

Who are the American people? What does it mean to be a fellow rather than a stranger in the collective that grounds the people of the United States? And most important in the context of this volume, is it necessary for one to be able to use the English language in transmitting bits of information to be a fellow in the collective—to be one of the people?

Wallace Lambert and Donald Taylor attempt to get a purchase on these questions. Their discussion does not, however, leave one with a clear and distinct image of what it means to be an American, to be one of the people of the United States. This should be expected, given the congeries of attributes that give form and substance to the people. The concept of the American people makes no sense whatsoever apart from the ideals mentioned earlier. Yet these ideals are not sufficient to define the people. Were they sufficient, Chief Justice Roger Taney would never have declared in the *Dred Scott* decision that people of primary African origin living in the United States, whether they were free or enslaved, were not a part of the people.

Questions of ideals aside, are the people of the United States those who are members of the sovereign body politic and entitled to all the benefits and the full range of protections grounded in the Constitution? Taney's Court drew very narrowly the bounds of the ones who could lay claim to such entitlement. Those bounds have been broadened exponentially since Taney's time. Still, nagging and troublesome questions persist. Is anyone who is entitled to the benefits and protections of the Constitution one of the people? And obversely, is one who is not entitled to such benefits and protections, but nonetheless has as the object of one's love the ideals mentioned previously, one of the people in reality though not in law? Put differently, was Frederick Douglass one of the people at the time of the Lincoln-Douglas debates, even though the Supreme Court had declared him not to be in virtue of his African ancestry? These are neither rhetorical nor academic questions. They are possessed of real blood-and-guts substance, for surely Douglass, as well as the many who shared his sentiments, was of the firm conviction that he was a part of the American people even though Taney thought contraiwise. One is thus forced to ask yet another time, what does it mean to be a fellow American, and is the use of the English language a necessary condition?

Minimally, the term fellow American entails an objective legal state as well as a subjective state of being. One is a lawful claimant to the cover of both constitutional law and statute law in virtue of one's objective legal state. One feels attached to the structure of ideals and values that ascribes meaning and purpose to human conduct in the society in virtue of one's subjective state of being. Neither objective legal state nor subjective state of being is by itself sufficient to make one a fellow American. Each is necessary but not sufficient; however, together they are necessary and sufficient to do so. In his subjective state of being Douglass no doubt felt himself to be a part of the American people, given his attachment to the structure of ideals and values in which he perceived the society to be grounded. Yet empirically he was not, given his objective legal state after the *Dred Scott* decision. Correspondingly, one whose objective legal state makes one a lawful claimant to the cover of both constitutional law and statute law, but who in his subjective being feels no attachment to the structure of ideals and values that give meaning and purpose to human conduct in American society, is not a part of the people. This much is clear and straightforward, but it all gets pretty tricky, and perhaps even vexing, awfully fast after this.

The idea of objective legal state is at first blush clear and unambiguous. But is it? When the president says "My fellow Americans", does he mean: only citizens of the United States; citizens and permanent residents; citizens, permanent residents, and those who are legally permitted to remain in the country pending the disposition of their application for permanent residency; citizens, permanent residents, those awaiting a grant of legal residency, and those who are in the country illegally but, wishing to remain in the society permanently, are in the process of taking the steps necessary to change their legal status? Are the persons residing in the United States illegally, but who are taking the steps required by law to change their legal status, lawful claimants to the cover of American law? If they are so entitled, do they satisfy the necessary condition of objective legal state to be counted among the people, even though they are neither citizens nor as yet legal residents? If they are not so entitled while they are in the process of becoming legal residents and possibly citizens, are they excluded automatically when the president says "My fellow Americans"? These are all tough questions in law and jurisprudence that cannot even be broached here. They are called out for the purpose of pointing to the intrinsic complexity of what appears *prima facie* to be a simple idea with easy empirical constructions in determining who are to be counted among the people.

Matters become even more complex when one turns to the idea of subjective state of being. If there were universal agreement on the form and substance of the structure of ideals and values that ascribe meaning and purpose to human conduct in the United States, each one attached by reason and emotion to such ideals and values would satisfy the necessary condition of subjective state of being to be counted among the people. No such agreement obtains. Where common agreement does obtain is that a structure of ideals and values ground American democracy, animate human conduct in the United States, and is in some way or other shared through reason and emotion by all of those who form the American people. Once one begins to decompose that structure in order to lay bare its essential and constituent elements, one runs into all sorts of trouble. This is due to the empirical fact that fellows at the level of the collective are often attached to ideals and values bearing similar names, but which are constituted dissimilarly in their minds' eye. Such dissimilarities tend to be the source of much friction and many vexations, especially when individuals and groups strive to make the conception of ideals and values that animate their conduct the only legitimate one for all the fellows at the level of the collective, for the people as a whole. But does this not contradict what was said earlier concerning every people having a common language, since it appears that all a people have in common in terms of ideals and values is a common set of names?

The putative contradiction raised by the preceding question is in reality no contradiction at all. The names represent ideals and values. What is shared are not just the names, but also what they represent. Individuals may and do differ about what is actually represented by the names, but they can and do agree about the necessity of that which is represented in guiding human conduct in the United States. A common language, then, does not mean universal agreement; it does mean a shared understanding of acceptable ways of determining the content of the abstract ideals and values that are shared by the people.[4] This is a point of the utmost importance, which serves to bring into clear and distinct focus yet another critical point, viz., the fact that neither universal agreement nor the use of one natural language need obtain where there is a common language. All too often bad common sense conflates the ideas of common language, universal agreement, and one natural language, something good common sense does not do. The presence of a common language which knits a people together in a given society thus does not mean that individuals need make use of one, and only one, natural language, nor that anything approaching universal agreement obtains pertaining to the peripherals, much less the fundamentals of right and proper human conduct.

If the preceding observations are sound, one cannot but lament as well as resist the activities of organizations such as U.S. English which seek to make the natural language, English, the one, and only one, official language of the United States. It is well at this juncture to return to the opening sentence of this epilogue. Rome endeavored to impose her natural language upon those whom she had conquered as a bond of peace. Her language, however, proved not to be the bond of peace that she desired. Could this also become true of the United States were English to be imposed as the sole constitutionally official language?

One who favors such a development may jump immediately on a word that has recurred in the references that have been made to Rome, namely, impose. The United States is a constitutional democracy. The minimal content of a well-ordered constitutional democracy is the participation of the citizenry in the activity of government through the opportunity of individuals to cast unfettered ballots at regular intervals for representatives, who are authorized to act in their behalf, by choosing among persons competing for public office. If this construction is sound, and assuming all the procedures for amending the Constitution were followed scrupulously, would it make any sense whatsoever for one to say that English was imposed upon the citizenry if there were an amendment which mandated it to be the sole official language of the United States?

This question evokes another which is even more fundamental in its political content: In a well-ordered constitutional democracy, is an amendment to the constitution an imposition either on citizens or noncitizens? As long as sound and proper criteria for citizenship obtain in the constitution, insofar as every citizen is afforded by right of citizenship the opportunity to cast unfettered ballots for representatives, and insofar as representatives act within the framework of the letter and the spirit of the organic law for making changes in it, one is really without good conceptual grounds for claiming that a given constitutional amendment was imposed on the citizenry. The amendment may be ill-tempered, misconceived, ill-thought out, unsound and unwise, but one should not construe from these that it was imposed if the conditions just mentioned were satisfied. It is thus the case conceptually that to the extent that the United States either is or approximates a well-ordered constitutional democracy, an amendment to the Constitution mandating English to be the one, and only one, official language of the land would not be an imposition on the ones who are citizens. But what of noncitizens? Are they also covered by the observations that have just been made?

This question invites one to reflect once more upon the idea of objective legal state. Noncitizens do not have the legal opportunity to cast ballots for representatives in our constitutional democracy. As such, they cannot participate in the activity of government through representatives, even though they are nonetheless bound by the decisions of the government insofar as they elect to remain in the polity. This exclusion does not, however, preclude all such persons from being counted among the people of the United States. Is a constitutional amendment enacted by representatives elected by those who are citizens an imposition on the ones who are noncitizens, their status in terms of being counted among the people notwithstanding?

Conceptually, no such imposition obtains. This is so in virtue of the fact that noncitizens either know or should know that the framework of American constitutional democracy is such that they are bound legally by the decisions of representatives for whom they are precluded from casting ballots. If they dislike strongly given decisions of representatives and particular outcomes of votes by citizens, they have three options: leave; take the measures necessary to become citizens in order to obtain the legal right to cast ballots; or change the framework of the constitutional democracy. Electing to remain in the polity voluntarily, and given what they either know or should know about the procedures and process by which the United States amends its Constitution, it is not the case conceptually that an amendment to the Constitution mandating English as the sole official language of the United States would be an imposition on noncitizens.

Still, there is no one-to-one correspondence between conceptual soundness and empirical soundness. In spite of what has just been said, many citizens and noncitizens alike would no doubt feel that a constitutional amendment which mandated English to be the official language of the United States was an imposition on them. And not just a benign imposition either, but one that is bad. This idea impresses itself upon one's mind as one reflects on Sau-ling Wong's use of Ruiz's construction of language-as-problem, language-as-right, and language-as-resource. If Ruiz's observations pertaining to language-as-right are correct, many of those who do not speak English, as well as the ones for whom it is not their mother tongue, could well perceive such an amendment to be designed to deprive them of a right to which they have a legitimate claim. True, "a substantial number of Hispanics," for example, voted in favor of the English Language Amendment to the constitution of the state of California in November 1986, according to Ruiz. Some portion of these were no doubt from households in which Spanish is the first language, since Spanish is spoken in four out of five Hispanic households in the United States, as Wong points out. In spite of this, many Hispanics living in California, for whom Spanish and not English is their first language, perceive this amendment to be an abridgement of the right to use Spanish—an imposition on them.

In the short run, this amendment, which falls within the tradition of what may be called the compel-them-to-learn-English syndrome (language-as-problem), may not have the sort of adverse unintended consequences that trouble both Ruiz and Larmouth. This could well not be true in the long run. As the racial, ethnic, and linguistic diversification of the society continues, and as more and more Americans for whom English is their first, and most likely only, language come to perceive ever increasing numbers of strangers who neither look not speak like themselves in their midst, the intrinsic tension between language-as-right and language-as-problem is likely to intensify. The more these Americans perceive the other Americans and would-be Americans to be strangers both at the level of the individual as well as the collective, and are impelled to treat them as such, the greater will be the press to mandate English as the putative unifying language of the body politic.

Everyone who contemplates this should read Donald Larmouth's chapter with the greatest care, and take to heart its admonitions.

Where, then, does all of what has been said lead? Kai Nielsen offers pointers, for he recognizes implicitly the value of Ruiz's conception of language-as-resource. The Enlightenment's impetus towards universality in our knowledge and understanding of human beings—their needs, wants, desires, hopes, fears, dreams of what can be, and visions of what ought to be—evokes images of a common language which transcends cultural barriers. The counter-Enlightenment's stress of the particular "hammer[s] home the importance in our very humanization of cultural particularities," says Nielsen. Striving to converge the best of the Enlightenment and the counter-Enlightenment traditions, Nielsen goes on to observe that

> [p]art of what makes us human is that we are each a particular kind of human being, a member of a distinct community with its own sense of how it is appropriate to live, and its own distinctive conceptual categories for interpreting and responding to the world. On the other hand, there is such a thing as cultural borrowing. There is the possibility for people to forge new tablets and to come to understand an alien culture well and to see that the ways that culture has of viewing and responding to things may be superior to one's own inherited ways of doing and viewing things.

One of the distinctive conceptual categories with which a distinct community interprets and responds to the world is language. It enables individuals to make some measure of sense of the congeries of phenomena that bombard their daily lives. Indeed, language is that indispensable resource without which one could not organize one's thoughts (perhaps one could not even think), make sense of the world outside of oneself, nor place oneself in relation to one's community. Through language one bridges the universal and the particular. It enables one to transcend the limits of cultural particularity and forge new tablets of cultural universality. It provides a means for one to see new sights, hear new sounds, think new thoughts, and sense new sensations. It can open the world to one, but it can also close one to the world. This is so because language is at once universal and particular. It is universal in its cultural transcendence; it is particular in its cultural confinement.

In its cultural transcendence language inclines one towards that which is human universally; in its cultural confinement it draws one towards what is human particularly. As such, it constitutes a resource most profound. Uniting man *qua* man in his universality and his particularity, language has the intrinsic potential of being a true bond of peace. The distinction drawn earlier between natural language and common language becomes crucial here. As natural languages converge in a common language, human beings transcend more and more the limits of the particularities of their own individual culture. One should not infer from this that the limits of cultural particularities can ever, or will ever, be transcended fully. Indeed, if one must possess at least some cultural particularities to be human, the transcendence of all such particularities would mean that one ceased to be human.

The transcendence of cultural particularity through a common language exposes human beings, who are limited by the particularity of their respective natural language(s), to different ways of seeing the world and doing things, opening ever increasingly pathways across the differences that divide them by making more clearly discernible the similarities they share. All differences are not intrinsically bad, and all similarities are not inherently good. What is critical to the well-being of a people is an abundance of good similarities and good differences, as well as a paucity of bad similarities and bad differences. The transcendence of good similarities over bad similarities and good differences over bad differences through participation in a common language is nurtured by the exposure of human beings to a variety of natural languages. And herein, perhaps, lies the ultimate value of language-as-resource: The melding of natural languages into a common language impels human beings to participate in a striving purpose to the end that what is truly human in each may blossom, even as individuals retain the vivacity of their respective natural language(s). Put differently, language-as-resource is made most consummate not in the dominance of one or more official or unofficial natural languages, but in the affect and effect of a common language that knits together the souls of a people in the order and tranquility of a well-ordered concord—peace.

NOTES

*I should like to thank my colleague, Thomas V. Tonnesen, for the range of ideas and observations he shared with me.

[1] *The City of God*, XIX, 7, trans. M. Dods in Whitney J. Oates, ed., *Basic Writings of Saint Augustine*, Vol. II (New York: Random House, 1948).

[2] Ibid.

[3] Ibid., XIX, 13. Author's italics.

[4] I should like to thank my colleague Carl G. Hedman of the Department of Philosophy, The University of Wisconsin-Milwaukee, for this idea.